DIGNITY *of* DUTY

THE JOURNALS OF ERASMUS CORWIN GILBREATH

| 1861-1898 |

ERASMUS CORWIN GILBREATH'S last formal military photograph (right) was taken sometime in 1897 or 1898, after he made the rank of major for the second time in his 37-year military career. During his time in the United States Army, there was no regular system for medals and awards because official medals were then seen as symbols of monarchical, aristocratic privilege (one exception being the Medal of Honor, which was established by the U.S. Congress during the Civil War). Thus the medals and cords he is wearing in the photograph are largely ceremonial. Gilbreath is wearing Palm Leaf Epaulettes, indicating the rank of major, and an Indian Wars Bullion Aiguillette (gold fringe and shoulder cord). His medals and badges include (top row from the left): Third Corps Union Badge, Society of the Army of the Potomac Medal, Military Order of The Loyal Legion of The United States Medal, Grand Army of the Republic Medal; (bottom row): Sons of the Revolution Medal.

It is interesting to note that the War with Spain, in which Major Gilbreath fought, marked the end of America's continental struggles and the beginning of America's use of its maturing armed forces for world power projection. Following Gilbreath's death, who died while stationed in Puerto Rico ten days after the cease-fire with Spain was signed on August 12, 1898, the U.S. military began issuing campaign medals. Posthumously he is eligible for the Civil War Campaign Medal, Indian Wars Campaign Medal, Occupation of Porto Rico Campaign Medal, and Spanish American War Campaign Medal, all of which are featured on the book jacket. Major Gilbreath is also eligible for a Purple Heart for the wounds he received during the battle of Fredericksburg. These medals, like the last war he fought in, are a reflection of the United States' shift from a continental power to a world power.

—*Colonel (IL) Jennifer N. Pritzker, IL ARNG (Retired)*

Erasmus Corwin Gilbreath, seated second from right, camp at Seneca, Arizona Territory, 1894. Son-in-law Oliver Edwards is on his left.

DIGNITY *of* DUTY

THE JOURNALS OF ERASMUS CORWIN GILBREATH

| 1861-1898 |

A personal odyssey of service
from the Civil War to the
Spanish-American War

Edited by Susan Gilbreath Lane • Introduction by Carlo D'Este

PRITZKER
MILITARY
MUSEUM & LIBRARY

2015

Library of Congress Cataloging-in-Publication Data
Names: Gilbreath, Erasmus Corwin, 1841-1898, author. | Lane, Susan Gilbreath, editor. | D'Este, Carlo, contributor.
Title: Dignity of Duty: The Journals of Erasmus Corwin Gilbreath, 1861-1898, by Erasmus Corwin Gilbreath; introduction by Carlo D'Este; edited by Susan Gilbreath Lane.
Description: 352 pages: illustrated with black and white photographs, maps; cm. | Includes glossary and index.
Identifiers: ISBN 978-0-9897928-5-1 (hardcover) | ISBN 978-0-9897928-6-8 (e-book)
Subjects: LCSH: Civil War, 1861-1865 – Personal narratives. | United States. – Army. – Indiana Infantry Regiment, 20th (1861-1864). | Reconstruction (U.S. history, 1865-1877) | Indians of North America – Wars – Personal narratives. | Fort Custer (Mont.) – History. | Spanish-American War, 1898 – Personal narratives. | United States – History – 1865-1898.
Classification: LCC E601.G55 2015 | DDC 973.781

Executive Editors:
Colonel (IL) Jennifer N. Pritzker, IL ARNG (Retired), Kenneth Clarke
Designer: Wendy Palitz

Maps by David Cain © Pritzker Military Museum & Library:
Endpapers, p. 25, p. 44, p. 67, p. 82, p. 95, p. 119

Photographs and documents courtesy of Susan Gilbreath Lane:
Cover, frontispiece, p. 214, p. 216 (bottom).

Photographs and documents courtesy of William Sydnor Gilbreath III:
p. xvi, p. 215 (both), p. 216 (top), p. 217 (both), p. 218 (both),
p. 219 (both), p. 220, p. 221, p. 313, p. 321, p. 326.

This book was published in coordination with a companion exhibit at the Pritzker Military Museum & Library about the life and times of Erasmus Corwin Gilbreath. Visit www.dignityofduty.org or the Museum and Library in Chicago. The trade edition of Dignity of Duty: The Journals of Erasmus Corwin Gilbreath, 1861-1898, was preceded by a limited edition of 100 numbered copies with a unique tip-in page.

First Edition

...But the sense of fear on this and other occasions has been subjugated by a strong sense of duty and honour, or otherwise I should have slunk to the rear.

The brave man is not he who feels no fear,
For that were stupid and irrational;
But he whose noble nature dares
The danger Nature shrinks from.

—From *Reminiscences of the Sutlej Campaign*
by Colonel S. Dewé White

CONTENTS

PART 2. POST–CIVIL WAR

PART 3. THE SPANISH-AMERICAN WAR

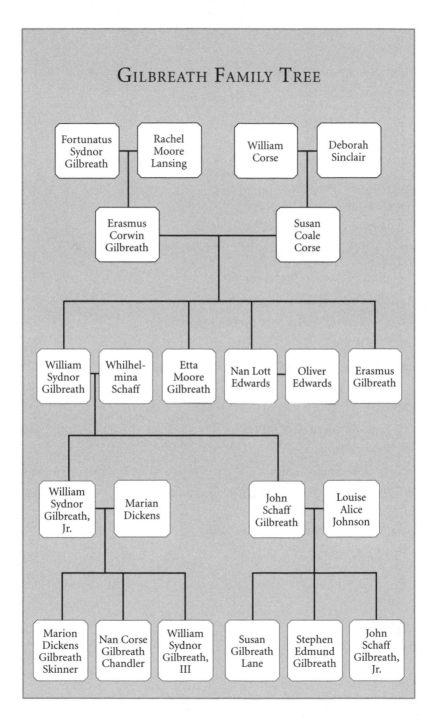

GILBREATH FAMILY TREE

Fortunatus Sydnor Gilbreath — Rachel Moore Lansing

William Corse — Deborah Sinclair

Erasmus Corwin Gilbreath — Susan Coale Corse

William Sydnor Gilbreath — Whilhelmina Schaff

Etta Moore Gilbreath

Nan Lott Edwards — Oliver Edwards

Erasmus Gilbreath

William Sydnor Gilbreath, Jr. — Marian Dickens

John Schaff Gilbreath — Louise Alice Johnson

Marion Dickens Gilbreath Skinner

Nan Corse Gilbreath Chandler

William Sydnor Gilbreath, III

Susan Gilbreath Lane

Stephen Edmund Gilbreath

John Schaff Gilbreath, Jr.

FOREWORD

AS A YOUNGSTER, I WAS FASCINATED BY THE STORIES my grandmother told with obvious pride and affection about her husband and his family. She was married to the son of Erasmus Corwin Gilbreath, the author of these journals.

Erasmus was born on May 13, 1840, in Guernsey County, Ohio, the eldest child of Fortunatus Sydnor Gilbreath, a physician, and Rachael Moore Lansing. Sometime in the 1850s the family set off for Chicago, traveling by canal to Cleveland, by steamer to Detroit, and by railroad to Michigan City, Indiana, where they were met by relatives who convinced them to settle in Valparaiso, Indiana. Just after Erasmus finished his last term in school, his father died, in 1853. My great-grandfather worked to support his family, studied law, and when the Civil War broke out "begun work raising a Company" and signed on as a volunteer with the 20th Indiana Regiment.

In support of his widow Susan's application for a military pension, Erasmus's attending officer General Schram wrote, "The immediate cause of his death was apoplexy...The campaign in which Major Gilbreath's regiment took part, though a brief one, was exceptionally arduous and trying to the officers and soldiers engaged in the expedition... It was a few days later when Major Gilbreath received the stroke which in the course of a few days resulted fatally." He died on August 22, 1898, in Puerto Rico; he was 59 years old. Susan was awarded a monthly pension of $25.

Susan was born in 1843 in Maryland to William Corse and Deborah Sinclair. They were Quakers, raised their large family in Baltimore, and lived in their home, Furley Hall. William was a "nurseryman," a business he took over from Deborah's father, Robert Sinclair. According to family lore, the family assisted escaping slaves, giving them safe haven as part of a link in the Underground Railroad. This is elaborated upon in a novel, *The Green Rose of Furley*, written by Helen Corse Barney, the daughter of Susan's brother, Frank. Susan died in 1919. Erasmus, Susan, and their daughter Etta are buried in Arlington National Cemetery.

I can only guess how Susan and Erasmus met. I know, however, that one of the first stops for the 20th Indiana was Baltimore, Maryland. The two were married on April 24, 1866, leaving that same day for Philadelphia then on to Chicago where his family was living. What challenges they would face together!

Erasmus and Susan had four children: first, William Sydnor, my grandfather; second, Etta, who never married; third, Nan, who died a tortured death from complications of childbirth; and fourth, Erasmus, who died in infancy. Only my grandfather and grandmother, Wilhelmina (Minnie) Schaff, had children: first my Uncle Syd (William Sydnor, Jr.) and second my father (John Schaff). Syd's children are Marion, Nan, and William Sydnor III (Bill), my cousins. My father's children include me and my twin brothers, Jack and Steve.

By the time I was born in 1942, my grandfather had died. I knew my grandmother very well. She lived to be 96 and died when I was in college.

Grandma told me many tales of her life with William Sydnor, including having danced with Henry Ford. But mostly I remember her description of his intoxicating recipe for eggnog, love of books, and adventurous pioneering spirit.

My father also had stories to tell about his father's adventures in the West: going down a river and being attacked by Indians who were shooting at the family using bows and arrows. To a city kid it all sounded very exotic and full of hyperbole. Somewhere along the way, I vaguely remembered hearing that his "papers" were in both the Detroit Public Library (DPL) and a special collection at the University of Michigan.

In the late 1970s, I updated and had reprinted a family tree, "Unser Stammbaum," written by my grandmother's father, John Adam Schaff, a German immigrant who came to Chicago. I was visiting the DPL's Burton Historical Collection to give them a copy of the thin volume when, acting on my vague recollection, I looked in the card catalog for listings under Gilbreath. To my surprise and delight, I found volumes of material about my grandfather.

William Sydnor had been an active and innovative force in the creation of the Dixie Highway and the Good Roads Movement during the early 1900s and came to Michigan to work for the fledgling Detroit Motor Club. In some haste, I perused the scrapbooks that had been brought to me, discovering a treasure of pictures and, in one instance, an album that was my father's and had his name on the back cover. The entire collection seemed to have been donated en masse with little consideration to its content. In my father's scrapbook there were some personal items that I wish I had. But, as someone pointed out to me, if they hadn't made it into the Burton Collection, I may never have seen them. The more I looked at the dozens of pictures of my grandfather, the more I felt a connection with the handsome and flamboyant person I had only heard and wondered about.

At the same time, in the same card catalog, I found another treasure which neither I nor any member of my family had any knowledge of: the Civil War Journal of my great-grandfather, Erasmus Corwin Gilbreath. When the librarian brought it to me, I could hardly believe what I had in my hands. It was a yellowed, legal-size, multicolored typed document that included his handwritten notes.

Another 20 years passed before I returned to the DPL for a more careful look at their collection of my grandfather's papers. On that visit, I found stuck in a folder another typed copy of the Civil War Journal in which my great-grandfather's edits had been incorporated into the text, a post–Civil War Journal, and a Spanish-American War Journal. It was the Post–Civil War Journal that confirmed the reality of what I had once thought was hyperbole.

I have never found a handwritten copy of the journals. However, I do have copies of letters that Erasmus wrote, and his writing is a challenge to read. I am therefore grateful that he produced a typed copy of the materials. Recently, with my family present, I passed out copies of a letter he had written to his mother. Working together, we couldn't completely decipher what he had written, but we had some good laughs trying.

Erasmus stated on the first page of the Civil War Journal that it was for his descendants and not for publication. However, his son donated the journals to the DPL, exposing them to public scrutiny. Because my great-grandfather was an educated man, I can well understand that he would not have wanted an unedited manuscript in the hands of a broad population of readers. If he had been satisfied with the original document, he would not have begun editing the journals.

In my grandfather's papers, I found responses to letters Erasmus had written to a person in Virginia seeking information about his family. Therefore, I'm convinced of his interest in family history and am not surprised that he wanted to pass on his personal story. But I also feel that he wanted to correct what he felt was a poor historical record of his regiment. He laments that record at the beginning of Chapter 5 in the Civil War Journal. I believe that his journal is, in part, a response to that regret.

Of course, when working on the project at least 30 years after the events occurred, Erasmus couldn't possibly have remembered all the details he ultimately wrote about. Evidently, he researched some facts and figures that he combined to create a narrative from the notes he had kept at the time. We have a glimpse into how he kept a journal by what remains of a sketchy record of his involvement in the Spanish-American War.

For years I resisted reading the Civil War Journal because I thought it would be disturbing, but at the urging of both my brother Steve and cousin Tom Chandler, I finally took the plunge. It was indeed disturbing, and even horrifying and appalling. But I was riveted. Here was my great-grandfather telling his great-granddaughter his accounting of history, breathing life into the textbook version I had read in school.

When I discovered that my great-grandmother was Susan, I asked my father if I had been named for her. Curiously he said, "No, I didn't know that was her name!" Since she died in 1919 when my father was 17, I found that a bit surprising, but presumably he only knew her as "Grandma." I'm delighted to share her name.

As I immersed myself in this effort, there were times when it seemed I felt Erasmus's presence, working with me and discussing his life. I only wish he had known how thrilled his family is to have his record of the events in his life beginning when he first signed on to volunteer to fight in the Civil War.

What a privilege that dumb luck led me to these journals. As my husband suggested, it was like finding a bottle stuffed with a message that washed up on a shore, and I was the fortunate one who found it.

This has been a true labor of love. My version of my great-grandfather's journals is dedicated to Erasmus Corwin Gilbreath's memory. It is also dedicated to the first Susan Gilbreath, my namesake even if only by chance, who braved the challenges of marriage to a pioneering military man.

—*Susan Gilbreath Lane*

Note

I respect that historians value firsthand accounting of events in their original states, as mistakes in such documents can also reveal information about the writer. But my great-grandfather Gilbreath did not leave unedited material. He began the editing process himself, and so I continued it. My guiding principle has been to retain the character of his writing and aim for clarity, without changing his content or style of writing.

The author's punctuation, paragraphing, usage, and spelling of place names, proper names, and military ranks were made consistent throughout. Where the absence of punctuation made his account difficult to understand, for example, where the beginning of Chapter 1 of his Civil War Journal was written as one long sentence devoid of punctuation, the addition of two commas clarified his meaning.

Obvious typographic errors were corrected. Where a word was clearly missing from a sentence, it was added in brackets. When the author's sentence seemed to make no sense, or his meaning or intention was unclear, the sentence was left unchanged.

Based upon Gilbreath's indicators, I created a table of contents. He gave titles to only three chapters in the Civil War Journals. I named the others, using a phrase from his text. I also added the year in which the events occurred, in keeping with his Post–Civil War Journal indicators.

In the last chapter of the Post–Civil War Journal, Gilbreath wrote about events he had not included in the earlier material. I inserted those entries where I thought they were chronologically appropriate.

—*S.G.L.*

*Erasmus Corwin Gilbreath wrote this letter to his mother on
May 7th, 1863. He wrote of the Union's loss at Chancellorsville
and of being slightly wounded during the battle.*

INTRODUCTION

THE MOMENTOUS CIVIL WAR that lasted from 1861 to 1865 was the most traumatic event in American history. A recent study estimated that as many as 750,000 soldiers on both sides died in a clash of ideas that left scars on the American psyche that a century and a half later have yet to fully heal. As the Civil War Trust notes, "Approximately one in four soldiers that went to war never returned home," in what was "the largest human catastrophe in American history."

In the spring of 1861, a call went out from Washington for volunteers to join militias for what was originally thought to be only three months of service to help put down what President Abraham Lincoln initially called the "insurrection."

One of those who came forward to volunteer to fight for the Union was an unusually gifted 21-year-old from Valparaiso, Indiana, named Erasmus Corwin Gilbreath, who served initially as a lieutenant in the 20th Indiana Volunteers.

Although not much is known of his early life, we do know he was born on May 13, 1840, in Guernsey County, Ohio, and that, prior to the war, Gilbreath had worked under a civil engineer building a railroad in Indiana.

Gilbreath was typical of the young men who fought the in Civil War. Although he came from a background ill suited to a sudden transformation from an ordinary citizen into a combatant, he quickly learned the art of soldiering. Fortunately, his natural curiosity and great intelligence resulted in these journals through which we experience not only many of the major battles of the Civil War but also an illuminating journey through much of 19th-century America that reveals the growing pains of a nation seeking its identity in the wake of the most devastating event in its history.

This book is first, and foremost, a tale of war in which there is no glory, only carnage and death. We get a sense of what war was like from the point of view of a young field officer rather than from the perspective of high command, strategy, and maneuver.

In Gilbreath's journals death is as routine as the dawning of a new day. Through his eyes we learn firsthand of the true horror of the Civil War: of the boredom, the fatigue, the death of so many on the battlefields, of the crude nature of caring for the wounded in the 1860s, of the blood and the amputations in the aid stations and primitive field hospitals.

Although seriously wounded by a Rebel bullet at the battle of Fredericksburg in December 1862, Gilbreath was one of the lucky ones who miraculously survived his wound to record his extraordinary tale of life and death, pithily noting that "my right leg would not do its duty." He lay on the battlefield for nearly seven hours before help came. It is a measure of his grit and determination that he refused to permit his badly injured leg to be amputated.

Another revelation of these journals is how little the participants in the Civil War actually knew of the politics that lay behind it. Gilbreath and his fellow soldiers were cogs in a great war machine, men who fought for a cause that, in retrospect, few fully understood. These were young men who simply responded to a call to duty, without regard for or knowledge of its myriad political and social elements.

His years of soldiering turned a country boy from Indiana not only into a professional soldier but also into a self-taught student of history who carefully chronicled what he saw and experienced into a fascinating journal of his life and those who served with him.

Gilbreath was the quintessential good soldier who learned to lead by example. Like so many other citizens in the more than 200 years of America's history, he almost seamlessly evolved from an ordinary citizen into an exceptionally capable and dedicated soldier.

His later journals paint a vivid picture of a nation recovering from a devastating war. Rural America of the post–Civil War years was a harsh and unforgiving place, where lawlessness, bloodshed, and disorder often reigned and where none of the amenities we take for granted today existed. After the war, Gilbreath remained in the army where his duties during the years of Reconstruction resulted in extensive travel in the war-torn South and throughout the vast wilderness of the western United States.

He takes us on a fascinating and hazardous journey by stagecoach in the Texas frontier that took him 175 hours to travel 175 miles, where the plains were rife with raids by warring Indians and filled with herds of buffalo that extended for 200 miles. We learn about the revolting food he was obliged to eat, and how this crude and thoroughly rough means of travel bore no resemblance to the romantic images depicted in Hollywood films.

The reader will also learn what it was like to experience a shipwreck off the Gulf coast, travel in a wagon train pulled by mules with pet names, and steam aboard a riverboat for more than 700 miles to the Montana Territory to establish Fort Custer, where his daughter was born in a tent with his cook acting as a midwife.

Gilbreath also witnessed events such as the great Chicago fire of October, 1871, that burned $200 million in property, killed some 300 people, and left another 100,000 homeless.

His amazing journey through America ended tragically on August 22, 1898, as a result of his service in the Spanish-American War. It is likely that, while stationed in Puerto Rico, he was a victim of an illness that led to what is thought to have been a stroke at the age of 59.

Major Gilbreath is buried in Arlington National Cemetery among fellow comrades-in-arms of America's wars. We are indeed fortunate that his legacy lives on in the pages of these remarkable journals.

—*Carlo D'Este*

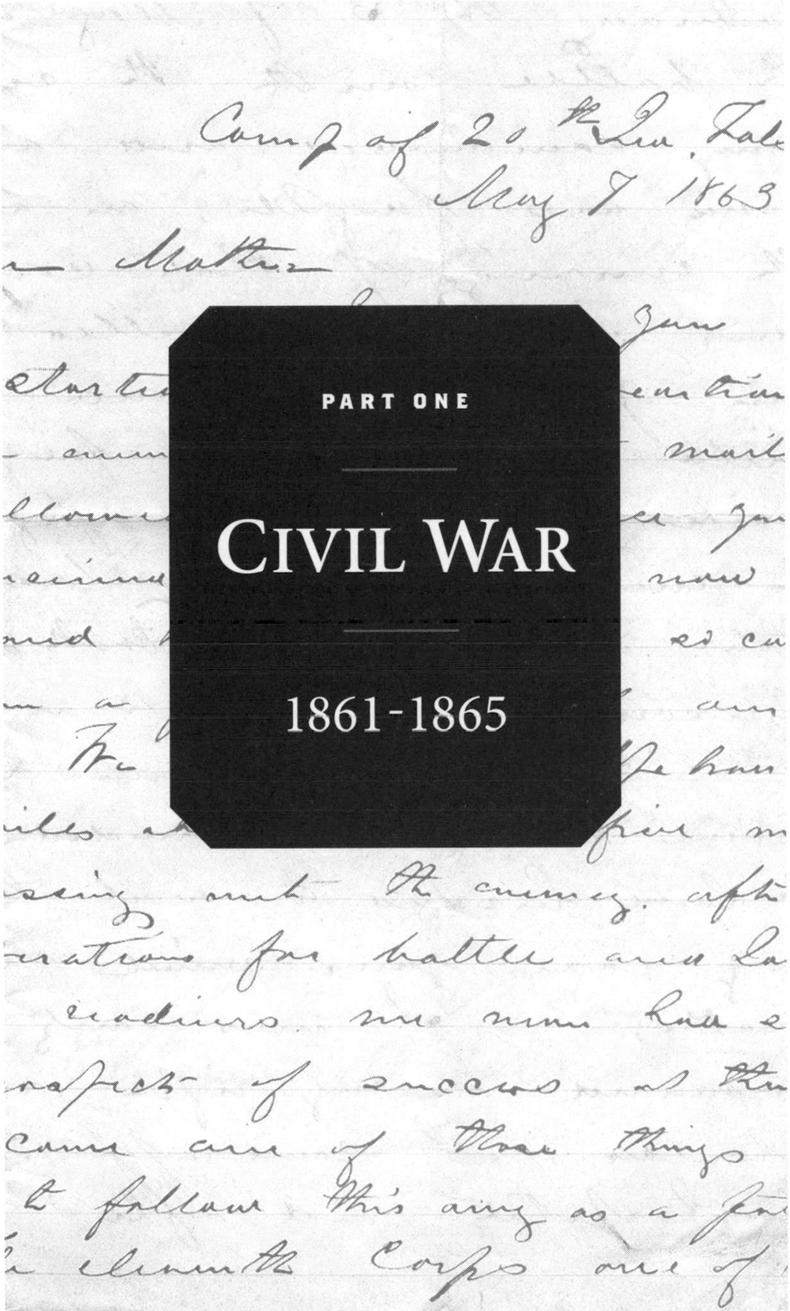

PART ONE

CIVIL WAR

1861-1865

*There is no pretense to originality in these pages as
I have consulted all the reports and books on these events
I could lay my hands on to help me make a connected
story with the hope that it may be slightly interesting.*

*I have tried to relate my own experiences and to tell of
what I saw so that it is all more personal than a general
history of either the Twentieth Indiana Volunteer
Infantry or of the events in which we took our part.*

*So too, with regard to battles, I have only written of
my part or the part of my Regiment and have not tried
to give a full description of the affair. There are numerous
stories of these battles fully describing all of them.*

—E.C.G.

CHAPTER 1

Raising & Organizing the Regiment

1861

I n a country like ours was in 1861, accustomed to a long series of years of peace and composed of a people not at all habituated to the performance of any military duty, the mobilization of a large force in a short time was a problem not easily solved.

History relates the story of the arousing of public sentiment in the North on the attempt of the Southern States to withdraw from the Union. I shall confine this narrative to the more personal story of the raising of the Volunteer Company and the organization of the Regiment to which I belonged, the 20th Indiana Volunteers, and shall follow this with an account of the Regiment's experiences, the whole intended to be my own personal experience as well as the movements of the Regiment during the War.

The story of raising one Company or one Regiment from county districts was like the story of each one so raised.

In 1861, I was living at Valparaiso, the County seat of Porter County, Indiana. Like the majority of the great mass afterwards formed into the gigantic Volunteer Army of the War of the Rebellion, the people of this county were living with no thoughts of the possibility of such events as came to them in the following four years.

We, who became members of the Volunteer Army from that county, were entertaining only hopes for the future bounded by friends, neighbors and our immediate surroundings.

I wished only for a light which would guide me to a way by which I could care for my mother, her daughter and other son.

I had begun to study law in the office of Mark L. DeMott, Valparaiso, Indiana, who later became Colonel in the Volunteer and held many offices including that of member of Congress. My law study had progressed to such an extent that I had hopes of being admitted to practice at the Bar after a few more months' work.

The War alarm was sounded. President Lincoln called for 75,000 Volunteers. I paid little attention to the matter except to keep posted by the newspapers as to the excitement of the country, and certainly had little thought of going into the Army myself.

On the 4th of June, 1861, J. W. Lytle, a personal friend of mine and of my mother, came to Valparaiso from a visit to his old home and the home of his father at Logansport, Indiana. At the latter place, he had come in contact with W. L. Brown, a Mexican War Veteran, and had been asked by Brown to help raise a Rifle Regiment which Brown had authority for from the Secretary of War at Washington.

Lytle had been a Civil Engineer and I had worked under his orders for some time while he was building a railroad from Logansport to Valparaiso, Indiana. I met him quite by accident, as he stepped off the train at Valparaiso. His first exclamation was, "You are just the one I wanted to see, for you are going to War with me." I was surprised, and refused. I pass the personal and affecting incident following his arrival, and say that on the 5th of June, Mr. Lytle and myself begun work raising a Company.

To do this, we simply rode through the country, informing everyone of our desires and sending out information that we had fixed on the 15th day of June for a grand meeting at the courthouse for the purpose of organizing a Company for the War under the call of the President for 75,000 men.

On the day fixed, the 15th day of June 1861, nearly everybody in the county came to Valparaiso, and so great was the enthusiasm that, in an hour after the meeting was called, we had enrolled 150 men or 50 more than we needed. So little did we know about military affairs that we supposed we could keep all of these men with us.

When the time came at that meeting for the selection of Officers, everybody was good-natured and Lytle urged me for Captain while I urged him to take it. Either one of us would have been satisfied with any position in the Company.

Lytle was made Captain by vote of the 150 enrolled. I was elected 1st Lieutenant. The 2nd Lieutenant and 1st Sergeant, Sergeants and Corporals were also elected, and, after a day of pleasurable excitement, we began our preparation to leave home.

We had fixed on the 4th day of July as the day for starting for the rendezvous. This day was fixed by Col. Brown for each Company to start from home.

Lafayette, Indiana was the place at which all the Companies were to assemble and the Regiment was to be organized.

On the 4th day of July, the day fixed for the men to get together, almost every man, woman and child in Porter County was at Valparaiso.

The only music in town was a fife and drum. The former was played by M. Cook, the Sheriff, and the latter by Jacob Brewer, the blacksmith. These gentlemen played all day and were only too anxious to march us to the railroad Station and to go with us to Lafayette.

The crowd at the Depot was very extensive, and we had plenty of time to say good-bye to all our friends. We went without change of cars to Lafayette, and so on the 5th of July marched into camp.

Other Companies came in from time to time until on the 6th all had assembled.

The Col., W. L. Brown, had some experience of war and, being a very energetic man, began at once to get his men in shape as well as he could. It was no easy matter to form the Regiment, as so few had any notion of what was to be done.

The number of the Regiment was given from the office of the Adjutant General of the State of Indiana.

The Colonel gave the letters to the Companies, and the Captains, 1st Lieutenants, and 2nd Lieutenants each took rank from the place the Company occupied as to the alphabet. Captain & etc. of Company A, was senior Captain followed by Captain of Company B, and so to the last, or Company K.

The Colonel, Lieutenant Colonel, Major, Adjutant, Regimental Quartermaster, the Surgeon and Assistant Surgeon were all appointed by the Governor.

This form of organization was only for the first formulation of the

Regiment. As vacancies occurred, the Lieutenant Colonel was promoted to be Colonel, the Major to be Lieutenant Colonel and the senior Captain was promoted to be Major.

In Companies when a vacancy in the Captain's place happened, the 1st Lieutenant of the Company was promoted and he was followed by the 2nd Lieutenant and by the 1st Sergeant of the Company. The Captain promoted in his Company took his rank with the rest of the Captains according to the date of his commission, and was promoted to be Major in that order, without reference to the original letter of the Company.

Our Company was lettered I, next to the last of the 10 in the Regiment. This was given because Capt. Lytle called Logansport his home, and that being the home of Col. Brown, the latter thought best to give us a low place. He was confirmed in this no doubt because Logansport Company was F.

In the formation of the Companies at Lafayette, each Captain selected his own 1st Sergeant, Sergeants, Corporals, Musicians, and so on, making his choice generally of those picked out by the men.

———

THE CAMP AT LAFAYETTE WAS AN AMUSING PLACE to think of now after the lapse of years. There were 1100 untrained Hoosiers there who had camped out often enough, no doubt, but never before under any restraint whatever. Guards were stationed around the camp, but their old style Harper's Ferry smooth-bore muskets without any ammunition were of little avail to keep men in bounds. Everybody was good-natured and having too much fun to get real mad about anything. Sentinels did not yet know that such a thing as military dignity could be in existence.

The men had great bunks in sheds with one side open and plenty of straw. No clothing was issued, so they all had to depend on what they brought from home.

Company messes were formed, and each Company was drilled in such movements as the Officers had mastered. The Colonel even essayed to move the whole crowd out as for Battalion drill, but this did not amount to as much as the other.

The Officers were as zealous and enthusiastic as we could be, and were very busy preparing to be mustered into the U.S. Service. With all our efforts, however, I think of the camp at Lafayette is [as?] one of the greatest turmoil I can now imagine.

On the 22nd day of July 1861, we were gotten ready to be mustered in the United States Service. The Officers and men were not submitted to any medical examination. The Mustering Officer simply walked along the line of each Company, looked at the man's hands and general appearance, asked him if he were all right and sound in every way, and passed on. The Mustering Officer took his place in front of the Company after inspection and, calling on the Officers and men to hold up their right hands, read or administered to them the usual oath of enlistment.

Each Company was mustered in separately and was then dismissed.

The officer who mustered in our Regiment was Major Thomas J. Wood, 1st Cavalry, U.S. Army, a very dignified old soldier who had been in service since 1845. He was a graduate from West Point and from Kentucky.

As he passed around the line of Company I, he found a thin 6 footer in the second file from the right, in the rear rank, named John Smith. Smith had lost the index finger of his right hand. This was a serious defect. As Smith held out his hand, Major Wood said, "You can't shoot a gun with that hand." "Yes, I can," said Smith. Major said, "Do you think you could hit a man at 400 yards?" Smith replied, "I wish you would step out and let me try."

The Major went on. At the left of the Company he found a young boy with blocks placed under his heels to make him tall enough to pass muster. The blocks were taken away, and young Boulson went off crying like a child.

Smith was sworn in. Boulson went with me as sort of a servant until he became large enough to enlist, when he became a fifer of the Company and later the Chief of Field Music in the Regiment. He is now a prominent physician in Jackson, Michigan.

It may be well observed at this place that the 20th Indiana Regiment was composed of quite young men, most all from life in the country. I, myself, was only 21 years old in the month of May 1861. All trades were represented in the Regiment. The Captain of Company F was a Methodist Minister, while the Captain of Company A was a shoemaker; Captain of Company I was a Civil Engineer.

There were no strictly town or city Companies in the Regiment, but each Company represented some County. There was a Company from each of the following Counties: Marion, Tippecanoe, Porter, Lake, La Porte, Carroll, Cass, Marshall, Jasper and Howard.

The Officers of the 20th Indiana at the time of the Muster in were as follows:

Field and Staff
William L. Brown, Colonel, Logansport
Charles D. Murray, Lieut. Colonel, Kokomo
Benjamin H. Smith, Major, Logansport
Israel N. Stills, Adjutant, Lafayette
Isaac W. Hart, R. Q. M, Attica
William C. Porter, Chaplain, Plymouth
Orpheus Everts, Surgeon, La Porte
Anson Hurd, Asst. Surgeon, Oxford

Company A
John Van Valkenburg, Captain, Peru
William B. Rayburn, 1st Lieutenant, Peru
John Hoover, 2nd Lieutenant, Peru

Company B
John Wheeler, Captain, Crown Point
Charles A. Bell, 1st Lieutenant, Corydon
Michael Sheehan, 2nd Lieutenant, Crown Point

Company C
Oliver H. P. Bailey, Captain, Plymouth
William C. Castleman, 1st Lieutenant, Plymouth
Joseph Lynch, 2nd Lieutenant, Plymouth

Company D
George F. Dick, Captain, Attica
Charles Reese, 1st Lieutenant, Attica
James A. Wilson, 2nd Lieutenant, Attica

Company E
James H. Shannon, Captain, La Porte
John W. Andrews, 1st Lieutenant, La Porte
John E. Sweet, 2nd Lieutenant, La Porte

Company F
John Kistler, Captain, Danville
John H. Logan, 1st Lieutenant, Logansport
Edward C. Sutherland, 2nd Lieutenant, Logansport

Company G
Nathaniel C. Herron, Captain, Delphi
William C. L. Taylor, 1st Lieutenant, Lafayette
William H. Brittingham, 2nd Lieutenant, Lafayette

Company H
George W. Geisendorff, Captain, Indianapolis
George W. Meikel, 1st Lieutenant, Indianapolis
William O. Sherwood, 2nd Lieutenant, Indianapolis

Company I
James W. Lytle, Captain, Valparaiso
Erasmus C. Gilbreath, 1st Lieutenant, Valparaiso
William I. Carr, 2nd Lieutenant, Valparaiso

Company K
Alfred Reed, Captain, Monticello
John I. Richardson, 1st Lieutenant, Monticello
Daniel D. Dote, 2nd Lieutenant, Monticello

CHAPTER 2

EQUIPPING THE REGIMENT & LEAVING INDIANA

1861

The two days of July 23rd and 24th, 1861, were rather slow to pass, and rather solemn ones for all of us. We had been sworn into the service of the United States, and possibly felt the serious side of really being soldiers for the Government.

On the 24th of July, we left Lafayette by rail for the city of Indianapolis. We numbered 1200 men, and every man carried with him his grip sack or carpet bag. As no uniforms had been issued to us, the variety of dress was very great, and it was a motley procession.

Arriving at Indianapolis on the 25th, we camped at Camp Morton just outside of the city. The camp was in a beautiful place and well situated to facilitate the work of completing our organization. Clothing was given out to the men. Officers procured their uniforms, swords, & etc. The uniform of the men consisted of a jeans suit, gray in color, the coat or jacket was of Zouave shape with round corners and a braided edge. Thus our first suits were the gray color which the Confederacy adopted as their own. The material was of the worst possible quality and soon wore out. The Officers wore the blue of the Regular Army.

Everything about the Capital was haste and hurry, and the energy displayed by Oliver P. Morton, the Governor, and his assistants was quite wonderful, as not one had had experience in such affairs. He soon collected about him a number of Regular Army Quartermasters and other Officers, and everything moved quite smoothly.

The time came a few days after our going into camp at Indianapolis for the issue to us of guns, belts, cartridge boxes, & etc. This was done in this way. The various articles were placed in a large store building. We were marched on the side street and entered the back door through an alleyway. The Officers required the men to equip themselves as they passed to the front door. Each man picked up a belt, cartridge box, haversack, canteen, & etc., and the last thing at the front door was the gun. One Company followed another rapidly, and the entire Regiment was soon equipped.

The Companies were formed on the main street of the city by the Company Officers as fast as they arrived with their equipments.

As I have said before, the Regiment was raised to be a "Rifle Regiment," and in getting men together, we were told to induce them to enlist for a "Rifle Regiment." This plea had its effect, as the idea of carrying a smooth-bore musket shooting buckshot with a round ball in each cartridge was repulsive to all who gave the matter any thought. It will thus be readily imagined how intensely indignant every man was when he found that he was in possession of an old-fashioned smooth-bore Harper's Ferry Musket.

It may be well to explain at this time that a smooth-bore gun for foot troops was manufactured by the Government at Springfield, Mass. from 1795. It was fired by means of a flint and pan, and was called a musket after a French Model.

In 1842 the Government adopted the use of percussion caps, and old muskets were changed at Harper's Ferry so that, instead of the flint and steel, the percussion caps were used. These altered muskets were called Harper's Ferry Muskets because altered there. All muskets used a round ball and three buckshot in each cartridge.

In 1846 there were not enough of the altered muskets to arm the troops taking part in the Mexican War, and Genl. Scott preferred to use the old flintlock musket to using an untried gun (like the musket altered to use percussion caps), and the Mexican War was fought with the 1795 gun. After the Mexican War, the altered musket became of general use in the Army.

In 1855 the new gun, called the Springfield Rifle, was adopted and placed in the hands of the Regular Army, but the Government had not arms enough at the beginning of the war for so many troops, so they were compelled to use the old altered musket the caliber of which was 69, the diameter of the ball being 69 one-hundredths of an inch.

These rifles of 1855 were what our men supposed they were to get while the old musket was what was issued. All the guns given out by the Government were muzzle loading.

When our men were formed in the street after receiving their equipment, there was a groan of indignation which increased to loud expressions of dissatisfaction and, before the Officers knew what was going on, all Companies had piled their guns on the sidewalk.

There was great excitement, and the Governor came out and wanted all the Officers arrested. After a good deal of persuasion, we coaxed the men to carry the musket to camp and the Governor promised to explain things to us.

The following morning on looking out at Reveille, we found that the men had gone to the guard line and had thrown the guns in a heap outside the camp.

The Governor came to our camp, but when he tried to speak, the men hissed him. He arranged with the Colonel to show good faith in the promise to give us rifles, so that Companies A and B on the right and left flank of the Regiment should at once receive the rifles, and that the other Companies should be supplied at an early day with rifles. The men accepted of the situation, and we had no more difficulty.

Having completed our equipment and organization at Indianapolis, we were ordered out of the State, and left the State on the 2nd day of August 1861. The journey was delightful, as at every farm, village and town on the way we were received with every demonstration of patriotism.

We went by way of Pittsburgh and Harrisburg to Cockeysville, Maryland, thirteen miles from Baltimore, and there had a beautiful camping place.

Our first duty consisted of guarding 65 bridges on the Northern Central Railroad running from Baltimore to Harrisburg. We drilled a great deal and worked ourselves into a fair state of discipline.

During our stay at Cockeysville, the Officers and men made frequent trips to the city of Baltimore. These visits were probably the first time many of the Regiment had seen a city.

Our stay at Cockeysville was short, as the Regiment was ordered to Baltimore and Fortress Monroe. We left Cockeysville about the first of September, 1861, and on our arrival at Baltimore by the Northern Central Railroad, we were disembarked from the cars at the old Fulton Depot near where now stands the Union Depot.

We were feeling that Baltimore was still very hostile to all Union people, as it was no doubt, so that the Colonel ordered all the muskets loaded. It was an awfully dangerous thing to do, as I look at it now, as the slightest accident might have precipitated a fearful disaster.

After disembarking, we marched through the city of Baltimore, passing down St. Paul [Street] to Baltimore Street and to the wharves where we took steamer and were landed at Fortress Monroe next morning.

We were marched to the mainland, and went into camp at what was called Camp Hamilton; Genl. J. E. Wool commanding the Department, and Genl. Joseph K. Mansfield commanding the Camp. There were several Regiments of Volunteers in this camp, and we were kept hard at work drilling and marching for practice.

About the 26th of September, we took the steamer S. S. *Spaulding*, and on the 28th entered the inlet of Fort Hatteras. Most of us had never seen the ocean before, and as the passage was stormy, we had wonderful experiences.

On reporting to the Commanding Officer at Fort Hatteras, we were ordered to change from the ocean steamer to smaller vessels and ordered to proceed inside the Hatteras Island in Pamlico Sound to the extreme northern end of the Island where there was a small inlet. This place was called Chickamicomico Beach, and the object of sending us there was to establish a camp from which to demonstrate against Roanoke Island.

COMMENTARY: *When the first shots of the Civil War were fired on Fort Sumter in Charleston harbor, at dawn on April 12, 1861, the total strength of the U.S. regular army was just over 16,000. But by early May, as the battle lines emerged between Confederacy and Union, President Lincoln had called for over 150,000 volunteers. Many states responded quickly, as did Indiana, and volunteer regiments were raised. Initially, the units had the character of town meetings, with basic democracy prevailing over anything like military discipline in selection of officers and decisions about uniforms and weapons. Some drilling occurred, but there was little in the way of basic training. Neither side was prepared for the scale, ferocity, and duration of the war that had begun.*

CHAPTER 3

Horrors on Hatteras Island

1861

Hatteras Island is a long narrow spit of land with Pamlico Sound on the west. It is about 45 miles long, extending from Hatteras Inlet to Loggerhead Inlet on the north end. The former inlet is only about 12 hours' sail from Fortress Monroe. The island is as wide as 2 miles in one place, but is generally much narrower.

Chickamicomico Beach is about 40 miles from Hatteras Inlet by water, and only a few hours steaming from Roanoke Island.

The surf of the sea beats upon the east side of the island and over it in many places in cases of a storm or strong east wind. The Sound, on [the] west side of the island, is quite still and the bottom shoals for a long distance into the Sound, and there are only a few places where a steamer could reach the shore. In fact, I believe that at Hatteras Lighthouse, ten miles north of the inlet, is the only place, and there only if an expert pilot is at the wheel.

To get to Chickamicomico, we transferred at once from the ocean steamer to several small gunboats which drew only 6 to 9 feet of water. In them, we were taken north through Pamlico Sound and were compelled to anchor about 3 miles from shore, and to disembark in lighters. This we accomplished with 7 Companies, or about 500 men, on the 29th of September.

The Officer in command at Fort Hatteras was in such haste to send us north that we carried little baggage and very few rations. He wanted to send all of our baggage on a separate boat. Our Regimental Quartermaster was left at the Inlet to bring up the baggage.

We were without tents or rations on landing. Capt. Isaac W. Hart, our

Quartermaster, did not leave the inlet until 6:00 A.M., October 1st, and we were rejoiced to see the *Fanny* come to anchor about 2:00 P.M. that day, opposite our camp.

We got off one lighter loaded with tents and supplies when, a little after 4 P.M., we saw in the northwestern direction three great lines of black smoke. They grew blacker and, within an hour, our little gunboat, the *Fanny*, was attacked by three Rebel gunboats. After a short resistance of 35 minutes, the *Fanny* was overpowered and, within four hours of her coming to anchor, she was a captive and on her way to Roanoke Island.

Capt. I. W. Hart and 47 men were prisoners, all our tents, rations, camp equipage and records of every kind were taken. News of the disaster was sent by an Officer to Fort Hatteras, and, on the 3rd of October, the steam tugs *Putnam* and *Ceres* landed five days' rations at Chickamicomico for us. For two days we had had little to eat. I remember that the watery oysters we found on the Sound side and the sweet potato pies we got from the people living on the Island tasted very good. I have not wanted any of either since, however.

Thus it was that the first sight we had of the hostile flag was on the coast of North Carolina. It was far away, and the time passed so soon that we could scarcely believe our eyes.

—————

ON THE MORNING OF THE 4TH OF OCTOBER 1861, about 9:00 o'clock, we were attracted to the highest points of the land by seeing dense clouds of the same black smoke coming from the direction of Roanoke Island.

As it came into view or closer approached, we counted a fleet of nine steam vessels and smaller boats, and they were coming directly toward us. Everything was excitement in our camp. We were 500 men armed with smooth-bore muskets, which when they fired at all were effective at 100 yards or so. We had no artillery at all.

A more hopeless and frightened crowd was seldom seen.

To add to our discomfort after the fleet had come to anchor about 3½ miles away, one of the largest of the Rebel vessels was detached and sailed southward. We at once decided that they were going to land below us, and thus cut us off from help from the Fort at the inlet and make us prisoners.

Col. W. L Brown called all the Officers together and, after explaining the situation as he understood it, informed us that he had decided to retreat to Fort Hatteras. We fell in at once and started. As we were about to leave the Camp, 1st Sgt. Brown of Company K took position on a sand dune and sang "Our Flag Is There." After the song, which was the only defiant thing we did except shake our fists, we started on the march.

The entire island was only a sand pile, but by walking along the ocean side close to the surf, we found hard sand which made easy marching. We kept it up during the day without much rest, and felt that it was a race with the boat we had seen go south to get past the landing place before they could come on shore. We could see with our glasses too that they were landing men at our Camp at Chickamicomico, which was an additional spur to lively action on our part.

In the evening we formed a skirmish line across the Island to guard against running into the enemy should he succeed in landing. I was in charge of a part of the line, and never did harder work.

There was no water except as we dug for it. We had no tin cups (all captured) but had found some large shells which answered the place of cups, and we used them in digging for water. We thus supplied ourselves with enough. Between 10 and 11 o'clock at night, we arrived at Hatteras Lighthouse.

On the march down, we met Major Jardine of the 9th New York with orders to fall back to Hatteras. This Officer served with prominence and lost his leg in the New York Riot in 1863.

As we had no transportation of any kind, not even a horse at Chickamicomico, we left everything we had there. Soon after daylight, we discovered the U.S. Frigate *Minnesota* off our camp at sea. Her Officers saw the black smoke of the Rebel vessels, and they kept their grand old ship abreast of us as we marched. Their guns were old pattern, and they were of little help to us, but the companionship of such an escort was cheering.

Beautiful as our glorious flag is at all times, it seemed never so beautiful as when displayed on the water, especially if on one of the old-fashioned Men of War. The *Minnesota* accompanied us to Hatteras Lighthouse, and the first thing solid we got to eat there was hard bread and dried apples sent to us from her stores.

We camped about Hatteras Lighthouse the night of October 4th, and in the morning of the 5th found that we had not only been followed by a Georgia Regiment, but that they had succeeded in landing during the night, four or five miles from us, soon after we had passed the point or landing place.

They captured 3 Sergeants, 2 Corporals and 24 Privates who had gotten tired out and straggled. We afterward learned that there were 2000 troops on the Rebel transport; only 500 landed at Chickamicomico, and the vessel *Cotton State*, which tried to get into shore to land troops near the Lighthouse to cut us off, ran into the soft bottom offshore some 4 miles and could not move for a long time, so that we owed our escape to an accident.

On the morning of the 5th of October, we again started on the march for Fort Hatteras at the inlet where we arrived at an early hour. We were without tents and so camped our men under old sail cloths which had been taken from the Rebels at the time the Forts were captured.

We found that there were two Forts at Hatteras Inlet, Fort Hatteras and Fort Clark, and that from Fort Clark 1200 yards up the Island, there was not a stick or shrub of any kind. High water washed the floor of Fort Hatteras, and it was desolate enough. These Forts had been captured from the Rebels on the 29th of August 1861 by the action of the Army under Genl. Butler, and the Navy under Commodore Stringham.

We remained in Camp near Fort Clark which was a mile from Fort Hatteras. The latter was on the point at the inlet, where the sea swept into the Sound, and Fort Clark was simply an outpost for Fort Hatteras.

Time dragged along slowly until the 4th & 5th of November, which became stirring days for us. On the 3rd, the Steamer S. S. *Spaulding* came from Fortress Monroe with supplies for the Hatteras command, and brought to us regular U.S. blue clothing of all kinds, new Rifles for the entire Regiment and many Commissary Stores. On the morning of the 4th it begun to rain with a driving east wind so that the unloading, although most finished, was stopped. The storm increased with the approach of the night, and about 3 o'clock in the morning of the 5th of November, we were called up by a soldier crying, "You better get out; your trunks are gone." We jumped up and into sea water. On looking out we found that the sea had cut a new channel through the Island and that the Regiment had been left on an Island away from the main Island. We also saw our stores rolling off into the flood. All sorts of clothing, arms, commissary stores and everything were fast disappearing into the waters of Pamlico Sound. We rolled as many things away from the channel as we could. Far as the eye could see up the Island, the surf was beating over into the Sound.

The storm abated during the 5th, and on the 6th we were ordered to move our Camp up the Island 6 miles. We had no means of crossing the new channel, which was 30 feet deep, so had to march the men around on the circular bar which had formed as the waters of the new inlet had checked their force in those of the Sound.

We camped at the new place called Camp Wool, and were quite comfortable, but in need of almost everything for our men. This portion of the Island was quite its widest part. There was little timber there, the water good.

The entire Hatteras Island was inhabited only by wreckers, a wretched class of people who lived almost solely on the misfortunes of those who go down to sea in ships. Their houses were built of material taken from wrecked ships and filled with all sorts of things appertaining to a ship's equipment. The beach was strewn for 40 miles with wreckage. Near our camp was a small church, which the people had put up of the same stuff as that composed their houses.

About the 10th of November we were ordered to proceed to Fortress Monroe, and on receipt of this order we were greatly rejoiced to close our chapter of horrors on Hatteras Island.

CHAPTER 4

The Most Remarkable
Naval Combat

1862

Arriving at Fortress Monroe we were camped on the mainland at what was called Camp Hamilton. We had a Brigade of six Regiments encamped with us, and we kept up a round of drills and miltary duties. We were supplied with complete equipment of everything, Springfield Rifles and blue clothing, and the spirit of all in the Regiment arose in due time to the highest mark for drill and discipline.

Sometime in January 1862 we were moved by steamer to Newport News, where we were placed under the orders of Genl. J. K. F. Mansfield in a camp of some 8000 men. It was a delightful place for a camp, and we all enjoyed it to the fullest extent. Everything was calm and peaceful. Our camp was high above the water and fronted on the James River, as it debouches into Hampton Roads.

We were about a mile and a half from Newport News Point, and from our tents we could see far across James River, which is 4½ to 6 miles wide at this place. We could see up the Elizabeth River towards Norfolk and to Fortress Monroe and the sea beyond.

We had little thought of our nearness to most remarkable events, and the 8th of March 1862 promised to be one of the most delightful of all our days as it came so balmy and dreamy. But this day we were to witness the beginning of the most remarkable naval combat of any age, and within the hours ending with 12 o'clock noon on the 9th of March, we were to see a new era opened in the history of maritime warfare in the closing of the first battle of ironclad ships.

Armored vessels were used since the 12th Century. In 1815 Fulton built an armored defense vessel and there were constant improvements on the idea. From 1847 the French Government constructed in ironclads and in 1855 had quite a fleet — all, however, built after old forms of their wooden ships. But the initial test or trials of the value of iron vessels and of the advance in Naval Construction was in the battle of the 8th & 9th of March 1862 between the *Congress, Cumberland* and *Monitor* against the *Merrimac* and her consorts.

The lesson was given progressively and forcibly.

On the 8th of March ironsides against wooden walls, while on the 9th of March ironsides met ironsides, and the end of it all was that old-fashioned wooden line of battleships ceased to be used forever in battle.

Hampton Roads in Virginia is a broad sheet of water forming an arm of Chesapeake Bay. It receives the waters of the James River [and] of the Nansemond and Elizabeth. The general shape of the Roads is that of an irregular parallelogram with the long side to the east.

The Elizabeth, on which is situated Norfolk, Portsmouth and the Gosport Navy Yards, empties into the Roads at the southeast corner of the parallelogram. Sewell's Point, 6½ miles from Norfolk and only 5½ miles from Fortress Monroe, is on the east side, and it is five miles across the Roads from Sewell's Point to Newport News Point, which occupies the west side of the square.

The James River empties from the west and is 4½ to 7 miles wide. Rebel batteries were located at Sewell's Point to command the entrance of Elizabeth River and Norfolk.

The Gosport Navy Yards had been seized by the Rebels at the breaking out of the war in 1861, though not before all the vessels had been sunk and the buildings burned.

Norfolk is about 12 miles from Fortress Monroe. It is not visible from Hampton Roads or Fortress Monroe, but from Newport News about 12 miles away looking up the Elizabeth River, we could distinguish the spires of the town and the movements of the shipping.

Within this amphitheater, we witnessed most beautiful pictures and were observers and participants in sublime events. This locality has great historical interest. Around no part of the United States does there cling

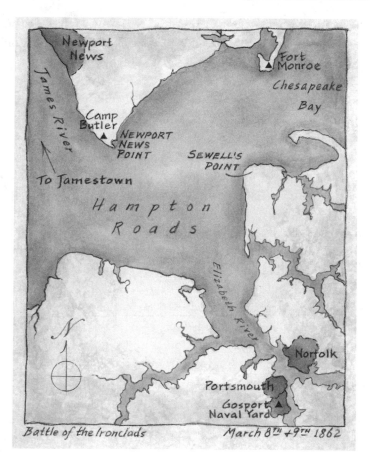

Battle of the Ironclads   March 8ᵀᴴ +9ᵀᴴ 1862

so many or such attractive memories of adventures, chivalry and military glory. The placid waters of this great estuary welcomed the peaceful prow of the first English settlers on the Continent. At Jamestown, some 40 miles away up the James River, were built the first homes in America. There the redoubtable John Smith led his life of adventure and by his prowess saved the infant colony from destruction. Nearer and only 20 miles away at Yorktown, Washington received the surrender of Cornwallis ending the Revolutionary War.

Every landing place, point, island, and creek in the vicinity bears a name supplied by early Colonists, given for some reason quaint and interesting. Old Point Comfort, where now stands Fortress Monroe, was so called because they there found comfort after stormy voyages. Newport News was named for Sir Christopher Newport, a Governor of Virginia. The Colonists gave him up for lost because of his long delay in returning from England. They there first saw his ships and sent news of his coming.

In 1861 and 1862 Hampton Roads was the dividing place between opposing armies of the Civil War. The Union Army held Fortress Monroe and Newport News and established great camps, forts and hospitals. The Rebel Army held Sewell's Point, Norfolk and all of the east and south sides.

Amongst the vessels sunk at Gosport Navy Yards in 1861 was a large steam frigate of 3500 tons and 40 guns. She was called the *Merrimac*. In the summer of 1861 the Confederates raised this vessel and rebuilt her as an ironclad. They cut down both ends and covered over 170 feet at the middle of the vessel with iron. Thirty-five feet at each end were so arranged as to be just under water when she was ready for action. The middle roof was built at an angle of 45 degrees and 7 feet high. Both ends of the middle iron roof were rounded.

The ironclad roof was made of 20 inches of pine covered by 4 inches of oak and four inches of iron. The outer iron shield was composed of plates made at Richmond. They were 2 inches thick and 8 inches wide. The first course of plates was put on horizontally, and the outer course was laid vertically. All were bolted through the 24 inches of wood.

For ramming purpose, there was placed on the stem a prow of iron. It was wedge shape and weighed 1500 pounds. It extended 2½ feet beyond the stem.

The smokestack was in the center with the pilot house at the extreme front end of the shield. The sides of the iron wall came within 20 feet of each other at the top, and this open space was covered with a heavy iron grating, allowing the ready escape of smoke when in action and serving as a promenade at other times.

This floating fort was armed with two 7-inch breech-loading rifles in the bow and stern. She had two 6-inch rifles and a broadside battery of six nine-inch smooth-bore guns, or a total of 10 guns.

Commodore Franklin, whose brother served on the *Congress* and who had been an Officer of the U.S. Navy, was in command. Lieut. Jones who built the new ironclad was the second in command.

This vessel was called the *Virginia*, but we always retained the old name of *Merrimac*. She drew 23 feet of water and was very slow, taking 30 to 40 minutes to turn.

The United States Government had all the time kept informed of the Confederates' progress in the rebuilding of the *Merrimac*, and had contracted for a vessel to meet this one when she should come out. The Navy Department expected to have the new boat finished in January, 1862, but the novelty and magnitude of the undertaking caused delay. The vessel, [named the *Monitor*,] was completed early in March, 1862, just 100 days from beginning the work, and she at once left New York.

The story of the *Monitor* was about as follows: John Ericsson, a Swede by birth but an American citizen, had long been planning an ironclad ship. He adopted the revolving turret of Theodore R. Timby of Duchess County, New York, and which was patented by Timby in 1843.

Instead of building a clumsy floating fort, he planned a small battery of only two guns. She was of light draft and armor clad. He named his vessel the *Monitor*. She was 172 feet long, 41 feet 6 inches broad and drew only 11 feet. The deck was one foot above the water line. There was nothing whatever above the deck except the pilot house and a revolving turret with two guns side by side. The turret was 20 feet in diameter, 9 feet high and 8 inches thick.

The side armor of the deck was 5 inches thick and overhung the wall of the vessel. The deck was covered with iron 1 inch thick. The pilot house was simply an iron box 4 feet high made of iron blocks 9 inches thick, and there was room inside for the wheel and three men. The only lookout from the pilot house was through a narrow opening ¼ inch wide between the blocks.

When ready for action she had smoke pipes 6 feet above the deck, and blow pipes 4½ feet high. The Flag, pilot house and turret only showed when ready for action.

The armament was two 11 inch smooth-bore guns, firing a solid shot weighing 180 pounds. The portholes of the turret were covered with a heavy iron pendulum which required the whole force of the gun crew of 8 men to raise for firing.

The pilot house, where the Commanding Officer remained during a battle, was connected with the turret, which was under charge of the second Officer, by a simple speaking tube.

Capt. Worden was 44 years old and had been 28 years in the service. His second officer was Lieut. Greene, 22 years old, and the crew was composed of 56 men.

The *Monitor* passed Cape Henry at 4:00 P.M., March 8th. The situation at Newport News was about as follows on that day. Anchored in the James River off our camp were two sailing warships. The *Cumberland*, 30 guns, was furthest upstream, while the *Congress*, 50 guns, was ½ mile lower down. She was a sister ship to the *Merrimac*. Each was about 700 yards from shore, and both swung at their anchor as the tide ebbed and flowed, being sailing vessels only.

At eleven o'clock we were informed by the Signal Station at Newport News Point and the Officers of the *Congress* and the *Cumberland* that vessels were coming out from Norfolk. The long roll was sounded to collect all of our men and, stacking arms on Company streets, we all sought high grounds from which to see.

Off toward Norfolk we observed dense clouds of smoke and soon were able to distinguish a large vessel and two smaller ones drawing out toward Sewell's Point. Reaching a position off that place, they followed their leader, turned west and steamed for the James River. It seemed a long time but was only a few minutes till we could plainly see the *Merrimac*. She was black and moved slowly. When ¾ of a mile away, she opened the battle by firing at the *Congress* with a bow gun. She was answered at once by a broadside from the *Congress*, and the battle was on. Our batteries on shore joined in, the gunboats with the *Merrimac* fired as rapidly as they could. The roar of the guns, the smoke and the whole scene cannot be described, but it was forever fixed in our memories.

The *Merrimac* passed the *Congress* about 200 yards away, receiving broadside after broadside from that vessel. She did not pause, but sailed slowly on, turned when opposite the *Cumberland*, and steamed slowly into her side. It had only been 15 minutes since she fired the first gun of the battle. She cleared and turned upstream, and as she slowly swung around, her stern guns and her broadside played on the Union vessels and the shore. The troops of the camp lined the shore, and we kept up a constant hail of lead hoping to strike someone at a porthole or do some damage at a vulnerable point.

The Rebel vessel's smokestack was often pierced by shots from our batteries, and as the smoke and flames poured out of these openings she looked more demoniacal than before. She advanced on the *Cumberland* a second time, and one shot from a bow gun killed 9 men on that ship. Following this with a broadside, Capt. Buchanan demanded the surrender of the *Cumberland*. Lieut. Morris who was in command yelled back, "Never! I'll sink longside."

The decks of the *Cumberland* were covered with the killed and wounded. She settled, filling, and soon her portholes gave entrance to the water. Her crew, driven from deck to deck, worked the guns left unsubmerged, and at 3:30, as she lifted her bow for the plunge, they with ringing cheers gave a final shot with their after pivot gun, and the *Cumberland* with a roar quickly sank. Her colors were flying, and her flag was submerged where it hung. She had fought 45 minutes. All that remained to be seen was 6 or 8 feet of her top mast. Some of her crew who had gained the shore went out under fire and nailed a large flag to this top mast. It was never removed.

The *Merrimac* now turned her attention to the *Congress*. That helpless vessel had slipped her cable and tried to maneuver or get away. As she used only some of her top sails and floated with the tide, she turned and, her bow toward the shore, she struck and was fast grounded with her broadside upstream.

The *Merrimac* steamed downstream and, fearing to ram on account of the shallow water, stood off and fired shot after shot into the side of the *Congress*. The Officer in command, Joseph B. Smith, was killed and Lieut. Pendergast hauled down the colors. The news flashed to Washington rapidly as each event occurred, and as brave old Commodore Smith read the message, "The *Congress* has surrendered," he only said to those about him, "Joe's dead."

Buchanan attempted to send his men in a small boat to take possession of his prize. He repeated the attempt three times, but we on shore kept such a firing that we drove them back to their vessel.

Genl. Mansfield said that we had not surrendered, and he paid no attention to the white flags on the *Congress*.

The Confederate Officer gave up his attempt to board the *Congress*, and sent the *Raleigh* and the *Beaufort* to the lower side of the *Congress* to receive the surrender and take off the Officers.

Lieut. Minor and Commodore Buchanan were both wounded severely by small balls from the shore. The latter had to have his leg amputated on account of the severity of the wound.

Most all of the crew of the *Congress* escaped to shore, but the Confederates took off 20 prisoners.

The *Merrimac* now selected a raking position astern of the *Congress* while one of the smaller steamers poured in a constant fire. Three other steamers kept up a fire on the shore or on the *Congress*. She was set on fire by the Rebel shots, and they then began to withdraw. The firing at this part of the battle lasted from 2 until 5 P.M.

The men of the 20th Indiana, with others, worked faithfully in assisting the wounded beyond fire and to the shore, and in firing from shore on the enemy.

Other events were occurring on a different part of the field. When the *Merrimac* made her appearance, the vessels at Fortress Monroe were gotten ready for action. The *Minnesota*, *Roanoke* and *St. Lawrence* got under way and proceeded toward the scene of the battle. They followed each other by the North Channel, and the *Minnesota*, arriving at the place for turning into the James River at Newport News Point, grounded hard and fast. The *St. Lawrence* grounded not far away and so did the *Roanoke*. None of those vessels got out far enough to enter battle.

The *Merrimac*, on leaving the *Congress*, gave her attention to the *Minnesota*'s 50 guns and gave and received several shots, but it was now having become dark and the Rebel vessels all withdrew to Sewell's Point and to Norfolk.

The losses of the day were: on the *Cumberland*, 121 killed or wounded; on the *Congress* 100 killed, 26 wounded and 20 prisoners; on the *Minnesota* 3 killed, 16 wounded; 286 in all. The Confederates lost 6 killed and 20 wounded.

We went to our tents worn out with excitement, as it was our first experience of the horrible sights of war. While the terrible and bloody incidents of the day could not be forgotten, the sublimity of the scene was indelibly impressed on our minds. At times during the day all about Hampton Roads, we heard the roar of artillery and saw white clouds of smoke from the batteries. No picture could be more imposing and impressive.

Night came upon the scene with a pale moon. Its silvery light seemed paler in light of the burning *Congress*. She burned slowly, and for hours the flames seemed to be playing with the huge vessel whose hull stood forth so massive and black.

Now a tongue of flame would spring from her portholes and spin up the long ropes to the furled sails. A spar would fall or a sail unfurled by the fire would fall over the side on fire. Again a great tongue of flame would spring aloft as the deck burned through, or a burning mast would fall. And during all this mournful conflagration, as all the guns were shotted, the fire would ignite the charge and some gun would fire sending a ball up or down the river. So slowly and almost regularly did these explosions occur that they seemed like signals of distress or that the noble vessel was firing her own death knell.

The fire extending, our men were taken back from the shore to avoid injury when the magazines should explode. This finally occurred at about 2 o'clock in the morning when a column or fountain of burning matter appeared high in the air to be followed by the stillness of death.

All about the shores were cast bolts, nails or burning bits of timber. In our camp for a thousand men there was scarcely a tent but was riddled. The *Congress* burned to water's edge. This day's events cast a gloom over the country. At Washington the Officials were almost terrified, and we in our camps could see no gleam of hope for relief.

Within the sounds of the last guns fired on the 8th of March, the *Monitor* was coming to the rescue of her weaker sister ships. She reported at Fortress Monroe at 9 o'clock and, almost guided by the flames of the *Congress*, she passed up Hampton Roads, and at 12 o'clock Worden reported to Capt. Van Brunt commanding the *Minnesota*, which was still fast in the mud.

Worden had had no rest since leaving New York, and his crew were well nigh exhausted with their labors. They had not been able to cook on the voyage and had been compelled to work every moment after entering Chesapeake Bay to get their vessel in fighting trim. Everything as to her fighting quality was, of course, uncertain. The *Merrimac* had been tried successfully, and her crew had rested after their triumph.

Early in the morning of the 9th of March, the *Monitor* steamed up past our camp and the scene of the fighting on the 8th. She passed the resting place of the *Cumberland*'s silent crew and around the smoldering timber of the *Congress* and then back to the *Minnesota*.

I first saw her within about 400 yards, and in common with all, saw little to inspire confidence. The men at once named her the "Cheese box on a raft," and her appearance warranted the description. Almost every man in our camp of thousands went to Newport News Point to see what would next occur. Our place of observation was excellent, as we could see across the wide expanse of water to Sewell's Point to the right toward Norfolk, and to the left to Fortress Monroe. At the latter place a vast mass of shipping was collected with many foreign flags interspersed. The vessels there lined themselves seemingly across the water so as to see well up the Roads.

It was 8 o'clock. The dense clouds of black smoke up the Elizabeth River appeared again as yesterday, and the *Merrimac* with five consorts steamed out to Sewell's Point and turned as before toward the *Minnesota*.

At once the *Monitor* went out from her place beside the *Minnesota* and moved directly to meet her foe.

The day was perfect, and we almost stopped breathing in the interest in the occasion. We all seemed thrilled as we thought of Worden in the pilot box or of the boy Greene with his 16 men in the turret. Worden showed that he was as anxious to get as far from the *Minnesota* as possible, and he had not progressed very far when he was recognized by the enemy who sent a shot dancing over the water and sinking beneath the waves near her. This shot was apparently fired with such low depression that it looked as though touching the water near the muzzle of the gun, and as it danced along on its journey, it cast up a great fountain of water at each contact.

She fired again and again; still no reply from the *Monitor*. The latter vessel placed herself alongside her larger foe and at close quarters when she fired her first gun, and then the battle raged for four hours; a broadside from the *Merrimac*, with two guns from the *Monitor* in reply. The former tried to get closer to the *Minnesota*, but the *Monitor* was always ready to dance in ahead of her more unwieldy antagonist.

We watched each discharge of the guns, fearing the worst, but as the smoke raised, our little friend was still visible, and after the first interchange of shots, we breathed easier as the *Merrimac* had found an equal and the *Monitor* was no longer an experiment.

The vessels about Fort Monroe came a little nearer. The *Monitor* steamed around her foe at will, she seemed in close contact at one time, again far away. We were less than a mile from the fighting.

Genl. Mansfield, our Commanding Officer, was so deeply interested that he forgot all else. At one shot from the *Monitor*, he would exclaim, "D - d it you're firing too high," or to the *Merrimac*, "You cussed Rebel, you didn't hurt us a bit."

Worden tried to foul the propeller of the *Merrimac*, and the latter tried to ram the *Monitor*. As the latter attempt was made, Greene on the *Monitor* planted a 180 pound shot fair on the shield of his enemy. At another time both 11 inch guns on the *Monitor* were fired at once, and the shots struck against an angle of the corner and forced it all in two or three inches.

The *Monitor* was using only 15 pounds of powder, or ½ a charge, because the durability of her Dahlgren guns was not known. The Navy Department had fixed 15 pounds as the charge, and if 30 had been used, there is no reason to suppose that the *Merrimac* would not have been destroyed.

The *Merrimac* fired several times at the *Minnesota*. One shot exploded a boiler of a vessel alongside.

The ammunition for the turret of the *Monitor* growing too small in amount, she withdrew to replenish. Worden climbed out on the deck, but we thought he had lost the fight. He returned to the pilot house and renewed the battle which continued until 12 o'clock. About this time, a shot from the *Merrimac* struck the pilot house of the *Monitor* and Worden was wounded by flying splinters, & etc. He was stunned and blinded, and ordered the vessel to be sheered off. Greene took his place and again started toward the *Merrimac*, which had begun to withdraw.

After firing a few shots, the *Monitor* left for Fortress Monroe, and the *Merrimac* went into Norfolk. The *Minnesota* was thought to be lost, and preparations were made for her abandonment, but this idea was given up and she was gotten off and served for a long time. The injuries on the *Monitor* amounted to nothing except the shot which struck the pilot house.

The *Merrimac* lost 2 men killed and 19 wounded. She lost her prow, her stem was twisted, and she leaked. She lost all her boats and an anchor. The armor was damaged somewhat. The steam pipe and smokestack were riddled. The muzzles of two guns were shot away, and she needed extensive repairs. She came out in April but the *Monitor* did not meet her.

This contest of such worldwide importance seemed like the battle of the intelligent beings.

The *Merrimac* was run ashore and burned on the 11th of May 1862, and the *Monitor* foundered at sea off Hatteras on the 30th of December, 1862. Worden was promoted and was twice voted the thanks of Congress. He died October 9, 1897.

In the years which have passed, great changes have taken place about the scene of this fighting. The Union restored Norfolk, and the Navy Yards are again filled with life and activity. Newport News is becoming a great city with extensive docks, wharves and railroads, and peaceful vessels plow the waters of the James.

The dead of the victorious Army and Navy sleep beneath their flag near Fortress Monroe, cherished in death amidst their tufted mounds. At Portsmouth their foremen lie none the less tenderly cherished although above them hangs the shadow of defeat.

We each and all put the incidents of life away in a great storehouse, and as I wander through the halls of my memory, I find no picture of the past more strikingly beautiful or grandly impressive or before which I more fondly linger than my mental picture of the battle between the *Merrimac* and her foes.

COMMENTARY: *On a spring morning in March 1862, the 20th Indiana Regiment, camped at water's edge, witnessed—indeed, joined with rifle fire—the battle between the Confederate* Merrimac *and several Union ships at Hampton Roads, Virginia. Lieut. Gilbreath was fully aware of the decisive historic nature of the engagement. A discerning reporter, Gilbreath repeatedly demonstrates the eye for vivid detail that characterizes the entirety of his journal. He sets his eyewitness account of that day's fight, the night's fires and explosions, and the second day's clash between the ironclads* Merrimac *and* Monitor, *in a larger narrative derived later from historical descriptions.*

CHAPTER 5

First Brush with the Enemy

1862

I t was not until long years after the close of the War that the Government published a Record of the Rebellion and thus rendered accessible the reports of Officers on the many engagements. There was no way to know previous to the publication of these Records what such written history would show of the battles. As those of us who participated in the War for the Union look over this collection of reports and correspondence, we are impressed with the great deficiency there is in these papers.

The reports from the Headquarters of the 20th Indiana as published are distressingly meager as to very many important, and in fact, most all the events in which we took part. It is hence a very difficult task to compile a history of the Regiment.

Of the events related in the foregoing pages, there is not one word published as coming from the Head of the Regiment. Not one word is given to show that we occupied any place at Hatteras or that our men gallantly covered the hillside on the banks of the James and participated in the contest of the ironclads.

The Rebel Genl. Magruder, stationed at Yorktown, came to within one mile of Newport News during the fighting of the *Merrimac* and her foes, and a position of the 20th Indiana on picket opposed him. There was no battle or firing to amount to anything, still, there is no mention of our having had that service.

The 20th Indiana remained in camp at Newport News until the 19th of May, 1862, when it was taken to Fortress Monroe by steamer and transferred to the land at Willoughby's Bay, which was directly across the water from Fortress Monroe. The object was to march into Norfolk from the Bay.

Genl. McClellan's army was being transferred to the Peninsula, and the Rebels decided to evacuate Norfolk. Genl. Wool was in command, and had about 5000 troops. As we marched toward Norfolk at the crossing of Tanners Creek, we encountered a Rebel battery which fired a few shots, destroyed the bridge, and left hurriedly for Norfolk.

We marched into Norfolk on the 10th day of May, 1862, crossed the Elizabeth River, and camped first in the grounds of the Marine Hospital at Portsmouth. Later we camped on the outskirts of Portsmouth and in the old Rebel Camp where, to our surprise, we found some of our tentage standing which we left at the camp at Chickamicomico.

We had little to do at Portsmouth, but after the Battle of Seven Pines, the 20th Indiana with several other Regiments was sent to the Army of the Potomac in front of Richmond. We left Norfolk by boat and steamed up the York and Pamunkey Rivers to White House Landing, from which place we went by railroad to the camps of the Army of the Potomac about six miles from Richmond. We were 999 in number in the Regiment on joining that Army. The 20th Indiana was assigned to Robinson's Brigade (1st), Kearney's Division (3rd) of the 3rd Corps, which was commanded by Genl. Heintzelman.

As we marched to our camps from the railroad, we passed over the ground on which the Battle of Seven Pines had been fought and saw many of the bodies of the slain. We began at once the regular work of soldiers in the performance of all sorts of rough duties: picket, guard duty and drill occupied our time fully.

The Brigade was made up of the 87th New York Volunteers and the 57th, 63rd and 105th Pennsylvania Regiments. The 3rd Division had been under the command of Brig. Genl. Philip Kearney since April 30, 1862, and the strength of the Division on the 20th of June 1862 was 13,051 total, with 8323 for duty present.

Our newfound comrades were veterans of the Peninsula, and when we joined them, they had but just completed the experience of the Battle of Fair Oaks or Seven Pines, May 30th and June 1st, 1862. The loss of the Brigade in that battle was 419, while the Division lost 1091 men.

Genl. Phil. Kearney was an Officer of extensive experience. He lost an arm in a cavalry charge during the Mexican war. He went to France and there raised, equipped, and armed, at his own expense, a troop of Cavalry for service in Algiers. He resigned from the French Army on the breaking out of the Civil War, and made a gallant Officer.

With battle-tried comrades and a brave leader, the spirit of emulation, pride and ambition to be good as the best was awakened within us, and it never died.

At the time of the battle of Fair Oaks or Seven Pines, May 30th 1862, Genl. Philip Kearney found that the Officers and men of his Division were dressed alike on account of everyone's being compelled to get clothing from the Quarter Master's Department. To distinguish them, he directed by order that the Field and Staff Officers should wear a red patch on top of the caps, and the line Officers the same in front.

After Kearney's death, his successor in the command of the First Division, 3rd Corps., Genl. Birney, ordered this habit to be continued in memory of Kearney and, also for the same purpose, that the rank and file should wear a red patch on the side of their caps. This custom was continued, except that all placed the lozenge shaped red patch on top of their caps. The Officers and men of Kearney's Division were thus easily distinguishable at a glance.

The idea took throughout the Army, and each Corps adopted a badge of a different shape from the rest. The 1st Division in each Corps had a red patch, the 2nd white, and the 3rd blue. The 3rd Corps always wore the lozenge; the First Corps a disc; the 2nd a trefoil; the 5th Corps a Maltese cross; the 6th a plain cross; the 11th a crescent; and the 12th a star.

When Genl. Joe Hooker was placed in Command of the Army, he ordered the seven Corps of the Army of the Potomac to be distinguished by a badge as above. This system extended to other armies, and every survivor of the war cherishes his army badge with fondness to this day

We were camped in or near Malarious Swamps and were troubled with much sickness arising from the locality. Roads and, in fact, the whole country were in a terrible condition, and the work of supplying the men was a great labor. We saw one bale of hay making the load for a six-mule team.

Our first camp was between the Richmond and York River Railroad and the Williamsburg Road. The entire Regiment was on picket on the

18th and 19th of June, 1862. Capt. Bell, with Company B, occupied the left post of our Regimental line of pickets. At 4:30 o'clock in the morning, some 300 Rebel Infantry and Cavalry attacked Bell very suddenly, but Bell proved himself a thorough soldier and speedily repulsed the enemy. Capt. Bell's Company B was supported by Capt. Dick of Company D and by Lieut. Andrews commanding 50 sharp shooters selected from the Regiment.

The last shot fired by the Rebels, as they were driven off, mortally wounded Pvt. Grant of Company F from Logansport, Indiana. As the Rebels were driven off on the left of the Regiment, they moved along the picket toward the right and came unexpectedly on an advance picket post commanded by 2nd Lieut. W. I. Carr of Company I. Both parties fired at once, and Lieut. Carr was shot through the hand while Pvt. John Smith of Company I was shot through the muscles of his right arm. This was the same Smith of Company I to whom reference has been made as being deficient in the loss of the index finger of his right hand at the time of the Muster in of the Regiment.

Lieut. Carr's capture was prevented by the prompt action of Capt. Rayburn with Company A and Lieut. Logan with Company F. These Companies fired a few rounds when the enemy retreated. Their loss is not known.

In this action Capt. Dick, Company D and Lieut. Andrew left the Camp of the reserve at 3 o'clock A.M. and passed over the same ground occupied by the Rebels in attacking at 4:30 on the left, and they returned to reserve camp just as the attack begun.

The 20th Indiana had good reason to be proud of the results of their first brush with the enemy in the Army of the Potomac. Pvt. Grant, Lieut. Carr and Pvt. Smith shed first blood for us. Following them came a crimson flood which 768 men of the Regiment helped to fill from the 19th of June, 1862, to June 23rd 1864; the average was more than one man either killed or wounded for each and every day of our service.

On the 25th day of June 1862, six days after our first skirmish as above described, we were again engaged with the enemy, this time more seriously.

It is necessary to give a short explanation of the situation of the Army of the Potomac on the 24th of June 1862, as such important movements and events followed that day. Genl. McClellan had taken the Army of the Potomac from about Manassas Junction and Washington to Fortress Monroe, Yorktown and up the Peninsula to within about six miles of Richmond. The army was supplied by the way of the York and Pamunkey Rivers, and from the White House Landing to their camps, about 20 miles, by railroad. Trains of cars were run across the Chickahominy at Savage Station and to Fair Oaks closer to Richmond.

The army at the time we joined it occupied a position extending from White Oak Swamps on the south side of Chickahominy to a point about Mechanicsville and Cold Harbor on the north. That portion of the army between White Oak Swamps and the Chickahominy was attacked at Fair Oaks or Seven Pines by the Rebel Army on the 30th and 31st of May and lost many guns and large quantities of supplies. Amongst the latter were some 200 barrels of whiskey as this was at that time a part of the regular ration of soldiers.

After a great effort, our forces held onto or recaptured the line of defenses which they occupied before the 30th day May, but in the reestablishment of this line, the Union picket line was not advanced as far as it should have been previous to the battle, and was very close to the line of the battle, or entrenchments. This was in consequence of the difficult character of the Swamp and the dense undergrowth.

Our pickets being so near to the camps necessitated keeping troops more on the alert than would have been necessary had they been out the usual distance, thus depriving them of much needed rest. Every effort to extend the pickets was strongly opposed by the Rebels in the most determined manner, causing daily losses to both sides.

On the 25th of June an advance of our picket line was ordered, preparatory to a general forward movement. Immediately in front of the most advanced redoubt on the Williamsburg Road was a large open field, beyond that a swampy belt of timber some 500 yards wide which had been disputed ground for many days. Farther in advance was an open field, and the railroad commanded by a redoubt and rifle pits of the enemy.

It was ordered that we push our lines to the other side of the woods in order to enable us to ascertain the nature of the ground and to place Genls. Heintzelman and Sumner in position to support a general attack. This advance was to begin at 8 A.M., June 25th.

At this hour, the three divisions were formed in position for the advance, and it began—Hooker's division on the right and Kearney's, in which our Regiment was, on the left. The hardest fighting was opposite Genl. Hooker's Division which was on both sides of the Williamsburg Road. Still, he pushed them slowly backward for half a mile and beyond three of their picket camps, while on our front, we forced them a mile farther away from our camps. Genl. McClellan telegraphed to stop the advance and finally came upon the field himself at 1 P.M., when seeing the situation, ordered the advance to be continued.

Genl. Heintzelman, commanding the 3rd Corps, brought up two guns under Capt. G. A. DeRussey and shelled the Rebels out of their camps across an open field and to the woods beyond. Measures were now taken on all our fronts to establish a picket line. While this was being done, at about 5:30 P.M. the enemy made a sudden attack on the right of Robinson's Brigade. A portion of the line, the 87th of New York, gave away. This occurred just as the 20th Indiana had been ordered to charge across an open piece of ground to drive away a line of the enemy advancing, and with the enemy rushing into the opening left by the 87th New York, we were flanked on our charge. The firing was very heavy, and the 20th Indiana suffered severely. Our loss being 11 men killed, 3 Officers and 79 men wounded, and 32 captured, or 125 all told. We were thus compelled to give away, and fell back in great confusion a short distance in rear of the intended line of pickets. The Regiment was soon rallied on its Colors, and again advanced to the attack. Our line was reestablished, and on it we three times repulsed the attacks of the enemy.

The total loss in the 3rd Corps in this battle was 626 of which 67 were killed. It will thus be seen that the 20th Indiana casualties amounted to one fifth of all the loss in the Corps of 31 Regiments of Infantry and 2 Batteries of Artillery having been engaged. The Confederates had 14 Regiments engaged and reported a loss of 441.

We halted and laid on our arms during the entire night of the 25th of June within 400 yards of the field on which we had been flanked and had suffered such a loss. It was our first battle; 100 of our comrades lay on the field either dead or wounded.

Col. Brown of the 20th Indiana sent a flag of truce at dark to ask to be allowed to relieve our wounded, but the Confederates refused to give such permission, and their pickets controlled the field. Who can depict the horrors of that night to us, untried by loss of comrades in battle? All night long we were compelled to listen to the heartrending cries and groans of our friends. The mournful wail of suffering comrades was unbroken during the long dismal night. Amongst those wounded and left on the field was Capt. James W. Lytle of Company I. During the night some of the members of Company I crawled out through the darkness and brought him within our lines. He was sent to Washington where he died on the 20th of August following. As I had known Capt. Lytle for a long time and he had been a friend of our family for years, his loss was a very great one to me personally. He was a man of education, a Civil Engineer by profession, and had many of the instincts of a soldier to a great degree. He was brave to a fault and died as he lived, a Christian gentleman.

I regret that I cannot give the names of each and every one of our men killed or wounded, but it is impossible to do so now.

In this battle Capt. N. A. Miles, afterwards Maj. Genl. U.S.A., Commanding the Army, greatly distinguished himself.

The 20th Indiana was highly praised for its action.

Genl. Heintzelman, Commanding the Corps, says, "The 20th Indiana distinguished itself and bore the brunt of the attack." Genl. Robinson reported the gallantry of the Regiment, and Col. W. L. Brown was especially commended for his good conduct and efficient service.

On the morning of the 29th of June we returned to our camp within the line of works.

COMMENTARY: *The 20th Indiana was sent in June to join the Army of the Potomac and then settled into a line just six miles from Richmond. With McClellan's army threatening the Confederate capital, Genl. Lee realized the city could not withstand a siege and that he must attack McClellan.*

Genl. Jackson's three divisions were to join Lee's planned attack on Genl. Porter's corps. A week of sharp skirmishing preceded the Seven Days Campaign. The 20th Indiana was assigned to Genl. Heintzelman's III Corps, which led the Union attack on June 25, and in the 20th's first real battle, the regiment took significant casualties.

CHAPTER 6

SEVEN DAYS FIGHTING

1862

The Army of the Potomac was composed, on the 24th of June, of 105,000 men, while it was opposed by 90,000 Confederate, including Jackson's Command.

Genl. McClellan had been compelled to occupy 16 days in marching 52 miles from Williamsburg to Chickahominy. He had fought the battle of Fair Oaks or Seven Pines; had there lost 5031 men, and had inflicted a loss on the Rebels of 6134. We had fought the fight at Oak Grove and, at its close on the 25th of June, were lying within four miles of Richmond.

The Army of the Potomac had been astride the sluggish Chickahominy, imbedded in its pestilential swamps for 39 days. Genl. McClellan says that he had decided that on the 26th day of June, 1862, he would make a general attack on the army opposing him.

Genl. Fitz-John Porter with the 5th Corps was the only Command on the north side of the river. On the 24th of June, Genl. McCellan was informed of the approach of Stonewall Jackson of the Confederate Army from the Shenandoah Valley where he had been operating. While McClellan was observing our fight at Oak Grove on the 25th, he was called to his extreme right by the intelligence of Jackson's nearness. This, he says, took his attention off of the proposed advance and to his communication and depot of supply. He remained at the right. Genl. D. H. Hill attacked the advance force of the Union Army at Mechanicsville on June 26th, and on the 27th the Confederate Army attacked Porter and defeated him. The 5th Corps was withdrawn to the south side of Chickahominy and the concentrated army consisted of the 2nd Corps, Sumner; 3rd Corps, Heintzelman; 4th Corps, Keyes; 5th Corps, Porter; and 6th Corps, Franklin.

Genl. McClellan decided on the 27th of June to withdraw his army to the James River. He had always wanted to advance toward Richmond by the way of the James River and was withheld from so doing by orders from Washington and the hope that McDowell would be sent with the 1st Corps to join him from Fredericksburg. So that now, when disaster came upon the right of his army, he turned gladly toward the James River. He sent off his Cavalry sometime before on the 19th of June, and they found at the James River several supply boats which Genl. McClellan had caused to be sent up the James River, loaded with supplies, on the 13th of June.

By noon on the 28th of June, Keyes' Corps had crossed White Oak Swamp and taken position toward Richmond to cover the the crossings of our immense trains. On the same day the Confederates began an attack on Franklin and Sumner about the Golding Farm, and were repulsed.

We of the 3rd Corps still occupied the advance position we had taken on the 25th of June beyond the upper portion of White Oak Swamp.

On the 29th at 6 A.M., we were moved back across the head of the Swamp and within the old line of works, and still beyond there to a line back of Savage Station. In withdrawing from our front line to the line of breastworks, we were followed cautiously by the Rebel skirmishers, who took possession of our camps as fast as we vacated them, as they did also of the line of breastworks. We remained here at Savage's and were witnesses to the attack on Genl. Sumner at Savage Station. Great quantities of stores had been placed there, and there were very extensive Hospitals established. We saw the stores destroyed, fire was set to the immense piles of rations and stores, and great clouds of smoke filled the atmosphere.

About 4 P.M. of the 29th the Corps was ordered to retire across White Oak Swamp. The 20th Indiana was directed to remain in the works at Savage's with Battery G, 2nd U.S. Artillery, Capt. Thompson.

The Regiment remained in those works until dark and until our troops on the right had all withdrawn. Twice the enemy approached us and were driven back. Genl. Kearney reported that Col. Brown, 20th Indiana Volunteers, greatly distinguished himself. The Regiment lost several killed and wounded, and the enemy shelled the works. This Regiment and Thompson's Battery formed the rear guard and maintained their position until dark to prevent the enemy from hurrying the rest of the Corps. After dark we withdrew following the battery, and we crossed the Swamp at White Oak Bridge and arrived on the new line at Charles City Cross Roads about 12 o'clock midnight of the 29th. The fords above this bridge were in the hands of the enemy.

We had thus marched from our camps at Oak Grove to the breastworks in the rear of Savage Station and thence to Charles City Cross Roads, a total distance of about 12 miles. The members of the Regiment had been moving from 6 A.M. to 12 at midnight on limited rations. They had maintained a cheerful front amidst the trying movements indicating that the Army was defeated and retreating. They had been attacked at Savage Station and had marched at night to cross the White Oak Swamp. There were a few stragglers, but as a whole, the men maintained a cheerful front.

Charles City Cross Roads, or Glendale, is about 2½ miles from White Oak Swamp Bridge. It was the place at which several roads south of White Oak Swamp crossed, and its possession secured our march to the

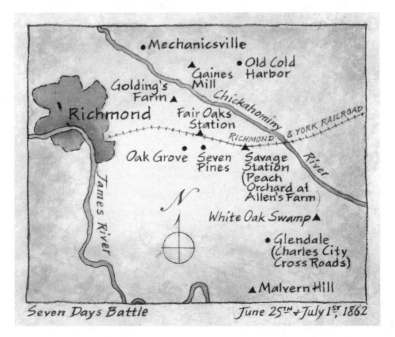

James. If the enemy got possession of this road, our trains and the march of our army would be cut off.

The Confederates had appreciated the importance of the position as it would enable them to pen us up, and they had sent Genl. Holmes to Malvern Hill and Genl. Huger to the fords of White Swamp, but Genl. Holmes was deaf and Huger was slow so they accomplished nothing before we got Keyes' 4th Corps across White Oak Swamp at daylight on the 28th of June.

At Glendale, our Brigade occupied the extreme left of the 1st Division and was joined by McCall's Division of the 5th Corps, and on the left of McCall was Hooker's Division of the 3rd Corps.

The attack began at 2:30 P.M. when Longstreet assailed McCall, broke up his Division, and captured him. Longstreet was attacked on the flank by Hooker and forced back, and then at 4 P.M. the attack began on us of Kearney's Division. It continued for five hours and a half. Genl. Kearney says the attack was with such vigor and in such masses as he had never seen. About to lose his guns by a Rebel charge, Genl. Kearney, having but one arm, took his bridle reins in his teeth and seized the Colors of the 63rd Penn. Volunteers, charged with that Regiment, the 37th New York, and the 20th Indiana broke the Rebel line and saved his artillery. For this act, Kearney was made Major General on the 6th of July 1862.

The Confederates charged three times and were each time driven off, but the firing was continuous until 9:30 P.M. Two Companies of the 20th Indiana were deployed in the woods in front and were suddenly assaulted, being driven in haste. We lost one Officer, 1st Lieut. Andrew of Company E, killed; Capt. Alfred Reed of Company K, captured, and 34 enlisted men. Col. Brown had directed that the men construct a breastwork of logs and rails, and this saved many lives. He reported that "The Regiment behaved with great coolness," the men engaged jesting, cracking jokes, loading and firing deliberately as if at target. We were joined by the 2nd Michigan, and maintained our position until the firing ceased.

Glendale was the hardest fought battle of the seven days.

It was after 12 o'clock midnight when we were ordered to move to a new position at Malvern Hill. This move was effected quietly and rapidly, and by dawn of July 1st, we were again in position to receive the attack of the enemy.

The battle of Malvern Hill began about noon, and we were under fire of Artillery and lost more or less from the Division, although we ourselves were not engaged. Our total loss was 13.

It was at midnight again that we were called upon to move in retreat, and tired as all were, the march was executed with much regularity and we arrived at Harrison's Landing at 10 A.M., July 2nd, 1862.

To recapitulate the seven days battles were as follows:

Oak Grove	June 25th	Regiment lost	126
Mechanicsville	June 26th	"	
Gaines Mill	June 27th		
Golding's Farm	June 28th		
Peach Orchard	June 29th	"	15
Glendale	June 30th	"	34
Malvern Hill	July 1st	"	13

The total losses were:

Union forces:	**Confederate forces:**
1734 killed	3823 killed
8062 wounded	15,909 wounded
6053 missing	980 missing
15,849 total	20,712 total

The great numbers missing were of men left on picket or lost in the night marches, having lost the roads, etc. Many of those counted as missing were only stragglers. The column of stragglers was one of the sights to see to last one's lifetime. There were thousands of men tramping the road in an immense column without any organization or any form of regularity. Every man in the column was his own master. There were field Officers, Captains and Lieutenants, and all classes of enlisted men, wagons, ambulances, caissons, and cattle, all hurrying on to the river. Tired, they would stop to rest until a distant boom of artillery warned them, and again they hurried on. This column was interspersed with the slightly wounded.

All in all it was a mass once seen never to be forgotten.

The whole of the seven days fighting was a contest by Division Commanders more independent of higher Officers than many of the battles of the war. Especially was this the case at Charles City Cross Roads. This battle was called by various names in accordance with the location occupied by various bodies of troops as: White Oak Swamp, Nelson's Farm, Frazier's Farm, Willis Church, New Market Roads, Quaker's Road, Charles City Cross Roads, and Glendale.

The line of battle was about six miles long, and troops fought as in this order: Franklin's 6th Corps opposite White Oak Swamp Bridge, next Smith's Division, Richardson, Slocum, Kearney, McCall, Hooker, Porter, and Keyes. The main fighting fell on Slocum, Kearney, McCall and Hooker as they occupied the ground extending from the right of the Charles City Cross Roads to the left about 3½ miles.

Everything was at stake at this battle, as a break would have lost much of the large train and caused no end of damage. The fight was won by the skill of the Officers and the bravery of the men, and their task was not a small one.

The wheeled carriages and the train belonging to the army if stretched out in one line would have extended not far from 40 miles. A Southern writer says that "with consummate skill McClellan's Army was withdrawn. He had crossed his vast train of 5,000 wagons and his immense parks of Artillery safely over White Oak Swamp, and then was more exposed than any time on his flank march. Escape seemed impossible for him but he did escape, and at the same time inflicted severe damage on his pursuers. His army was attacked by three columns, yet their attack as an obstruction amounted to nothing."

It is hardly possible to fully imagine the feeling of almost every officer and man in the Army of the Potomac on our arrival at Harrison's Landing. The nervous excitement of being under fire every day for a week, of marching every night only to receive the fire of the enemy during the day and often without being able to return it, caused great exhaustion or prostration so that the relief of a quiet camp was fully appreciated by all.

Harrison's Landing was the home of William Henry Harrison, President, and it was a lovely spot. It was 19 miles from Richmond, 25 miles from Williamsburg, 37 miles from Yorktown, 57 miles by land from

Fort Monroe. It was 20 miles from Mechanicsville where the extreme right of the Army had been.

At the time of the fighting of the Charles City Cross Roads, Genl. Mc-Clellan was on the ironclad *Galena*, so that there was no directing head, and the different Corps Commanders withdrew their Commands at such time as they saw fit.

After the fighting on the night of the 30th of June, many of the Corps and Division Generals collected at Genl. Heintzelman's Headquarters at Willis Church and had a sort of an informal Council of War as to the better way to maintain the morale and spirit of their men as well as to know what was best to do next. Each General gave his opinion and discussed Genl. McClellan's action in leaving his army.

Genl. Heintzelman expressed the opinion that if Genl. McClellan did not return from the boat, he could not hold himself responsible for the effect of the 3rd Corps. Maj. Genl. Kearney is said to have made a speech in which he said, "I, Phil Kearney, who am an old soldier and a member of the Legion of Honor of France, do say (and I am personally responsible for what I say) that George B. McClellan is either a traitor or a coward."

The feeling in the Army was intense against McClellan when it became known, as it soon did, that he had left us to our fate, or rather the care of our own Generals.

COMMENTARY: *In repeated attacks over seven days, Genl. Lee's forces drove Genl. McClellan's larger Army of the Potomac away from Richmond. McClellan had planned a major assault on the Confederate lines for June 26, but his initial attack by III Corps was stopped. McClellan decided to move his base back to the James River. Lee, though still without the support of the tardy Genl. Jackson, continued to attack the retreating Union army over several days—though Confederate attacks were confused, poorly organized and costly. McClellan's withdrawal was dubbed the "Great Skedaddle." Lee's final attempt to sever the Union line at Malvern Hill failed, broken by Union artillery in a 5000-casualty slaughter.*

After hard fighting on both sides, Lee secured a strategic victory in saving Richmond, while McClellan remained in a position to attack Richmond from the James River, until President Lincoln ordered the Union Army's withdrawal.

CHAPTER 7

POPE & MCCLELLAN

1862

At Harrison's Landing we had Picket Duty Drills and inspections. On the occasion of an inspection, Genl. Heintzelman came to our camp along the line of breastworks and very carefully inspected each man. He told one of the men to open his blouse. The man did so, and disclosed a well worn, even ragged made shirt. The General looked at it, and seeing how clean the old shirt was, said, "That's right, that's right, we can have clean shirts if we cannot have new ones." The General had lost his palate, so that all he said sounded peculiarly and very droll.

The men came back to the Regiment slowly from Hospitals and from simple straggling, and the Corps was soon in good shape again. The spirit of the men of the 20th Indiana never sank, and they were always cheerful.

It was decided in Washington that the Army of the Potomac should be moved from the Peninsula, and orders were sent to Genl. McClellan on the 3rd of August to withdraw the Army. He did not like the idea of the change, and so protested and argued with Genl. Halleck about it and succeeded in delaying the move until the 14th of August. The idea was to place the Army of the Potomac along the Rappahannock and in front of Washington where Genl. John Pope was in command, his army being called the Army of Virginia. The Army of the Potomac was to act under or with Pope.

On the 17th of August, everything was removed from Harrison's Landing and the place was abandoned. We had been in camp there 45 days.

The 20th Indiana, with the rest of the 3rd Corps, marched by way of Jones Bridge across the Chickahominy, and thence across the Diascund

Creek and to Williamsburg and Yorktown, 59 miles. It was a most delightful march as we passed over roads and through a country which had been undisturbed by the movements of the armies. We were away off to the left of the Army on the march, as the other Corps crossed the Chickahominy lower down and closer to the James River. The enormous train of wagons, & etc. crossed the Chickahominy at Barrett's Ferry, and on the 17th of August, all the Army was north of the Chickahominy.

We camped on the first day's march on the 15th of August across that stream at Jones Bridge, at Brahardsville on the 16th, at Williamsburg on the 17th, and we arrived at Yorktown on the 18th of August. On the 20th, we went on ship board and sailed on the 21st of August for the Potomac. The other Corps of the Army were embarked at Yorktown, Newport News and Fortress Monroe.

It had been the intention to disembark the 3rd Corps at Aquia Creek, but the order was changed so that we went to Alexandria where we were placed on board the cars and carried by rail to Warrenton Junction, where Kearney's Division, 3000 men, arrived at 12:20 P.M., August 22nd.

There was now great confusion, as the intention had been to have Pope, commanding the Army of Virginia, and McClellan, commanding the Army of the Potomac, act in conjunction under the orders of Genl. Halleck. But the delays caused by McClellan and his sympathizers changed the plan so that Halleck was compelled to remain in Washington. Parts of the Army of the Potomac were placed under the orders of Pope as they arrived on the field of the campaign in front of Washington. As the campaign progressed, the Officers of the Army of the Potomac showed readily where personal preferences overcame their patriotism. Many not only gave no more support to Pope than they were compelled to, but actually threw every obstacle they could in the way of his success.

The worst foe that Pope had to encounter, in fact, was McClellan and his henchmen. This was especially noticeable in the fact that not one of the strong supporters of McClellan gave Pope any willing assistance. The only troops of the Army of the Potomac to join Pope and to act under his orders were the 5th Corps, Porter; the 3rd Corps, Heintzelman; and Reynolds's Division of the 2nd Corps. Pope reports that only 20,000 men of the Army of the Potomac were in position to pull trigger out of all its 90,000 men.

The Corps of Sumner, Franklin, Keyes and Burnside never came upon the field of action at all except Reno's Division of Burnside's Corps.

McClellan was repeatedly ordered by Halleck acting for the President to send forward Franklin and others from Alexandria to Pope, but he did not do it, and left Pope to shift for himself.

The demoralization of Officers was intense on account of having to serve under Pope instead of McClellan, and their every act and word seemed to be intended to break down the spirit of the men. In consequence of this feeling amongst ranking Officers, straggling was very great indeed, and effective strength was reduced in consequence.

The 3rd Corps Officer did not share in the feeling of dislike for Pope, but loyally supported him, and Heintzelman, Hooker and Kearney all did their best to help him obtain a victory. Pope's plans were good, but he was hampered by McClellan and was defeated.

As we of Kearney's Division went out on the railroad, we passed Catletts Station where, on the 22nd of August, Stewart of the Rebel Army had made an attack and captured some of Genl. Pope's trains, papers, & etc.

After halting at Warrenton Junction on the 23rd, we were pushed forward day by day toward the Rappahannock until, on the 26th of August, our Regimental pickets were along the banks of the stream.

COMMENTARY: *Maj. Genl. Henry W. Halleck was promoted to general-in-chief of the Union army in July, 1862. On August 3, he ordered Genl. McClellan to withdraw from his James River position on the Peninsula and move north of the Rappahannock River to reinforce John Pope's Army of Virginia in defending Washington, D.C. McClellan's opposition to this move, his arguments against Halleck and his delays in deploying his forces bordered on insubordination. Many of McClellan's loyal Corps and Division commanders also failed to join or support Pope, who was engaging Confederate divisions under Generals Jackson and A.P. Hill.*

By mid-August, it was clear that Pope meant to launch a major offensive. He was joined by several of McClellan's Corps, including III Corps, but Lee's army moved aggressively in the Cedar Run/Gordonsville area, compelling Pope to pull back to the Rappahannock and await reinforcement by McClellan—setting the stage for the major second battle of Bull Run.

CHAPTER 8

Second Battle of Bull Run

1862

The 20th Indiana arrived at the Rappahannock River on the 25th of August, and were placed on picket along that stream. The picket posts were close to the river, while the supports occupied higher points in the rear or away from the stream.

I commanded Company I, having been promoted to be Captain of it on the 20th of August on account of the death of Captain James W. Lytle by reason of his wounds received on the 25th of June.

The Company was on the picket line all day of the 26th of August, and its position was at Rappahannock Station where the railroad bridge crossed the river. There had been some buildings at the place, and a mill had been erected on the right side of the track looking south. Behind the mill was a high hill of about 75 feet, and several large rocks were scattered about on top of the hill. At these rocks I was stationed with all my Company not on picket post. The 4th Maine Volunteers occupied the line to the left of the railroad.

From my elevated position, I could see far across the river. About ¾ of a mile away were some high hills, and during the day several of our men were sent to the hills for observation. The river was fordable at several places on my front, as the water was low.

The army occupied the line of the Rappahannock from its mouth to the Blue Ridge. Burnside and Porter of the 9th & 5th Corps were below us, as they had landed at Aquia Creek, while McDowell and Sigel were off toward our right. The whole line fronted south while the Orange and Alexandria Railroad stretched back from our position to Washington and Alexandria. These cities were exactly behind us, and, of course, we had no feeling of insecurity in that direction.

The 26th of August passed in a sort of a restful way, and the duties of the night began. Officers visited the Sentinels frequently, and after my tour, I had put out my blankets on a big rock for a rest when I was aroused by the firing of cannon in the direction of Washington, or directly on our line of communication. Soon a Staff Officer came and ordered us all to abandon our posts and join the Brigade. We hurried off about 4:00 A.M. and, following along the railroad, overtook the Brigade near Bristol Station.

The cause of our change of front was that the Confederates under Jackson had passed around our right through Thoroughfare Gap and had taken possession of the Railroad at Bristol Station at about 8:00 P.M. He then sent a force under J. E. B. Stuart to Manassas Junction, seven miles from Bristol. This force attacked Manassas about 12:00 o'clock at night and took the place. On the morning of the 27th of August, Jackson had all his men united at Manassas and held the place with 25,000 men. He captured large quantities of stores and material of all kinds, several guns and a good many prisoners. Jackson was able to do this because of the fact that Pope relied upon troops from Genl. McClellan's forces to be at Manassas Junction for its protection. He had ordered a Division to be halted there.

Hooker of the 3rd Corps attacked Ewell of Jackson's Corps at Bristol Station in the afternoon of the 27th of August and drove him off the field toward Manassas.

Kearney's Division, in which the 20th Indiana was placed in the advance on the 28th of August at 8:00 A.M., pushed forward toward Manassas Junction. The Division was formed in three columns of attack with skirmishers between, and the 20th formed a skirmish line between the two columns on the right of the line. The day was awfully hot, and we advanced slowly through the woods. We met with no opposition and marched into Manassas Junction at about 12:00 o'clock noon. We were surprised to see that we were preceded by our stragglers. It was quite laughable, notwithstanding we were so tired.

We had advanced in due military form, with every movement expecting to hear hostile shots to announce that we had come in contact with the enemy when, as we advanced from the woods toward the smoking ruins, we saw our blue coated stragglers helping themselves to the eatables left scattered about. We were only a few minutes behind the last of Jackson's column as it evacuated the Junction and less than an hour after he had himself gone. The scene of destruction at the Junction was extensive. Thousands of packages of all kinds were broken open, trains of cars were on fire, and every sort of goods one could imagine as used by an army was to be seen about over the plains.

Jackson moved toward Centerville, and our Division followed him. We camped near the town that night, and on the morning of the 29th of August, we were moved by way of Stone Bridge to a position opposing Jackson on about the same ground as that on which the battle of Bull Run of the year before had been fought.

The position of the Union and Confederate Armies was reversed from that in the first battle. As when we faced east then, we now fought facing the west in the second battle.

Kearney's Division drove Jackson's rear guard out of Centerville and followed them to Bull Run on the evening of the 28th, and during that night we were ordered to push closely after the retreating enemy. We pushed forward on the morning of the 29th and joined on the right of Genl. Sigel, who had been fighting since daylight, at about the hour of 10:00 o'clock. The field of battle was about a mile from Stone Bridge over which we had crossed Bull Run. The Rebel line was formed along the line of an unfinished railroad, the fills and cuts of which served a fine purpose for a sort of a breastwork.

Genl. Kearney placed us in such a position as to make the 20th Indiana the extreme right of the Division and of the Army. This position relieved us from the hottest of the fighting which fell upon our comrades of the 3rd Michigan, [and] 63rd and 105th Penn. of our Brigade. All of the Regiments lost more men than we did, but not a much greater percentage. Next to Kearney's Division on our left was Genl. I. Stevens of the 9th Corps with his Division. Then came Genl. Hooker with the 2nd Division of our 3rd Corps.

After forming our line, we advanced and drove the enemy back about 1½ or 2 miles so that we crossed the unfinished railroad, and by a partial wheel, we halted in line on the left flank of the Rebel Army. Nearly all of our loss during the battle occurred in this advance. Lieut. Jonathan B. Harbolt was mortally wounded, and we lost three killed, and forty wounded.

The Regiment was very small at this time because of so many men being absent, sick, worn out, or straggling. Those to the left of us were driven out of the woods about 4:00 o'clock in the afternoon, and we held our place without fighting until regularly withdrawn. When Genl. Kearney saw the lines to our left disappear, he directed the 20th Indiana to change front on the left company so that we faced to the left of our former front, and our left rested on the unfinished railroad of which I have written. The men were all lying down and, as there was some undergrowth and the position was in rather heavy oak woods, we were not discovered by the Rebels.

The dense column of Johnnies passed us about 300 yards away, every man cheering or giving forth the Rebel Yell. The head of their charging mass had passed us about 600 or 700 yards, and still the crowd in front of us continued when an incident occurred to change the face of affairs.

Stray shots were flying about, and one of them, from off beyond the charging column, apparently came flying over and struck the knapsack of Peter Schwartz of Company I. It was caliber 54, so it jarred him up a good deal and made him mad. He got up on his knees, began swearing in German loudly and firing as fast as he could. The whole Regiment was on the anxious bench and at such tension that every man only needed something to start him, so that when Schwartz began to send forth his profanity and to fire, the whole Regiment arose as one man, their guns went off as for a volley, and they loaded and fired as rapidly as they could. Hit on the flank with such a fire and supposing from our Hoosier yells that there was a new army attacking them, the Rebels did not stop to fire or disturb us in any way, but withdrew as fast as they had entered the break.

A flank attack was always dreaded, and ours was one of the most effective I ever saw. We were relieved in mind, as it looked as though our little crowd was going to be captured. We did not have a man injured.

Genl. Kearney, who was with us, and Col. Brown tried hard to stop the firing, but it did not cease until there was not a Rebel in sight. Both were highly amused when told of the way that row begun, and the General remarked that we might now withdraw.

Col. Brown then moved the regiment by right of Companies to the rear, and after that we crossed the unfinished railroad. The Colonel was the first to ride up onto the old railroad bed, and he had no more than done so when he was shot through the head by a Rebel sharpshooter. He fell dead from his horse. His body was taken back to Centerville, and later home to Logansport.

Col. Brown was a remarkable man. He was highly educated, and had a fine presence and bearing. He had served as a 1st Lieutenant in the 1st Regiment Indiana Volunteers in the war with Mexico in 1846 & 1847, and had the instincts of a soldier, as shown in many ways. He was active and energetic, and received the praise of his superiors on every occasion of action. He was an unflinching patriot, and had no sympathy or patience with those who would temporize with the enemy of his country. His loss was mourned not only by his Regiment, but was highly commented on by all his superiors.

Maj. John Wheeler assumed command of the Regiment on Col. Brown's fall.

In Genl. Heintzelman's report, he criticizes Genl. Kearney for not attacking at an earlier hour, evidently not knowing the true situation as to the falling back of Regiments to our left, and the matter is not reported except by one Colonel, it probably being the intention to not give publicity to the fact. But the above is a true statement of what occurred near the 20th Indiana just before Col. Brown was killed. We were halted at the railroad embankment, and thus remained in possession of the ground won.

Genl. Kearney brought up Genl. Birney's Brigade, and putting in line the 4th Maine and the 40th and 101st New York, he advanced them against the first line of the enemy. The Rebels had drawn back their left after our unexpected fusillade so that Kearney had these regiments wheeled to the left and advanced. It was a gallant attack, and Stonewall Jackson reports that, at the time, Union volleys were fired upon his lines at ten paces and that assault after assault was made.

The 20th Indiana remained on the field all night of the 29th of August with the rest of the Division, and we occupied ground still at the unfinished railroads. It was as tired and worn out a lot of men as I have ever seen. We had marched onto the field early in the morning and had been under fire almost all the time from 10:00 o'clock A.M. to 7:00 at night, and then had a sleepy picket to perform. The regiment had little to eat and very little water.

We buried our comrades hastily.

———

AT DAYLIGHT ON SATURDAY MORNING August 30th, our Division was relieved by Pickett's Division of McDowell's Corps and was advanced to act as support for the right of our army. As such, we were placed by Genl. Kearney opposite one of the fords of Bull Run.

The ground we occupied was quite elevated, and we were in easy range of a Rebel battery station near Sudley Springs. We had a fine view off to our left for five or six miles, and could see all along our lines except as woods interfered with our vision.

We saw the lines and masses of advance on our left to the attack, we saw the dense clouds of smoke from the batteries and from the line and heard the cheering. And finally we saw from our vantage ground the flanking of our left, and about four miles of line give way, scatter and retreat in irregular crowds or singly. We saw the batteries attempt to check the foe advancing, and then wheel and off, or possibly fall prey to the Rebel hosts.

It was a wonderful and awe inspiring picture of disaster. It seemed to me that day passed in breathless anxiety. I do not remember to have eaten anything. I do not remember anything of myself, but of that field 4 miles by 3 miles, I seem to see every physical feature even now.

At the close of most all the fighting, 5:00 P.M., August 30th, seeing the enemy in full pursuit advancing, we were drawn back a mile or so to the Brown or Wier house, and a block of woods near that house. While halted at the Brown house, the broken masses passed us on all sides, and there was great excitement with some of them, others were depressed and marched with stolid indifference.

Of the excited ones, a Chaplain came back gesticulating and calling on the men to halt right there for further fighting. He called on them for the sake of their homes, parents and all they held dear to stop. No one paid any attention to him except to laugh at his earnestness.

A Rebel battery got the range of our hill, and sent a shot flying our way which killed my colored servant Zeke, and so startled the Chaplain that he bounded to the rear in more haste than any around him, and he was soon out of sight.

As darkness fell upon us, we were withdrawn a little to the rear and remained there in line of regiments until the masses of broken organizations had passed.

The Brown house was occupied by Rebels, and we were within speaking distance, and so remained until fully 10:00 o'clock. About this hour we, the Genl. Rene's and Genl. Gibbon's Commands, retired to the Stone Bridge and beyond toward Centerville. Thus we were about the last to leave that field.

While we were halted near the Brown house, we heard voices about the house, and Genl. Kearney and his Officers were greatly interested in finding out who they were. The General called his Aide-de-Camp Briscoe to him, and said, "Briscoe, I want to know if those are secessionists at that house. I order you to dash up to it hard as you can ride, and return soon as you can and tell me all you have discovered." Briscoe passed our regiment, and said, "Good-bye, boys." Away he went; in a moment, we heard shouts of halt-halt and loud swearing and language. He was captured, and we did not see him again for several months.

On the 31st of August, we were placed in position in rear of Franklin's 6th Corps to act as support, and we remained all day in the vicinity of Centerville. On the 1st of September at 3:30 P.M., we were ordered back on the Fairfax Road toward Washington.

The Corps had not proceeded far when it was ordered to go by the left flank into position to assist Genl. Reno in resisting an attack by a Rebel column from the west. We were only about one half mile from the Warrenton Pike, which was our line of retreat.

The 20th Indiana was placed in position on a high hill facing west. About 6:00 P.M., Genl. Kearney passed through the Regiment toward the front and informed us that he was going to see what he could find. He was killed on this reconnaisance, having suddenly come upon a Rebel squad or picket, being shot in trying to escape. We had no fighting at this place, which was called Chantilly.

This engagment closed the campaign. We held the battlefield until daylight on the 2nd of September, when we were ordered to proceed toward Fairfax Courthouse and thence on into the fortifications in front of Washington.

Our camp was first at Fort Lyon, near Alexandria, which we reached September 3, 1862.

The losses of the 3rd Corps from the 23rd of August to the 2nd of September were: 1st Division, Kearney's, 1029; 2nd Division, Hooker's, 1209; total 2238.

The 3rd Corps had on August 10, 1862, present 19,247 and for duty equipped 15,460. Its only losses in battle were 2238 as above.

At Fairfax Courthouse on the 2nd of September, there were but 5000 men to draw rations. This gives us a loss of 8221 men not accounted for from this Corps alone. They were those broken down by disease and fatigue, and those absent from no cause at all, as the stragglers.

As to the causes of the failure of this campaign, they arose from lack of patriotic cooperation with Genl. John Pope, commanding the forces in the field, more than from any other cause.

The grand total of the Army of the Potomac on the Peninsula on the 10th of August was: present for duty, equipped, 90,372. Of this number, only 20,500 men reached Pope or were under his control. This although all the Army of the Potomac were about Alexandria and Fredericksburg from the 25th of August.

Pope's own Army of Virginia had 45,000 effectives and he fought the campaign from August 16th to September 2nd with 65,500 men against 58,000 men in the army of his foes.

Pope reports a loss of 14,462 from August 16th to September 2nd, 1862, while the Rebels' reports show a loss of 13,922.

COMMENTARY: *The 20th Indiana fought in the thick of the Second Battle of Bull Run, from August 25 to August 31, when Generals Lee and Jackson outmaneuvered Pope. Jackson flanked Pope and destroyed his supply base at Manassas. Most of McClellan's army arrived just in time to be routed.*

FORCES ARRIVE
AT FREDERICKSBURG

1862

I mmediately following the 2nd battle of Bull Run, the Confederate Army was taken to the Shenandoah and then on a campaign of invasion to Maryland, and the battle of Antietam followed on the 17th of September and which resulted in a Union Victory.

The Army of the Potomac and the Army of Virginia and all the forces about Washington were placed under the command of Genl. McClellan and by him were moved to oppose Genl. Lee in his invasion of Maryland.

The 20th Indiana, as a part of the 3rd Corps, remained in camp on the south side of the Potomac for the reason that the Corps was so depleted by its losses as to be not available for active service so soon. It has been said before that only 5000 men were present in the Corps for rations at Fairfax Courthouse on the 3rd of September.

On the 5th of September, Genl. Hooker, who was temporarily in command of the 3rd Corps as the senior General in command of one of the Divisions, having received notice to be ready to march up the Potomac, reported to the Chief of Genl. McClellan's Staff that both Kearney's Division and his (Hooker's) own Division were in no condition to march, and from their great losses in battle, were in no condition to meet the enemy. On this account, the 3rd Corps was left in the defense of Washington to recuperate and did not take part in the Antietam Campaign.

In the 20th Indiana, Lieut. Col. John Van Volkenburg was promoted to be Colonel[, and] Maj. John Wheeler to be Lieutenant Colonel.

The Divisions of the 3rd Corps were filled up with new regiments so that on the 20th of September we had in the 3rd Corps 20,602 men. Our worn-out men, the sick and slightly wounded had returned and many other absentees also. Referring to the new regiments, their arrival created no end of curiosity on our part while, as we were regarded as veterans by their men, the curiosity was mutual.

The drilling of the 114th Pennsylvania by the bugle or tap of drum and, as skirmishers, was very interesting to us who knew nothing of such work.

On the arrival of the 141st Pennsylvania, our men gathered in crowds on the side of the way. Some of our men called out, "Say boys, what Brigade is that?" A man called back, "This is the 141st Buttermilk Regiment from Penn. by G-d." They proved good soldiers.

We had our pickets about three miles to the front on the road. In visiting the pickets one night with the Field Officer of the Day, we went to a reserve post and the Sentinel called, "Who comes there?" The reply was, "Brigade Field Officer of the Day" in solemn tones. The Sentinel fairly yelled, "My God boys, fall out! Here's that Officer of the Day again." The air became fairly filled with blankets as the reserve was sleeping around in the open air. This post had been visited only a short time before by some other Officer.

While camped on the road out from Long Bridge, we called our camp "Prescott Smith."

We heard rumors all the time that our wounded left in the houses and woods on the Bull Run battlefield were not well cared for. Fifty ambulances were sent for them under flag of truce. On the return of the Surgeons on the 10th of September, they reported the dead and wounded on the field still. It was decided to send a party out to bury the dead and to gather up the wounded. Five hundred men were sent. It will thus be seen that we had to bury the dead 17 days after the battle. We found a Rebel Cavalry and Infantry force of 500 to 600 men under Maj. Stewart who had been camped near Bristol. We went over the field from Bristol Station to Sudley Springs, and the recollection of the scenes we came in contact with on that ground seems even now, 35 years after the event, like a nightmare. No one can know what the debris of a battlefield is until he sees it. The dead men in all positions, and in every condition of decay and rottenness. The dead horses and scattered garments and equipments, broken wagons, caissons and artillery wheels, in fact, everything that an army carries with it, we saw.

The Rebels had marched away, as explained, to Maryland, and had not stopped to gather up the arms and materiel left by the Union forces. Their own and ours were not buried except some were lightly covered. As they returned from Maryland, they sent and collected these things. In completing our task, so offensive were most of the bodies that we could work only on the windward side to dig a trench into which the body was rolled. The bodies were afterward collected and buried at Arlington Cemetery.

The Rebel Officers were very cordial but would not allow us to go to their side of the battlefield at all. This visit was nauseating in many ways, but gave one a fine opportunity to study the ground once again. We buried all we could find, and returned to camp on the 23rd of September, 1862.

On the 16th of September, Genl. Stoneman, commanding the Kearney Division, was ordered to take Birney's Brigade of 6th Infantry Regiment of that Division on the north side of the Potomac to Poolsville for the purpose of guarding the fords of the Potomac from Point of Rocks to Great Falls. Other parts of this Division were sent up from time to time until, on the 13th of October, Stoneman had 10,000 men.

Sometime about the 5th of September, Genl. Hooker was placed in command of the Corps before commanded by McDowell, and Genl. Daniel E. Sickles was given Hooker's Division of the 3rd Corps. This 2nd Division did not go up the Potomac, but afterwards joined the Army of the Potomac on the Rappahannock.

On the 9th of October, the Rebel Genl. Stewart crossed the Potomac at McCoy's ford above Williamsport, for the purpose of a raid around the Army of the Potomac, encamped near Sharpsburg. This Army had remained in camp along the Potomac after the battle of Antietam waiting for supplies and reinforcements. An absurd plea for not following a defeated enemy.

Stewart caused a great deal of excitement. Robinson's Brigade, in which we were, was ordered to join Stoneman.

The 20th Indiana crossed the Potomac at Georgetown on a chain bridge and marched to Rockville where we camped in the Fair Grounds. We were alone, the rest of the brigade being in advance or behind us. On the 11th of October, we were ordered to march without delay to Poolsville to assist in heading off Stewart. The Regiment left Rockville at about 4:00 A.M., and arrived at Poolsville at about 4:00 o'clock P.M. on the 12th.

We were not halted, but marched to the Potomac and arrived there in time to see Stewart's last men go out of the water on the Virginia side. His main body had crossed at a ford above, but these flankers crossed at Conrad's Ferry. Stewart was enabled to accomplish this feat because he dressed his men in blue clothing he had captured in rear of McClellan's army, and so was passed by our forces, in many places. We had a slight combat with our cavalry near the river, but got off safely. After resting a short time, we had to go back to Poolsville for supplies. It was a weary six miles this last was, and made our total forced march about 32 miles.

The Kearney Division was camped—Robinson's Brigade at Conrad's Ferry on the 14th of October—with the rest about Poolsville. About the 17th of October, I was sent to Washington to visit the Hospitals and to bring from them all the convalescents I could get together for our Division. I spent four or five days in Washington and then started with 350 convalescents for the camp. My orders were to go by the Chesapeake and Ohio Canal to the nearest point to the camp. It was about the most restless crowd I ever took charge of. At every lock, some would get off to walk to the next lock, and while I was on the picket, I could see these men going into every house, barn and woodshed on the way. I was entirely alone with them, and neither moral suasion nor profanity had any effect on this crowd.

I got to Conrad's Ferry, but I never did know how many of my convalescents ever reached their Regiments. I guess all did, as I never heard anything more of the matter.

The Army of the Potomac began crossing at Berlin on the 26th of October, 1862, to follow the Rebel Army into Virginia. Genl. Stoneman was ordered to take our Division to Leesburg to hold the place. We forded the Potomac at Conrad's Ferry on October 27th and camped at Leesburg that day. Genl. Stoneman was given command of the 3rd Corps on the 30th of October, and Genl. Birney became commander of the Kearney Division. Capt. W. B. Rayburn, 20th Indiana, was made Provost Marshall at Leesburg by Genl. Stoneman.

The route selected by Genl. McClellan for his movement to the south was east of the Blue Ridge. He did this and began the movement 50 days after the battle of Antietam where he was victorious and after peremptory orders had been given him to move, also after a seeming decision to go up the Shenandoah and directly against the Rebel Army. The Kearney Division with the 9th Corps advanced from Leesburg to Bloomfield, Union, Piedmont, Upperville and Waterloo on the Rappahannock, where it arrived on the 6th day of November 1862.

On the 7th of November, Genl. McClellan received the order relieving him from Command of the Army of the Potomac. He went to his home, at Trenton, New Jersey, never held command again, and resigned from the Army November 8, 1864.

It is not possible to know now exactly what plan of Campaign McClellan would have carried out had he remained in command of the Army of the Potomac. He reported that he had hoped to interpose between the two wings of the Confederate Army and to fight them in detail. But he was so slow in all his movements, it is doubtful if he could have done this with such a wily and skillful foe. The chances are that he would have simply settled down on the line of the Rappahannock, or of the North Anna at most, and argued with the powers at Washington on various subjects.

Burnside took the command on the 9th day of November, 1862, and the Army was then encamped around Warrenton. It remained thus for a week or so, during which Genl. Burnside gave to the President his plan of campaign and arranged for a new base of supply. He also arranged his Army into what he regarded as a more simple organization. He divided it into three Grand Divisions called the Right Grand Division under Sumner, Left under Franklin, and the Center Grand Division under Hooker. Each of these Divisions had two Corps and their strength was as follows:

Right Grand Divison, 2nd & 9th Corps	22,736
Center Grand Division, 3rd & 5th Corps	39,984
Left Grand Division, 1st & 6th Corps	42,892
Total	105,612

There were 350 Field Guns.

The Rebel Army was composed of:

Longstreet's 1st Corps	35,806

Jackson's 2nd Corps	33,595
Total	69,401

250 Guns for Field Service.

Genl. Burnside adopted the plan of Campaign which changed his base from the Orange and Alexandria Railroad to that running from Aquia Creek to Richmond by the way of Fredericksburg, and he wished to seize the latter city by a quick movement. He would then be within 60 miles of Richmond.

The 3rd Corps and the Center Grand Division moved from about Warrenton, the last of all the troops, and camped first at Hartwood Church; moved thence on the 19th of November 1862 to a point where the railroad from Aquia Creek crossed Potomac Creek. Hartwood Church is about 16 miles from Fredericksburg, and our camp was about 8 or 9 miles back from the river opposite Fredericksburg. We camped in this place for a long time—in fact it was our home for all the winter of 1862 & 1863. It was later called Camp Pitcher, being named for Maj. Pitcher of the 4th Maine, who was killed at Fredericksburg.

Sumner's Grand Division was the first to arrive at Falmouth, opposite the city of Fredericksburg, where he encamped on the 17th of November. Burnside would not allow him to cross in the absence of pontoons, as the river was rising and the fords difficult.

Fredericksburg was occupied at the time of Sumner's arrival by only four companies of Rebel Infantry, some Cavalry, and a light battery.

On the 20th of November all the Union Army was about Falmouth.

Genl. Lee concentrated his Army very slowly and not until after the 26th of November did all his forces arrive at Fredericksburg. Burnside had called for pontoons on the 13th of November, but they did not arrive from Washington until the 24th. They could have reached Falmouth on the 15th of November by way of Aquia Creek, but parts of them were sent over land from Washington instead of by the river. This delay defeated the first part of Burnside's plan. There were no quick crossing and no seizure of Fredericksburg.

The press of the North clamored so for a move of the Army of the Potomac that Burnside yielded and determined to attack Lee in his stronghold. He arrived at this conclusion on the 10th day of December and moved the Grand Division into position near the river. They were in place Right, Center and Left, and the Center Grand Division was divided so that a part helped the 1st Grand Division, while two Divisions of the 5th Corps, Sickles and Birney, were ordered to report to Franklin on the left.

The Rappahannock River is 200 yards wide at Fredericksburg, and is tidal there. It widens as it flows toward the sea. The left bank of the river, occupied by the Union Army and called Stafford Heights, is 150 feet above the water and is much more elevated than the right bank which it commands.

On the right bank of the river there are three distinct elevations. First, from the river, is a narrow strip left by the water as the channel deepened. Second, about 30 feet above, is a broad alluvial plain dotted with farm houses and divided by fences of the plantation and by ravines. Third, there is a low ridge which touches the river above Falmouth and then curves gradually away until, at the Massaponax, four miles below Fredericksburg, the ridge is two miles from the river. One half mile back of this ridge are high spurs. Along the low ridge was the main portion of the Rebel Army.

The heights of the main spurs of the ridge on which the Rebel array lay overlooking the town of Fredericksburg are as follows: Marye's Hill just back of the town, 40 feet; Prospect Hill near the Massaponax was 40 feet high, while between the two mentioned was Lee's Hill, 90 feet high.

There was a long sluice way for a mill, which passed in rear of the town of Fredericksburg from a point on the river two miles above the town to about a mile below it. This had to be crossed to get to the bluff occupied by the Rebels, and at the foot of Marye's Hill, as the Telegraph road wound around to the left, it passed behind a stone wall which the Rebels had arranged for a defensive breastworks. They had dug out a trench on the lower side of the road, and had thrown the earth out, banking it up against the wall. This wall was half mile long and about 400 yards from the mill race and Marye's Hill; behind it was 40 feet higher and occupied with artillery.

The weakest part of the Rebel line was on the left, as we looked at it, and near the Massaponax. There, their line was one and a quarter miles from the nearest point on the Rappahannock and was not entrenched at all. Lee's entire line was 11,500 yards, and the proportion of the men occupying it was 11,000 to the mile or six to the yard.

Battle of Fredericksburg   December 11-14, 1862

It seems almost positive that Burnside's plan on the night of the 12th of December was to have his main attack made on the left by Franklin's Grand Division as expressed at a Council of War.

Sumner was in charge of operations on the right about the town, and he had in all 30,000 men and 60 guns. Franklin had 116 guns and 55,000 men.

There was no suggestion at any time during the battle that the original scheme should be departed from, but Franklin did not understand his orders for some reason on the 13th, and so brought about a failure.

On the 10th of December, the Grand Divisions moved into position and the pontoons were lowered to the water's edge. It was the determination to lay 3 bridges at the town of Fredericksburg for Sumner to cross, and three a mile below for Franklin's crossing. 147 pieces of Artillery were placed in position on the north bank. The bridge men commenced before dawn on the 11th of December.

At the city, the fog hung over the river, and protected the men so that the first bridge was more than half completed before its builders became visible to the Confederates occupying the houses along the bank. These houses had all been loop-holed and were occupied by Barksdale's Mississippians. These at once opened fire at the shadowy figures on the bridge, and the range was so short that the workers were almost immediately driven off. Thrice did they resume their labors and were forced to desist, as men could not live upon that bridge.

After several hours of delay, Genl. Hunt, Chief of Artillery, called for volunteers to cross in boats and drive the enemy from their cover in the houses of the city. The 7th Michigan and the 19th and 20th Massachusetts sprang into pontoon boats and gallantly crossed the river under a galling fire and drove away or captured the Rebel forces. Under the cover which their presence on the opposite bank afforded, the first bridge was soon completed, and at 4:30 P.M. all three were finished and the town occupied. On the left, Franklin was more fortunate, as he had no enemy to oppose him to any extent so that he had all his bridges done at one o'clock and he had crossed a small force.

The whole of the night of the 11th of December was lost as no attempt was made to increase the force on the south side of the river.

On the morning of the 12th it was again densely foggy and covered by the mist, so Sumner's Grand Division with 104 guns and Franklin's Division with 116 guns leisurely crossed and were placed in position, connecting with each other.

The general line thus formed was with the 2nd Corps in and above the town, the 9th Corps next, then the 6th Corps and then the 1st Corps. The line was parallel with the river and was about four miles long. The 3rd Corps was moved from its camps on Potomac Creek on the 12th of December and marched during that day and night to a position on the heights 150 feet above the water at the lower bridge. This night was dark and stormy, and the road was muddy and rough so that we reached our halting place ½ mile from the Franklin Bridges at dawn of the 13th of

December. Previous to crossing, the whole army was given three days' rations, and 60 pounds of ammunitions per man.

Like its predecessors, the morning of the 13th of December was dull and calm, and the fog which enveloped the river, the city, the plain, and the hills hid everything from view. The rumble of artillery, the roar of heavy guns, loud words of commands, or the occasional sounds of music came to our ears muffled by the fog.

Now and again as this obstacle was for a moment lifted and the gunners were able to see, the batteries on Marye's Heights, 3000 yards away, belched forth and were replied to four-fold by shrieking shells from our long range guns.

As the sun rose higher about 9:00 A.M., the entire fog screen was rolled away. The sun shone with almost September brightness and warmth, and before us from our fine vantage grounds was a scene impossible to fully describe. Our position so high commanded a view of it all.

Far away to our right, the south side hills closing in to the river above, the quaint old town with the red bricks of its houses and the steeples of its churches, the winding river with its bridges, the forsaken houses on the plain, with beyond this, the brown wooded hills where was hidden our enemy, and through the center of this picture, just past the silver ribbon of the river, the blue line showing the hosts of the Army of the Potomac with its flags and banners.

Cloud puffs from the guns of friend or foe enlivened the scene, and of the grand and glorious in war the picture before us was unsurpassed. There can be no doubt but that Burnside appreciated the fact that the Confederates' right was its weakest point and that by driving off his enemy there, he would gain more than by breaking the line any place else.

He wished Franklin to make a great attack on our left, and when success was assured there, he hoped by an attack with Sumner on the right to drive Lee from the entire ridge. The two attacks were not intended to be simultaneous. Burnside had placed over one half of his army under Franklin's command. He ordered that General to attack with not less than a Division well supported. Part of Franklin's orders he did not like, and the spirit of the order he never obeyed. He ordered the 1st Corps to do the work determined upon, and Genl. Reynolds, commanding that

Corps, directed Genl. George G. Meade, commanding the 2nd Division, to attack and to be supported by Genl. Gibbon's 3rd Division.

Meade with 4600 men and Gibbon with 5000 men were to advance in line with each other, and Doubleday's 3rd Division, 5000 men, to be in support.

The main attack was to be made by the smallest Division, and the line of the two Divisions was 1000 yards long when they deployed to advance. Their connection was soon lost, and Meade went on alone. At 9:30 A.M., with sun so bright, the view before us of 50,000 men was inspiring.

Meade began his advance at that hour and soon came under the enfilading fire of Rebel batteries on his left. Meade halted until Doubleday's Division was placed in position on the left. This was all the assistance this Division rendered to Meade during the day.

It was past 11:00 A.M. when Meade again advanced, and his line gained a point 800 yards from the foot of the ridge he wanted to take, when suddenly the silent woods before him awoke to life and the crash and roar of 60 hostile guns revealed the magnitude of the task. Under this fire, his men recoiled for a short space and halted, and for an hour and a half we beheld a duel between the Rebel artillery and ours on the plain.

At 1:00 P.M. Meade, supported by 51 guns on his right and left, again started for the ridge. They crossed the railroad and passed into the woods. His leading Brigade dashed up the hill followed by the entire Division. They broke the Rebel line, captured two Colors, 300 prisoners and drove away the gunners from a section of artillery. They surprised the second Rebel line whose rifles were stacked, and threw demoralization amongst them for a time.

Gibbon's Division, having lost connection was of no assistance [and] it never advanced as far as Meade. At this critical moment of the entire battle, Meade was 950 yards in advance of any other formed body of troops. His numbers were reduced, his men with strength spent in their effort, their ammunition gone. They could do nothing more alone. Thrice Meade asked for reinforcements, and to his calls the only answer sent was two regiments, where 20,000 men were needed. The two regiments sent Meade were the 65th & 114th Pennsylvania of Birney's Division of the 3rd Corps.

At 2:15 P.M., Meade had been driven entirely from the hills and behind the line of the army. In the second line of the Rebels he inflicted a loss of 41 killed, and 265 wounded, while the total Rebel loss by his attack was 2,122, while his own was 1,853 out of 4,600 men.

The Rebels followed Meade and attacked Franklin's main force, but soon withdrew, renewing their demonstration at intervals during the afternoon. Franklin still had 42,000 men and was opposed by 28,000. At 2:30 P.M. Burnside sent an order to Franklin to again attack, but to this order he paid no attention.

Gibbon's loss amounted to 1267 out of 5000, but it went for nothing on account of his losing connection with Meade.

An English Officer who served on the Confederate Staff during this battle says,

> *To their credit be it said the Northern Infantry never attacked more resolutely than at Fredericksburg, and had the capacity of their leaders been equal to the courage of the men, Lee's veterans would have been pushed to hold their own. Meade with less than 3,000 men was alone and unsupported within the hostile lines, swallowed up by the forest and surrounded by an overwhelming throng of foes. At this crisis of the fight when every available batallion should have been hurried to the front and poured through the still open gap, when a determined rush of the whole fighting line and supports would have driven Hill and Early back, Franklin incapable of a bold offensive made no effort to assist his Lieutenant and, despite all appeals for succor, left the gallant Pennsylvanians to their fate.*
>
> *Franklin holding in his hand 40,000 men at least saw those daring men who scarce 3,000 in number had so successfully cleared the way, destroyed piecemeal by his own violation of the first principles of war.*

This was just and scathing criticism from one of our enemies.

With sadness and disgust, we turn to the heroism on the right of the Army. The point attacked there was the stone wall at the foot of Marye's Hill.

As the history of the campaign contains all the story, I shall only need to summarize it.

Burnside had hoped for Franklin's success from 9 to 12 o'clock when he determined to attempt the taking of Marye's. First, French's Division of the 2nd Corps charged with 4500 men against that stone wall. They left 1200 killed and wounded and got no nearer than 175 yards of the wall. Then 15 minutes later, Hancock, "The Superb," with his Division 5806 strong of the 2nd Corps, advanced. His noble men of the Irish Brigade under Maher threw off their haversacks and blankets, and though only 1200, breasted the slope and faced the death-dealing storm from the Rebel batteries.

Swiftly they passed by the farthest point reached by French, shoulder to shoulder, upbearing their own green flag and the starry banner of the Union, and swept forward against the low stone wall where their foes awaited them. No shot was fired from the Rebel line.

At 75 yards, the Brigade, feeling that victory was theirs, sent forth a cheer from their shattered ranks. They were only 40 steps from the wall when suddenly a sheet of flame burst from the 1200 rifles behind the wall, and volley on volley sped with deadly precision.

The Brigade struggled on for a while, and at 30 yards from the wall they began to slowly and sullenly fall back, and beneath that smoke cloud the Irish Brigade ceased to exist. 545 of the 1200 were killed and wounded.

Hancock's Division lost 2032 out of 5006 and his charge lasted but twenty minutes. Men of Coldwell's Division were killed fifteen steps from the wall. Twenty minutes after this, Howard's 2nd Division, 2nd Corps, vainly assaulted and lost 914 out of 6000. Sturgis' Division, 9th Corps, 3500 charged the wall and lost 1007, and Griffin supporting Sturgis lost 926 out of 7500. Getty's Division, 9th Corps advanced and lost 296 men.

At 5:00 P.M. Humphries' Division, 3rd and 5th Corps made one of the most brilliant charges of the day. It advanced wih rifles unloaded and with bayonets fixed.

The pitiless terrible fire from the wall stopped them at 60 yards from it, and the men without orders began to load and fire as they advanced. Genl. Humphries says that "in one minute more they would have climbed the wall." They were bewildered by the carnage and fell slowly back, disdaining to fly. This Division left 1017 but little less than half its numbers, on that corpse encumbered slope.

Six times did our Divisions and Brigades dash themselves to pieces against that wall. Burnside wanted to, in person, lead the 9th Corps to a charge on the 14th of December, but was dissuaded. His army lost in all 12,653, while the Rebels lost 5322.

The 20th Indiana marched with the 3rd Corps as above described and crossed on the Franklin crossing. It had 19 Officers and 508 men for duty November 30th, and on the field we had 17 Officers and about the same number of men as above. About one o'clock in the afternoon, December 13th, we were hurried across the river, and at a double step into the general line of the Army and arrived in time to aid in the repulse of the Rebels who were closely following Meade after his repulse from their once captured line.

The 20th Indiana lost two Officers and twenty-two men wounded and three men missing, or twenty-seven all told. Our Brigade, the first commanded by Genl. J. C. Robinson, lost 146, the 1st Division lost 950 and the 3rd Corps 1179 men from all causes. The 3rd Corps was highly complimented on its firmness and bravery by Generals Hooker and Stoneman.

The Congressional Committee on the Conduct of the War censured Franklin very severely after a full investigation of his actions in this battle.

COMMENTARY: *Newly in charge of the Union's Army of the Potomac following the relief of Genl. McClellan, Genl. Ambrose Burnside had a workable plan to turn the tide of the war. He meant to march his three "Grand Divisions" to cross the Rappahannock at Fredericksburg, overpower its garrison and attack Richmond before Genl. Lee could arrive to save the Confederate capital. Genl. Halleck approved, and President Lincoln thought it could work if Burnside moved quickly.*

Burnside did move quickly, marching his army to a position across the river from the weakly defended Fredericksburg on November 17. But his army needed pontoon bridges to cross the Rappahannock, and none was present as promised. While Burnside waited for his bridges, which finally appeared on December 11, the Confederates under Lee, Longstreet, and Jackson, reached Fredericksburg and on its high ground built defensive fortifications that no frontal assault was likely to carry. But Burnside stubbornly stuck to his plan and ordered charge after bloody charge that gained nothing at a cost of 12,000 Union casualties. Valor was not the issue; poor logistics and witless leadership brought a catastrophic defeat.

CHAPTER 10

My Right Leg Would Not Do Its Duty

1862

As I was wounded at Fredericksburg, to illustrate the experiences of one of the thousands disabled on that field, I will fully state my own.

As the Regiment was going on the right by file into line to oppose the Rebel advance, we [were] going at the double. I suddenly found that my right leg would not do its duty. On looking down I saw a small hole, and I dropped onto the ground.

I had on boots with my trousers inside the tops, and as we had doubled from the river about a mile, I had thrown off blanket, haversack, and canteen, and so I found myself in the mud, helpless.

The spin or thud of Rebel bullets all about made me more uncomfortable, and after the heat and excitement, the sudden cessation of all exertion caused me to get cold mighty quick. From this cause and loss of blood, I got colder, hungry, and thirsty. I tried to crawl off, but that was too painful. The ball had taken off the entire front of the Tibia of my right leg at the point about 2 inches above my ankle joint, and every movement was very painful indeed. I laid there on the field from about 2:00 P.M. until 8:00 or 9 :00 o'clock at night.

At last I heard a voice way off to the rear calling my name. It was pretty husky work, but I stopped my grateful tears and wetting my throat as well as I could, gave back a weak yell. He called again and up came John French of Company I, a Sergeant who, with others, was looking for me.

He had gone back to where he last remembered seeing me, and then with the rest, had come forward as near as they could over our track.

I had thrown my blanket so that I might find it again and French had found it. He and another then got me up and somehow back to a brick house near the bridges where the field Hospital was. They put me on one of the mattresses of the mansion on the floor of the dining room, and after getting me a bite to eat, they went back to their duty.

Wounded from various organizations were taken to this house and from there to the various Corps Hospitals across the river. If operations were required at the time of the wounded coming into this house, the Surgeons there performed such work.

Soon after I had been placed on my mattress, I was examined by one of the Medical Officers there, and as he had cut off my boot and trouser leg, he found my leg and foot much swollen and badly discolored. He marked me with a ticket and went to the next man. My curiosity was excited, and to satisfy it, I enquired about the mark left with me and found that it was to indicate amputation. So I was to lose my foot.

Surgeons were so busy that I could get no hearing from any of them. An accident, however, gave me an opportunity.

This Hospital was in easy range of Rebel Artillery, and a shot from one of their guns passed through the roof of the building. It, of course, shook every part of it, and all of the Surgeons and attendants rushed out of the house.

As they returned to their work, many of them passed through the room in which I lay, and I happened to see one whom I knew. I hailed him with a Masonic sign, and as he stopped to see what I wanted, I explained to him the situation. He arranged so that I could be sent across the river to the 3rd Corps Hospital where I had friends.

Sometime during the night I was transferred by ambulance to the care of our own Corps Surgeons, one of whom happened to be a cousin.

On the 14th of December I was placed on a flat car to be sent by rail to Aquia Creek. We were transferred from the train at Aquia Creek to the steamer and placed on the deck on such mattresses as could be provided. On arrival at Washington, I was carried by an ambulance through the city and to a building formerly used for a young ladies' Seminary in Georgetown, on the second floor of which I was given a very good room.

There was only one other Officer, Capt. George Wallace of the 4th Ohio, with us.

Soon as I had been located safely in this comfortable place, the nurse for the ward came to me and began by exhibiting the utmost of kindness. Her name was Miss Washburn, and she married Judge Steele of Illinois after the War. Under her gentle care and the close attention of the Surgeons, my wound healed rapidly and I was able to go home on crutches at the end of three months, and the crutches I cast aside at the beginning of April. About the first of April, I reported back for duty, although I still limped and could not use my foot except side ways for two years.

Capt. Wallace of whom I have spoken above was wounded by a small ball from a shrapnel shell, entering his knee through the knee cap. He would not consent to an amputation which the Doctors said was necessary from the first. His fiancee [Miss Schneider] came on to see him, accompanied by Mrs. Brown of Canton, Ohio. This lady was the mother of the wife of Senator Manderson of Nebraska. She felt compelled to return to her home, and Miss Schneider thought she could not go away from Capt. Wallace.

He had grown weaker and weaker and the Doctors finally told him that he must either lose his leg or his life. He consented then, and his leg was amputated. He improved after this right along, and when Mrs. Brown decided to go home, they thought that if they [Wallace and Schneider] were married, it would afford the wife the protection of his name as well as if she had a Chaperone. So one bright sunny Sabbath, a Presbyterian Minister, Dr. Brown (a brother of our first Colonel), was called in, and at 12:00 o'clock noon they were married. The wife stayed that afternoon with Capt. Wallace and finally went to her dinner about 5 o'clock. The Captain was very calm and quite happy. He ate his supper and was smoking a cigar when he carelessly raised the cloth covering his stump and then looked at me across the room with a horrified glance.

There was a slight stain of blood on the cloth. I could hardly restrain my excitement as I said, "Oh, that was nothing, but I will send for the Surgeon." The man went out and returned at once, and as he did so more blood was showing. I gave the man my handerchief and told him to tie the stump, which he tried to do but before it was accomplished, the blood burst out over the side of the bed and Capt. Wallace said "Oh, I can't breathe," and died at once. The tying of the artery had sloughed off.

At this time in Washington about the Hospitals, there were a great many young physicians who were gaining experience. They did this at the expense of great suffering on the part of those wounded. They called themselves Medical Cadets and on Sunday would go about in crowds or parties of five or six and visit the interesting cases.

Capt. Wallace had suffered them to probe his wound and do about as they pleased. They probed mine also at first, but it hurt me so much that I got tired of this work.

One Sunday a party of about six came in, and after examining Wallace's wound they came over to my bed. Nothing was said to me, but they came up to the bedside and without a "Good morning," or "By your leave," or anything of that kind, one of them threw back the cover, opened his instrument case which he put down on the bed, and taking out a probe, was about to begin when I said, "Hold on there a minute, what are you going to do?"

He said, "I am going to examine your wound." I said, "Not by a long shot you ain't." He replied, "Well, I know my business," and acted as if about to proceed. I reached back to the corner of my bed and bringing into view my sword in the scabbard, and all covered with the Fredericksburg mud, I said, "Now if you touch that leg I will mash your head with this sword." He said, "I will report you, sir," and they left in great disgust. I told the Surgeon, and he laughed and said I was right.

Young Boulson, who was rejected by Maj. Wood when we were sworn in at Lafayette and had put blocks under his heels to make him look taller, had become a Musician in Company I. He was an expert fifer and finally became Chief Musician in charge of the fifers and drummer of the Regiment. He was at the Hospital when I was wounded, and was so very sympathetic that I said, "I would like awfully well to take you to Washington with me." He said, "I will go." So he got down under the blankets on the car and impersonated a wounded man and went through to Washington with me. He was a great help and returned very soon to the Regiment, being one of those missing in the report. He was only absent on a little trip for I had stolen him to help me.

One of the most enthusiastic and patriotic women who gave most of her time to the care of the sick and wounded during the war was Mrs. M. A. Livermore of Chicago. I had known her before the War, and she became a great friend to me. When I was wounded and in the Hospital at Georgetown, she wrote to her friend Miss Dix of New York to come and see me. The latter was one who gave all her time to visiting Hospitals and looking out for the unfortunate of the War.

Miss Dix came to the Hospital on the day that Capt. Wallace was married and died, and she found me in such excitement. However, she left her address and came often to see me. She gave a standing order that a bottle of wine should be sent to me daily. It came regularly, and was the sourest wine possible.

Mrs. Hooper, wife of the Member of Congress from Boston, came to see me every day and brought papers and good things of all kinds. Mrs. Lincoln, wife of the President, also came to see the son of a friend of hers who was wounded [and] in the next room to mine. She was liberal to all of us, and distributed boxes of the finest cigars from Havana with a liberal hand.

Members of Congress also made regular visits, and it was always a pleasure to me to see Schuyler Colfax, the member who represented the district in which was my home. He was always so bright and so cheerfully kind. [U.S. Senator, Indiana] Dan Voorhees also came to see us, and did all he could for us.

COMMENTARY: *Just as neither Confederate nor Union Army was prepared for large-scale warfare, neither side was medically prepared for the casualties that five years of combat would generate. In 1860, America had no general hospital; the U.S. Army had just 30 surgeons; and neither side had any ambulances.*

More than 600,000 men died in this conflict, and over 140,000 of them died of wounds. Of the quarter-million Union Army men reported wounded, all but a tiny fraction were shot. In a war fought largely with Napoleonic tactics, newly developed rifles like the .58 caliber Springfield with its power, range and accuracy, proved to be devastating. The majority of wounds were to the soldiers' arms and legs, and amputation was the most common battlefield operation—with mortal results 25%–50% of the time. Sanitation was primitive, and infections were common and often fatal.

CHAPTER 11

CHANCELLORSVILLE

1863

During my absence in the Hospital & etc., the Regiment had with the Corps joined in the attempt known as the Mud March, January 22, 1863. Genl. Burnside had come to the conclusion that he better attempt a campaign on new lines. So his army left its camps about the 18th of January and marched for the fords above Fredericksburg. The roads were simply horrible, and for miles the men labored to advance through the mud and falling rain. After every exertion had been made and it was seen that no good could come of the movements, the regiments all returned to their old camps and on the 25th of January, 1863, Genl. Burnside was relieved at his own request from the command of the Army of the Potomac and Genl. Joseph Hooker was assigned to his place.

Genl. Hooker at once displayed great energy in all his actions, orders, and so forth for the building up of the Army of the Potomac. On the 5th of February he abolished the Grand Division System, and he had new Generals assigned to command the different Corps.

Genl. John F. Reynolds was given the 1st Corps, Genl. D. N. Couch the 2nd Corps, Genl. Dan E. Sickles the 3rd Corps, Genl. (George G.) Meade the 5th Corps, Genl. John Sedgewick the 6th Corps, Genl. W. F. Smith the 9th Corps, Genl. Franz Sigel the 11th Corps, Genl. H. Slocum the 12th Corps, and Genl. George Stoneman was assigned to command all the Cavalry.

The spirit of the Army rose day by day. The Cavalry became effective from the beginning of Hooker's taking command, and the expression so common before that, "No one ever saw a dead Cavalryman," was no longer heard. Absenteeism was checked and desertion was to a very great extent stopped.

About the 5th of April the Army of the Potomac was visited by the President Abraham Lincoln, and Mr. Seward, the Secretary of State. While they were with us, there were reviews of the different branches of the service by the President and Genl. Hooker.

We had three Corps assembled for review on the day the 3rd Corps was reviewed, and I enjoyed the day very much as I was on such duty as excused me from marching with the troops and still enabled me to be present to see it all. The Infantry was closed in mass, and as they marched off to pass the President, they took full distance and went directly to their camps after passing.

All of the wagons of each Corps and their ambulances were parked in front of the line of soldiers, and facing with the heads of the teams toward the line. The teams of each Brigade formed a small square by themselves and still formed a part of a larger square of the Division and of the Corps.

The President rode down the line in front, and after he had well passed the center of the park of wagons, something startled the mules about the middle of the line and away they dashed, and team after team followed taking up the fright and making a dangerous charge on the Infantry line. Mules were killed and wagons destroyed, and it was some time before the march past could be made.

On the day following, the President reviewed the Cavalry and saw about 10,000 horsemen as they filed past him.

The strength of the Army of the Potomac on the 30th of April was:
Present equipped   133,708
Present   157,996
Present and absent   206,628

Genl. Lee's Army consisted of about:
75,000 present effective
90,000 present
121,000 present and absent.

Genl. Lee occupied all the strong line of bluffs on the south of the river Rappahannock, and as the bluffs came close in on both sides of the river above Fredericksburg, it was deemed impossible to approach any of the fords near the town and to get possession of them without great loss.

Genl. Hooker, therefore, decided on a wide turning movement to flank the Rebel Army out of position at the fords above. On the 27th of April he sent three Corps, the 5th, 11th and 12th, to cross the Rappahannock at Kelly Ford, 30 miles from Fredericksburg, and the Rapidan at Elys and Germania Fords. The Rappahannock was crossed on the 28th of April, and the Rapidan on the 30th.

The General had caused a diversion in favor of these three Corps by throwing bridges over the river at the Franklin Crossing below Fredericksburg on the 28th of April. The three Corps mentioned, having crossed successfully, moved down the river and drove away the Rebels about the fords so that Genl. Hooker was enabled to cross the Rappahannock at the U.S. Ford, and on the night of the 30th of April, he had the 2nd, 5th, 11th and 12th Corps with him near Chancellorsville.

The Third Corps was still opposite Fredericksburg, but we joined the others at Chancellorsville at 11:00 A.M. May 1st. At 5:00 P.M. the Regiment in Ward's Brigade was moved up the plank road toward Dowdall's tavern and thence by a road at right angles to the plank road. The Regiment, with the 37th New York, was sent to the front after considerable firing drove the enemy out of the houses at Hazel Grove, and we established our pickets along Scott's Run facing south, where we remained all night.

Off to our right and facing south also was Slocum's 12th Corps, and farther to the right, Howard's 11th Corps with but few of his troops facing west or toward the right flank of the Army, the general line of which was facing south and along the Orange Plank Road. Scott's Run was about one and a quarter miles south of the Plank Road.

About 2:00 P.M. May 2nd, as a party of our Officers on picket were looking south, we would see the glint of gun barrels, and the movement of wagons as they passed our road about two miles away. On this being reported, Genl. Sickles ordered us forward. The 20th Indiana as skirmishers advanced, and the 2nd Brigade, 3rd Corps followed.

We advanced step by step, and as Genl. Ward says, "the Twentieth

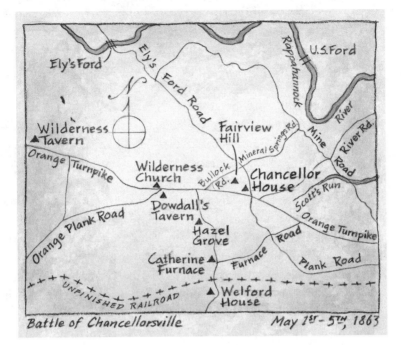

Battle of Chancellorsville   May 1st – 5th, 1863

Indiana continually sending prisoners to the rear, the last installment being 180 Rebels."

About a mile and a quarter from Scott's Run, we approached a railroad cut, and our skirmishers advanced on the right and left of the cut. We were amazed to see a great commotion in the cut, knapsack, haversacks, caps and everything went flying into the air.

One man on horseback dashed off, and when we got to the cut, we found that we had captured nearly the whole of the 23rd Georgia Regt. Only the Colonel got away with the flag of his Regiment.

The 20th Indiana Regiment continued to advance and finally arrived at the Welford House, about a quarter of a mile beyond the railroad cut.

This house was along the main road along which Jackson was marching his column to place himself on the right flank of the Union Army.

The Rebel column moved to a road farther south, and we, putting out pickets, prepared to stay all night. We were now nearly three miles in advance of the rest of the Army. While in this position, we heard the attack of Jackson on the right of Howard, and the rest of the Corps returned to the open field at Hazel Grove from which we had started.

The 20th Indiana and the 63rd Pennsylvania were left alone in the advance position.

Jackson's attack began at about 6:00 P.M., and from our position at the Welford House, which was on quite an elevation, we could see over the forest the progress of Jackson's advance, and as the darkness deepened, that progress was thrillingly marked to us by the shrieking and sparkling of shells and the roar of the musketry.

We watched the display of fireworks until very late at night, and then in low tones began to talk of how far it was to Richmond, expecting to be taken prisoners. The last of the firing looked to us to be about where we had started from, and it seemed as if we were cut off from all help.

It was after 12:00 o'clock at night when we heard the patter of horse's hoofs coming to us from toward Hazel Grove, and soon our picket halted the rider. (By this time we had pickets all around us.) The rider proved to be Capt. Fassett of Genl. Birney's Division Staff. He gave us the news that the Rebels had attacked Howard's right flank, defeating it, and that the 3rd Corps was cut off from the rest of the Army, and that only by the utmost silence could we expect even to get to the Corps.

We instructed our men about keeping quiet and, withdrawing our pickets, we faced to the left, and every man with his hand on his tin cup to keep it from making noise, moved off and succeeded in getting to Hazel Grove. But there we found that while we had faced south before our advance, we now had to face north. The Brigade had made a charge about midnight and had thus attacked Jackson's right flank and helped to stop his further advance.

We remained in line at the edge of the woods on the north of Hazel Grove opening, and could distinctly hear the calling of the Company Rolls by Rebel First Sergeants.

The night was passed under fire and excitement, and at dawn of day we moved by our right flank and soon joined the rest of the Army near Chancellor's House at a place called Prospect Hill.

Genl. Hooker had been hurt by the explosion of a shell at his Headquarters at the Chancellorsville House, and for a time was not able to command the Army.

When we got to the place called Prospect Hill, we first heard of Hooker's injury and the depression was very great. It seemed as though a large part of the Army was assembled in the open ground near the Chancellor House, and the immense field was filled with regiments lying in column of regiment, but in the cluster by Brigade or Division.

We were near the front when we heard the troops away off behind us cheering. On looking back we found that they were cheering for Genl. Hooker.

Fighting Joe, as he was called, was always very popular with the soldiers, and as that immense Army realized that he was well and riding toward the front, every man in sight rose to his feet and gave cheer after cheer. It was a fine sight. The General looked superb on a beautiful white horse, and the enthusiasm of all arose to the occasion.

We were soon moved back to a position rear of the Chancellor House, where we occupied a place in a new line of battle in support of Robinson's Battery E, 1st R.I. Artillery. We went into position at dark on the 3rd of May, and entrenched ourselves as quickly as possible. The Regiment remained in the trenches with about the thirty guns until Wednesday the 6th of May when we withdrew to the north side of the Rappahannock by way of United States Ford, returning to our camps near Potomac Creek on the afternoon of the 6th.

While supporting the batteries in rear of the Chancellor House, we were crowded in and about the guns. The Rebels attacked us quite often, and as the artillery had to open fire upon them, we had to get out of the way of burning powder from the cannon. The Gunners would call "Look out" when the men of the regiment would throw themselves back under the wheels of the guns. Soon as the shot was fired, we all threw ourselves forward again against the breastworks and kept up our fire from rifles. This, of course, was forced on us by the crowded condition of our line.

In the movement to the rear from this last position, Ward's Brigade was the rear guard for the 3rd Corps.

I was wounded in the shoulder on the 5th of May while lying under my rubber blanket. I was taken to the Field Hospital where, after having the wound dressed, I returned to the Regiment and remained with it, only having to be helped to march to the river which was done in haste.

During this campaign, Capt. George W. Meikel was acting as Adjutant General of the Brigade. Capt. W. D. Vatchet was acting Aide-de-Camp to Brig. Genl. Ward. First Lieut. Michael Sheehan was ambulance Officer of the Corps.

———

DURING THE CHANCELLORSVILLE CAMPAIGN, there were many new ideas put into execution, and all were good and stood the test very thoroughly. The total weight carried by each soldier was 45 pounds. It consisted of his knapsack, haversack, subsistence, and change of underclothing, overcoat or blanket, arms and accoutrements with one piece of shelter tent. Eight days' short rations were carried on the person stowed as follows: 5 days in knapsack, 3 days in the haversack, 40 rounds of ammunition in the cartridge boxes, and 20 rounds in the pockets of the men's clothing.

Each Officer was responsible for his own outfit. It was to be carried by himself or his servant. Only shelter tents were taken. No wagons followed the Army over the river, except a few ammunition wagons were brought up. The men carried all the things through the campaign most necessary for constant use. On the 2nd and 3rd days many men abandoned overcoats or blankets as the weather was warm.

The impulse of the men was to throw off all impediments especially on going into action. In the entire army about every fourth knapsack was lost or thrown away, but in the 3rd Corps only one knapsack in every 30 was not in [the] possession of the men at the close of the campaign. The extra clothing carried by each man consisted of one shirt, one pair drawers, one pair socks, and one blanket or overcoat.

On March 10th, 1863, the wheel transportation, and etc. in the Army of the Potomac was fixed as follows: For each Regiment of infantry with 700 men and upward present, 6 wagons; for a Regiment with 500 men, 5 wagons; for a Regiment with less than 500 present, 4 wagons; 3 two-horse ambulances; three wall tents for field and staff Officers; one shelter tent, two pieces for each other Officer; and one shelter tent for every two non-commissioned officers, soldiers, servants and camp followers.

After [the] above date, we never had more than as specified, and they often left these wagons out after that.

The Union losses at the battle of Chancellorsville were:

Killed	1606
Wounded	9762
Missing or Captured	5919
Total	17,287

The Rebel losses were:

Killed	1581
Wounded	8700
About prisoners	4500
Total	14,781

The 20th Indiana lost only twenty-four all told. It was highly praised for its conduct and actions by all the Generals above us. The Brigade and Division were also highly praised. The Regiment was commanded by Col. John Wheeler, he having succeeded Col. John Van Volkenburg after the end of the Fredericksburg battle. The latter was mustered out for disloyalty, he having written some letters to Indiana in which he criticised the demonstration and the conduct of the War. He was not disloyal, but was too enthusiastic a friend of McClellan, and was indiscreet.

The cause of the failure at Chancellorsville was no doubt the physical incapacity for command of Genl. Hooker. The cause of this disability arose from that General's own fault. It is true that he gave Genl. Howard particular orders as to guarding his right flank, which orders were not obeyed, and the surprise to the right resulted. Genl. Hooker, however, seems to have become so elated at his success in gaining a position at Chancellorsville that he celebrated this fact to his own discredit. Hooker was assigned to command at a time when there was great political activity at Washington and as a selection of Secretary Chase and his friends.

The Army of the Potomac was not whipped at all at Chancellorsville, and I never saw it in as good spirits as at the close of the Campaign. I well remember the feeling of disappointment on the part of everyone high and low when the orders were given to recross the Rappahannock.

Genl. Couch fell in command of the Army during a portion of the time when Genl. Hooker was said to be disabled, and he positively refused to serve any longer under Hooker and was relieved from the Army.

The Army was withdrawn to the north side of the Rappahannock to the surprise of everyone in Washington, and without their knowledge. There was much discussion as to the removal of Hooker after this, and Reynolds had good support for the command, but Hooker was retained until a later day.

Col. Wheeler, 20th Indiana, was called upon to report the morale of the Regiment before it recrossed the river, and his only reply was, "The 20th Indiana is gay."

I may add here that one of the causes of failure of the campaign was the same error which Lee committed later in the year.

Hooker sent off all of his 10,000 Cavalry under Stoneman for a raid in rear of the Rebel Army just before the campaign began. It was no doubt considered as a part of the Campaign, but it caused him to be without "his eyes" to discover the presence of Jackson on his right flank.

The raid of the Cavalry lasted until the 10th or 12th of May, and while the experience for the Cavalry was of vast benefit to them, the movement accomplished nothing else and it rendered one half of the Cavalry of no service.

Genl. Stoneman was relieved, and Genl. Pleasanton placed in command of all the Cavalry, and it was always very much better after this raid.

COMMENTARY: *Again maneuvering in the Fredericksburg/Wilderness area, the Army of the Potomac, now under the command of Genl. Joseph Hooker following Ambrose Burnside's departure, sought in early May to move between Genl. Lee and Richmond. Again, a good Union plan was undone by confusion and timidity at the command level. Hooker sent forces under Genl. Sedgwick to threaten the Confederates in Fredericksburg.*

But Lee, though threatened from two sides, surprised and unnerved Hooker by staying on the offensive: he divided his army, and with Genl. Jubal Early defending Fredericksburg, sent Genl. Jackson with 26,000 men on a stealthy swing through the Wilderness to fall on Hooker's vulnerable right wing at dusk. Jackson was fatally wounded in the attack, but his forces stampeded Hooker's army, which went on the defensive and retreated back across the Rappahannock, handing a stunning victory to the Confederates.

CHAPTER 12

GETTYSBURG CAMPAIGN

1863

T he Field of Operation on which the Gettysburg Campaign took place is filled with every kind of interest to the military student. The subject of terrain is illustrated in this Campaign on so vast a scale as well as in such minute particulars that interest in its study increases as the investigation extends. The Army of the Union was many months in learning the full value of terrain and many more in learning to fully comprehend systems by which the various features of the country could be best used to advantage or overcome if encountered as an obstacle. As one studies the feature of any country, it is of vast interest in a military sense to try to apply the relation of the various points in the terrain to each other and to any supposable problem placed therein for solution.

At the beginning of the campaign, we have hostile armies reposing in their camps on opposite sides of a nonfordable stream. Arousing their lethargy, one army proceeds on a march of invasion securely hidden by the natural feature of the country. It is soon followed by the other army on shorter and more interior lines. Each with a separate object uses every feature of the country to its advantage and progresses as rapidly as possible until at the end of thirty days the campaign closes after one of the bloodiest battles of modern times. Even the terrain of the battlefield itself gives the advantage now to one, then to the other.

Let us look briefly at the country through which these armies passed on this campaign, first explaining that by terrain I mean every feature of the country; applying the term as well to the location of a picket post as to the Army position where thousands fell in battle.

At the close of the Chancellorsville Campaign, May 6, 1863, the Union Army returned to its camps on the north side of the Rappahannock River and the Confederates occupied the strong position about Fredericksburg on the south of that river.

The river is tidal at the city, and about 200 yards wide. In the ordinary stage of water, there are but six reliable fords to cross the Rappahannock River in 35 or 40 miles above Fredericksburg, the first being some two miles away. The country on the south side of this river is densely wooded. It was strongly picketed by each army with heavy forces about the fords. The Rapidan flows into the Rappahannock about ten miles above Fredericksburg from the southwest. The Rappahannock heads in the eastern slope of the Blue Ridge and flows southwesternly.

Genl. Lee's Cavalry was camped about Brandy Station and Culpepper, and he moved his infantry from its position at Fredericksburg behind the Rapidan and the Rappahannock, and marching through a country entirely under control, he entered the Blue Ridge at Rockfish Gap, 50 miles from his starting point. Marching 30 miles further, but now in a northernly direction, he arrives at Staunton.

This place is at the beginning of the Shenandoah Valley, and being the last station he will find on the railroad from Richmond, [it] is Lee's base of supplies. A part of his army is now west of the Blue Ridge. This mountain chain extends from near the Susquehanna north of the Potomac to the James near Lynchburg.

The range affords a natural covered way for an army occupying its western slopes. It can be crossed by Infantry almost any place south of the Potomac, and there are 16 gaps through which good roads pass. It is called the Valley of Virginia, 20 to 50 miles wide, and it is 110 miles from Staunton to the Potomac. The country is exceedingly fertile, and at the time of this Campaign it was called the granary of the Confederacy.

Lee took advantage of this terrain in this way. He sent Ewell, commanding his 2nd Corps, through Staunton and to attack Berryville, Winchester and Martinsburg where there were Union Garrisons. He marched Longstreet's 1st Corps and Stuart's Cavalry, crossing the Rappahannock about Warrenton on the east side of the Blue Ridge. They thus created an uncertainty as to his objective until he had rid the Shenandoah Valley of impediments in the shape of Union forces. Here again he made good use of terrain, as east of the Blue Ridge and parallel with it, running from north to south, is a smaller range called the Bull Run Mountains. Between these and the Blue Ridge, Longstreet and Stuart marched. The Union Army proceeded north generally east of the Bull Run Mountains.

By this skillful use of his forces and the physical features of the country together, he so far covered his real designs that the Army of the Potomac did not discover them until Winchester fell on the 14th of June, or until Ewell's forces had reached the Potomac at Williamsport on the 15th of June.

Crossing the river at Falling Waters and Williamsport, his army entered Maryland at the southern end of the Cumberland Valley and still west of the Blue Ridge. This valley is wider and richer than the one south of the Potomac. The Blue Ridge range is higher, more difficult to cross and with fewer fords. The towns are more frequent, larger and better.

The valley south of the Potomac had to a great extent been overrun by both armies, but the one north of that stream had been undisturbed by warlike sounds or deeds except during the short invasion at the time of the battle of Antietam in September 1862.

It is 25 miles from the Potomac to Chambersburg, 35 miles from that town to Carlisle, and 15 miles from the latter to Harrisburg. The whole 60 miles from Williamsport to Carlisle was west or behind the Blue Ridge. At Chambersburg good roads passed in all directions. Passing through the mountains to the east 25 miles from Chambersburg was Gettysburg. Lee's Army passed north in this covered passageway for one hundred and seventy miles alone except his Cavalry. He made the mistake of allowing Genl. Stuart sort of a free commission, so that he lost the services of this [Stuart's Cavalry] to him, a very important aid, until it was too late to do any good.

Let us now observe the movement of the armies. The Union Army was composed of the 1st Corps, Genl. Reynolds; the 2nd Corps, Genl. Hancock; the 3rd Corps, Genl. Sickles; the 5th, Genls. Meade and Warren; the 6th, Genl. Sedgewick; 11th Corps, Howard; and the 12th, Slocum.

The Confederate Army had but three Corps commanded by [Generals] Longstreet, A.P. Hill and Ewell.

The position of each Army at Fredericksburg was such that neither could flank the other without a wide movement, and Lee decided that he would force the Union Army out of position by an invasion. He begun his movement on the 3rd of June. This was discovered by Genl. Hooker on the 4th of that month, but he did not know how far this movement was to be on its objective.

On the 9th of June Hooker pushed all his Cavalry over the Rappahannock at Kelly and Beaverly Fords, and endeavored to penetrate Lee's screen to find out what was going forward. From information gained, he pushed his Corps forward toward the Blue Ridge and as soon as the news of Ewell's taking Winchester on the 14th of June reached him, Hooker moved all of his Army Corps away from the Rappahannock and fixed his Headquarters at Centerville.

Hooker's handling of the Army of the Potomac was very masterly. As it marched, he had to cover Washington, and to keep his Corps within supporting distance of each other in case of attack. The Cavalry on both sides had frequent combats, and both behaved well.

Genl. Hooker was relieved from command of the Army of the Potomac on the 28th of June, and Genl. George G. Meade was placed in command. The former had never acquired the confidence of the authorities at Washington after his misfortune at Chancellorsville, and they were all afraid that a bad habit would again come to the front at the wrong time, and bring about a disaster again. Officers grew more and more nervous as the armies progressed toward the Susquehanna, and every effort was made to bring from Hooker a resignation of the command. He had handled the Army magnificently on all of the marches from Fredericksburg, but they were fearful that this very success would cause the loss of the Army.

Hooker wanted to send Reynolds with the 1st Corps through the Blue Ridge to attack Lee's communications about Williamsport. The Secretary of War or the authorities said, "No." Hooker wanted to take away the Garrison's 12,000 men of Harper's Ferry to act as a reinforcement of his Army. Again they said, "No," and this brought about the resignation of Hooker.

Genl. Meade, not knowing Hooker's plans, determined from what he knew of the enemy to march directly toward Harrisburg extending his wings as much as possible in order to force Lee to fight a battle before he should cross the Susquehanna. Meade was determined to fight any place he could bring Lee to bay, either by attacking or forcing Lee to attack.

On the 19th of June, Ewell was encamped about Hagerstown, Maryland. Longstreet and Hill followed Ewell, and the whole of Lee's Infantry was camped in the Cumberland Valley on the 21st.

The Army of the Potomac crossed the Potomac at Edward's Ferry on the 25th and 26th of June, and on the 27th the Headquarters of that army were at Frederick, Maryland, east of the Blue Ridge.

On the 21st of June, Lee, elated by his success up to this time, ordered Ewell to take Harrisburg and that General sent Early with his Division through from Chambersburg to York, and at Columbia he burned a bridge over the Susquehanna. Genl. Ewell himself moved with two Divisions to Carlisle. Thus on the 28th of June 1863, the Confederate Army was situated in this way as regards Gettysburg.

Genl. Lee with Longstreet's Corps and that of A.P. Hill was at Chambersburg, 25 miles west of Gettysburg. Ewell at Carlisle, 30 miles north of Gettysburg. Early at York, 30 miles east of Gettysburg. Lee still supposed the Army of the Potomac in Virginia. York was 30 miles from Carlisle, and that town was about 35 miles from Chambersburg.

Being without his Cavalry, Lee did not know until the 28th of June where the Army of the Potomac was. On that day a scout brought him the information that the Union forces were all in the vicinity of Frederick. Lee at once cast aside the old and decided on a new plan of Campaign. The Army of the Potomac now threatened his communications, and Lee ordered, on the 28th, that all his scattered Divisions should unite at Gettysburg to prevent the Union progress further north.

As Early was 60 miles away, Lee moved slowly. Hill's Corps moved nine miles on the 29th and eight on the 30th of June. The leading Division of Hill's Corps under the command of Major Genl. Heth bivouacked at Cashtown on the latter date nine miles from Gettysburg.

On the 29th several Corps of the Army of the Potomac were camped at Emmitsburg and Taneytown 10 or 12 miles from Gettysburg, and on the 30th of June the Headquarters of the Army of the Potomac moved to Taneytown.

On the 30th of June, Buford's Cavalry also moved to Gettysburg via

Emmitsburg, and the 1st Corps under Reynolds moved to Marsh Run five miles from Gettysburg. On this day also happened one of those accidents of war which gives rise to no end of fiction.

As Heth's Division camped only 9 miles from Gettysburg after a march of eight miles, Genl. Pettigrew, commanding one of Heth's Brigades and learning that there was a much needed supply of shoes in Gettysburg, proposed that he go with his Brigade and get them. He was ordered to do so, and not knowing anything of the whereabouts of the Army of the Potomac, he marched down on the town. When arriving near Willoughby's Run he ran into Buford's Cavalry and at once fell back to Cashtown. Heth, with the approval of Hill, then concluded to lead his whole Division into the town the next day, July 1st, and make sure of the shoes.

He too got to Willoughby's Run and attacked Buford. A murderous battle followed. Buford's Cavalry was relieved by the 1st Corps under Reynolds, the latter was helped by Howard and the 11th Corps. The Rebels soon had Rodes from Carlisle on the north, Early from York on the east, and Pender from the west to help them.

Reynolds was killed and the Union forces were forced back to and through the town of Gettysburg, and the battle was a very severe one.

I cannot believe that Gettysburg was an accidental selection for a battleground. Lee's Army was not drifting about aimlessly in the heart of an enemy's country, but I believe it was a machine, an engine controlled by the hand of a master.

On the 28th of June, he ordered a concentration at Gettysburg, and he predicated his order on the movement of his enemy. Had Lee had his Cavalry, he would have known of movements of the Army of the Potomac and so hastened his movements as to have chosen his own ground on which to fight. He had campaigned but little in a country where the people were all hostile to him instead of where every person was a ready scout to bring him news.

On the 1st of July nearly 150,000 men were intent on moving to Gettysburg, and by the dawn of July 2nd, these two armies were facing each other in line of battle. At the end of one day, more [than] 40,000 of these hosts will have shed their blood upon that soil. Within these three days, Rebellion's highest tide had been reached, and from this corpse-laden field, the flood recedes until passing away at Appomattox, and peace again reigns over all our Country.

======

GETTYSBURG IS A STRONG STRATEGIC POSITION, owing to the fact that 14 different roads extend in every direction. All the passes into the Cumberland Valley are easily controlled by the force holding the town. Its possession also to a great extent controls the country east and south toward the Susquehanna and the Potomac.

On the west of the town distant one half mile, there is a somewhat elevated ridge running north and south called Seminary Ridge from the Lutheran Seminary standing there. The ridge extends way off to the south, and at the Peach Orchard the Emmitsburg Road crosses it. It was covered with open woods. To the north it terminated at a distance of one mile from the Seminary in a commanding knoll, bare on its southern side, called Oak Ridge. From this Seminary Ridge, the ground slopes gradually to the west, and again rising, forms another ridge 500 yards from the first upon which stands the McPherson farm buildings. Oak Hill commands both of these ridges.

The McPherson farm slopes away for 600 yards to the west to Willoughby's Run and west of this run is Marsh Creek flowing parallel with Willoughby's Run. Along the McPherson Ridge the battles of the first day took place. Genl. Reynolds arrived on the grounds at an early hour with the 1st Corps, and placing his general line along the McPherson Ridge, advanced a portion of his forces across Willoughby's Run. The Cavalry relieved, retired to the south protecting the left flank.

The battle at this point was murderous, the heaviest losses in any single regiment of either army occurred along the banks of Willoughby's Run. Genl. Reynolds was killed at the corner of the McPherson woods by a Rebel sharpshooter.

Genl. Howard, with the 11th Corps, arrived on the grounds at about 10:00 A.M., and assumed command. He left one Division of the 11th Corps under Steinwehr at the Cemetery back of the town and advanced with the other two Divisions to the side of the 1st Corps. The line was held until Genl. Ewell approached the field from Carlisle.

He took position on Oak Hill, and caused the withdrawal of the Union

Troops first to Seminary Ridge, and then hastily through the town to Cemetery Ridge.

At 4:00 P.M. July 1st, the Confederates made the last attack which forced back the Union Troops. As the men of the 11th Corps arrived on the Cemetery Hill, they took position on the right of Steinwehr while the 1st Corps, under Doubleday, was placed to his left. Steinwehr's position was behind a stone wall along the Emmitsburg Road, and it was very strong. Buford's Cavalry occupied the open ground to Steinwehr's left and presented a firm front against any further pursuit.

The east side of Cemetery Hill is commanded by Culp's Hill, which is a little higher. On this Genl. Howard placed the 7th Indiana Regiment,

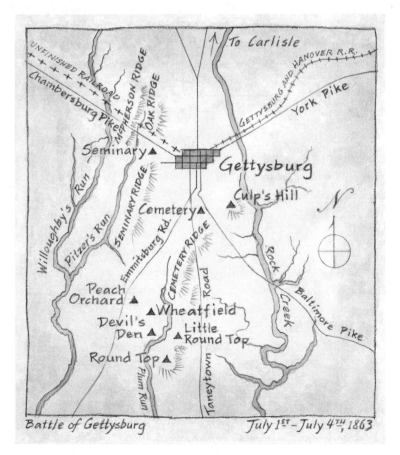

Battle of Gettysburg   July 1st – July 4th, 1863

500 strong and entrenching; they made it secure, their Brigade soon joining them.

This first day's battle was fought by 18,000 Federal Troops against 25,000 Rebels. At its close the Union Army for the first time during that day had the advantage of position.

As those defeated men came onto Cemetery Hill, they found Genl. Hancock there. His presence inspired new confidence and new courage as his person was well known, and he gave assurance that his Corps was near. He had been sent forward by Genl. Howard to take the command of all the forces there as soon as Genl. Meade heard of Reynolds' death.

The matter of the selection of a place for a continuance of the battle was left entirely to Genl. Hancock, and he at once sent a message to Meade saying that this was the best place to fight. Meade then hurried forward the rest of his Army.

Genl. Lee had witnessed the last battle on the 1st of July from the Cupola of the Seminary, and he ordered Ewell to take the Cemetery if practicable. The latter, having been severely handled, was in no condition to make the attack that day.

We, of the 20th Indiana, were camped at Bridgeport and Taneytown on the 30th of June and 1st of July. In the afternoon of the latter day, our Division, commanded by Genl. Birney, was ordered to the front and to march rapidly.

We had about 12½ miles to march and arrived on the grounds near the Cemetery at about 10 o'clock the night of the 30th of June. The other Divisions of the 3rd Corps did not arrive until 8 or 9 o'clock, July 2nd. The other Corps of the Army arrived at Cemetery Ridge during the 1st, the last to get there being the 6th Corps, which marched 32 miles in 30 hours and arrived about 4:30 P.M.

The 12th Corps was placed at Culp's Hill and the [1st] Corps near them. The 3rd Corps was left of the 2nd facing west, and the majority of the Corps was about Peach Orchard and extended from there to the Devil's Den near Little Round Top.

The Regiment occupied a place facing west at the edge of Plum Run and the Devil's Den. Plum Run was a small ravine running in the front of Round Top and 500 yards away. Its winding through the rocks is called Devil's Den.

Genl. Lee decided to attack our left and ordered Longstreet to make the attack on the 2nd of July. This attack was so long delayed that all the Federal Army had arrived on the ground. It did not begin until 4 P.M. The first point of contact was near the Peach Orchard, but the host advancing toward little Round Top soon came upon our Brigade line at the Devil's Den, and we were very hotly engaged.

Our Brigade was composed of the 20th Indiana, the 86th New York, 124th New York, 99th Pennsylvania, 4th Maine, and the 2nd United States Sharpshooters. The line of the 99th Pennsylvania was on our right until the battle begun, when they were taken to the left. To fill the space occupied by the 99th Pennsylvania, two of our Companies under Capt. Bell were extended from our right flank as skirmishers. Capt. Bell had under his command Company B, his own Company, and Company H, Capt. Meikel's Company. Capt. Meikel was absent from the fight.

Capt. Bell handled his men well. He had no breastworks or protection of any kind, our men standing up, loading and firing as cool as possible to imagine.

The Rebels advanced against us over a slight ridge about 600 yards away, then down into a ravine and up against our line. We did not fire from either side till they were about 200 yards away, when both began to fire at once. We had 268 men in line of battle, and in 25 minutes we lost, killed and wounded, 146. Ten men were missing after the battle making our total loss 156. Over one half of all we had were killed and wounded.

The Brigade lost 490, killed and wounded, and 119 missing. Many of the latter were wounded.

The Rebel Troops opposed to our Brigade were the 7th, 8th, 9th, 11th and 59th Georgia Regts., and their loss was 663 killed and wounded.

Amongst our killed was Col. John Wheeler, who was shot by a sharpshooter through the right temple. He was a fine Officer and a brave man. He was killed early in the action, and rather before the Regiment had had much firing. His death was noticed in the most complimentary way by his superiors. At the time of his death the Regiment was in line and he was riding behind it. Soon after he fell, the Major named Taylor came up to me and said, "Gil you will have to take charge of the line, as I am wounded." With that he rode off. I was senior present so took charge of the Regiment and commanded it through the severe firing which followed the absence of Taylor and until the close of the fighting at this point.

On looking about, I found that the Adjutant John E. Luther had left the field with the body of Col. Wheeler. I at first mounted Col. Wheeler's horse but as he became so restive, I could not hold him. I dismounted and let him go.

I sent someone, I do not know who, back to Genl. Ward to request ammunition and with the notice of Col. Wheeler's death. Soon Capt. Alfred M. Raphall, an Aide of Genl. Ward, came to me on the gallop, and as he rode up behind the line firing fast as it could, he said, "Hello Gilbreath, I am sorry Wheeler is gone, but as you are in command, Genl. Ward directs me to say that you must hold this line long as you can using ammunition of the killed and wounded, and when you can stay no longer, fall back toward the small cabin we passed coming in."

Capt. Raphall had no more than completed this instruction when a ball from a Rebel rifle struck him in the left arm. He asked me to help him off his horse, which I did, and putting [him] in my blanket, I sent him to the rear to a Hospital. Raphall had his arm taken off, and later was appointed to the Regular Army. In the changes of the Regiments, he was finally assigned to the 11th Infantry and to my Company.

Twenty-one years after the battle, I was in Chicago one day and picking up the *Chicago Tribune* found that Raphall was stopping at the Palmer House [Hotel]. I went to see him, and we had our first meeting since I lifted him off his horse at Gettysburg.

Among those mortally wounded was Lieut. Ezra B. Robbins. He was shot fairly in the breast. I was just behind him and helped him to the rear to a tree about 10 feet away and left him behind it.

The enemy had begun firing at about 200 yards from us and kept moving slowly forward, checked by our fire. As our losses were so heavy and ammunition gone, I ordered the men to fall back and follow the flag closely.

The Rebels laughed at us as we marched back, and their fire was concentrated on our color.

Sgt. William I. Horine, the Color-bearer, was shot through the right leg and fell. As he did so, the flag went down when it was seized by a boyish

Corporal who carried it to the rear. As the flag fell, the Rebels laughed out again and thought they had it, but we soon met the 5th New Hampshire Regiment and the Regulars and stopped behind their line to collect our men. The Rebels advanced no further then.

We stopped at the edge of the woods to collect the men and call the rolls of the Companies. This was being quietly done when Capt. Bell came to us. He ranked me and so took command. His first act was to seize the Color and try to sing "Rally round the Flag Boys," & etc.

Now Bell was a fine man, and a brave one, but he could not sing at all, so his music had no effect. He rushed to the rear with the flag in his hand, and waving it hard as he could and trying to sing, made an amusing sight. The men seeing him run back with the flag, not understanding that his efforts were the most patriotic possible, they started themselves to the rear. We collected then, and the sorrowful little band went to a rocky prominence a little north of Little Round Top and were there placed for the night. This prominence was not so high as Round Top, but was on the line from the latter to Cemetery Ridge, and gave a good view in all the northern direction. Thus ended the second day of July for us.

The Rebels, 18,000 strong, had driven off Sickles' 3rd Corps of 10,000 men, but were stopped soon as they reached a stronger force. After dark, while at the rocks, the mail was brought up to us. There was for us a whole wagonload, and on opening mine I found my Commission as Major of the 20th Indiana.

I was not the senior Captain, and this new commission came to me in this way: Lieut. Col. J. H. Shannon resigned on the 6th of June while we were in camp near Falmouth.

The Captains were Meikel, Bell and myself as third. The Officers of the Regiments assembled when Col. Shannon's resignation went forward and drew up a petition to the Governor of the State of Indiana asking that I be appointed Major over the heads of Meikel & Bell. This was done by the Governor, and here at Gettysburg I got the Commission dated June 6th, 1863.

During the battle described, Meikel's Company H was on the right; Bell's Company B was on the left; and my Company I, in the center.

My Company was thus the Color Company. It lost all but 11 men of the 27 in it on going into the battle. Capt. Meikel was acting on the Staff of Genl. Ward, and Capt. Bell was detached with skirmishers.

The 3rd of July dawned with a glaring sun, and we were left alone in our rocky bivouac. From our position, we being considerably above the ridge on which our general line was formed, [we] had an unobstructed view clear off to the Seminary and up our line to the Cemetery.

Our men and our batteries were moving about and into position. We could also see that on Seminary Ridge from 1000 to 1400 yards from our line, the Rebels were active to a degree. Dust arose as their column or batteries moved about, and there was only an occasional shot as if to get the range from either side.

At 10 A.M. all sounds seemed to cease, and a calm almost appalling enwrapped the two armies. We could not rest since the dawn. The tension was too great, and several hours of this silence passed to be broken at 1:00 P.M. by two signal guns way off to the left.

At once all the batteries on the Rebel side, 150 guns in one long line, opened and sent a continuous stream of shot and shell against our line ½ mile from us toward the Cemetery. Our 80 guns in the position assailed, replied, and the sight was one never to be forgotten. So mighty an artillery contest had never before been waged. For two hours all the Rebel batteries continued this fire.

Our batteries gradually ceased firing. Finally, at 3 P.M., and soon as their firing ceased, we could see the Rebel column form for attack and Pickett's Charge began and our batteries at once begun firing again.

Pickett's column for the attack was about 200 yards wide, and 700 yards deep. They marched slowly, deliberately and seemingly indifferent to the fire of our artillery. The shot and shell from our batteries tore great gaps in their ranks and still they bore on. From where we were, we could see that far, full 1400 yards, they made no halt at all. Up the slight raise to the Emmitsburg Road, they walked down the little declivity on the east side of the road and on to our batteries. Many fell, of course, some fell away and returned to their rear. They had almost reached our guns when an Aide called us to attention and our Brigade under command of Col. Berdan faced to the right and started on the run for the batteries.

At the end of one half mile, the command was given by the left flank, march, and into the batteries we flew. As we approached, we saw our main line broken, Rebels were all in and around the guns. A Rebel flag was being waved by a man on a gun. There were men mingled in every sort of confusion firing, yelling, cheering, and the ground was covered with every sort of debris to be found on a battlefield.

The Rebels threw down their arms, and were prisoners. Pickett's Charge had passed into history. Our Regiment was placed into position at a stone fence in front of our batteries and there remained till dark.

Pickett's men had passed that wall, and 100 feet beyond had seized our guns. One hundred feet from where we lay that evening is an immense monument now in the form of an open book, and on its bronze pages lying open is recorded the fact that it marks the spot as that to which the high water mark of the Rebellion rose.

In our movement to support the batteries, we were accompanied by the 4th Maine and 99th Pennsylvania. These three Regiments were placed on picket along the Emmitsburg Road on the morning of the 4th of July. Our position was at a little orchard across the road from the Cadori House. We were here on the exact line of march of Pickett's charging column and had a fair chance to see the effect of our artillery fire on his advancing troops. The ground was well covered with dead singly, or in groups where shells had exploded.

The 4th of July was thus spent among these evidences of carnage, and the stench of the dead men and animals was almost unbearable. It was a showery day, but very hot so that we actually suffered from the heat and stench. We remained on picket until the morning of the 5th of July when we were relieved and joined our Brigade.

———

I DO NOT WISH TO ENTER INTO A FULL DESCRIPTION of all the battles of Gettysburg, but will point out some of the vital movements of this battle. These periods of time I regard as of such importance, that at any one of them, the Southern Hosts were near something else than a "Glorious field of grief."

First: Had Lee's Cavalry been with him, he could have selected ground on which to have fought instead of having aggressive action forced upon him.

Second: Lee should have seized Round Top early on the 2nd of July, and having once decided to attack our left with his right, he should have forced the attack earlier in the day, on the 2nd of July, rather than 4 P.M. Federal Troops were arriving on the field from 7 A.M. to 4 P.M. that day.

Third: Had Longstreet had a heavy reserve to follow up his break in the 3rd Corps line, there would have been no help for us.

Fourth: Early had been ordered to attack the Cemetery Hill as soon as he heard Longstreet attack on the 2nd of July. He took the Hill but Rodes and Pender did not advance to help, so Early was driven off. If he could have held the batteries he took, Early could have enfiladed our entire line from Cemetery Hill to Round Top.

Fifth: Johnson's Division of Ewell's Corps, instead of attacking with Earley on the northeast front of Cemetery Hill, was sent to attack on the east side of Culp's Hill. Johnson found the Hill occupied, but he took possession of the empty trenches where the 12th Corps had been, they having been withdrawn to assist the 3rd Corps. At dark Johnson was 300 yards from the Baltimore Pike, 800 yards from Genl. Meade's headquarters. He might have created great havoc had he known where he was. Only one half mile from him was all our ammunition train and reserve artillery.

Sixth: The sixth point was in Pickett's charge. No strong support helped him by following closely.

The comparative strength of the two armies is quite difficult to obtain.

The weather was hot and there was a great deal of straggling from both armies, but the best guess one could make is for the Union forces, 93,500 men of all arms; Confederate forces, 70,000.

The losses of men:

Union:

Killed	3072
Wounded	14,497
Missing and Prisoners	5434
Total	23,003

Confederates:

Killed	2592
Wounded	12,709
Missing and Prisoners	5150
Total	20,451

Total killed, 5664; Total wounded, 27,206; Total, 32,870.

The Rebels rule was to count only those as wounded who were so disabled as to leave the field, while the Union Army always counted all those hit in its reports.

On the 4th of July, Lee sent off all of his impediments and his Army began its march through the mountains that night. The Army of the Potomac began its march to follow Lee on the 5th of July.

The battlefield of Gettysburg has been made a beautiful park and over $800,000 have been spent for monuments and land. Each Regiment has a monument on the ground where it fought, and many of the monuments are very costly. The State of Minnesota had only one Regiment in the battle, and for its monument (the 1st Minnesota) the State spent $20,000.

The 3rd Corps in which the 20th Indiana was camped at Marsh Creek, six miles from Gettysburg, was engaged in burying the dead from the 5th to the 7th of July, when it took up its march south. We marched to Mechanicstown to three miles west of Frederick [Maryland] to Foxes Gap in South Mountains, then to Boonsborough [Boonsboro] and Antietam Creek. We crossed Marsh Creek and were in position to attack Lee who was about Williamsport on the 15th of July.

On the 17th we crossed the Potomac at Harper's Ferry and camped three miles away on the Virginia side. On the 18th we marched to Hillsborough, thence to Wood Grove and to Happerville. From Happerville we marched on the 22nd of July by way of Piedmont to Linden, and to Manassas Gap, then to Salem and on the 26th of July we camped at Warrenton, Virginia.

The 3rd Corps was commanded by Major or Genl. W.H. French from the 9th of July. Lieut. Col. Taylor was promoted to be Colonel of the 20th Indiana from July 3, 1863.

On the march to Warrenton, the 3rd Corps was ordered to assist Buford's Cavalry in seizing Manassas Gap, and the First Division now commanded by Genl. Ward was sent to Linden where it took possession of the Gap at a place called Wapping Heights.

We were deployed and under fire all day, but lost only two men killed and six wounded. As we were in the midst of our preparations for an advance on Wapping Heights, we saw away off to our right a line of apparent skirmishers. Genl. French was very excitable. He was called "Blinky French" on account of a blinking habit he had. Soon as he saw the supposed skirmishers he concluded at once they were enemies and made dispositions to protect his right flank. It was no fun moving about in the hot sun, but we got into position in time to meet the skirmishers. On near approach, they turned out to be about 50 of our stragglers, who had gotten to some farmhouse up in the mountains and had there found a fine flock of sheep. Each man seized a sheep and tying its feet together came in with it on his back.

COMMENTARY: *Often called the "high tide of the Confederacy," the battle of Gettysburg in early July 1863 was indeed a decisive one, as Genl. Lee's bold, all-out effort to take the war to the north failed. When the two armies moved into battle lines, Genl. Sickles pushed his III Corps (including the 20th Indiana) too far forward on the Union left and neglected to secure the high ground at Little Round Top, exposing their position to a flank attack. Lee noticed and sent Genl. Longstreet's two divisions to attack Sickles's position. Much of Sickles's Corps was destroyed, but the Union line was held, thanks to rapid reinforcement by the reserve V Corps. Lee's frontal attack (Pickett's Charge) was preceded by a huge but ineffective Rebel artillery barrage. The massive infantry attack failed to break the Union line, and the costliest battle ever fought on American soil ended in a Union victory.*

CHAPTER 13

RIOTS IN NEW YORK CITY

1863

O n the 30th day of July 1863, the 20th Indiana was one of the four Regiments selected from the Army of the Potomac to go to New York City to aid in the suppression of rioters who wished to oppose any draft.

On our march into Virginia, after the battle of Gettysburg, we in the 3rd Corps camped along Antietam Creek from the 13th to the 17th of July. We camped at the Burnside Bridge for a few days and had a fine opportunity to examine that interesting field. Our march from there was by way of Foxes Gap to cross the Potomac.

On the 12th of July 1863, the attempt was made to make a draft in New York City and a great riot occurred in the streets. Provost Marshall's offices were sacked, and many persons were killed, amongst the rest a good many negroes.

It never was definitely known exactly how many people were injured in these riots. Riots also occurred about the same time in Boston and in Buffalo.

The Government decided to enforce the draft and sent something like 10,000 men from the Army of the Potomac for that purpose.

The first regiments sent to New York were the 1st and 37th Massachusetts, 5th Wisconsin and the 20th Indiana. They left the Army on the 31st of July 1863 [and] were under the command of Col. Oliver Edwards of the 37th Massachusetts.

We went by rail as fast as cars could carry us through Washington, Baltimore, Philadelphia and through New Jersey to Perth Amboy from which place we were taken by boat to Pier No. 1, New York City, and landed.

We had started from about Falmouth on the Gettysburg Campaign on the 5th of June, had marched to Gettysburg, and after fighting that battle had marched back into Virginia. On [the] beginning of the Gettysburg march, we had stored all our baggage not carried on our person in the train. I never saw my trunk again and all of the Regiment[s] were about in the same condition of having only the clothes they had marched 500 miles in through dust and heat and rain. I remember my coat was stiff with the dust, & etc. Most of us had only dreamed of a city like New York and few had seen such a place.

The sight on getting on the pier baffles description. The Battery was at that time all open, no elevated road and nothing, not even many trees to obstruct the view.

As we tied up, we found the pier and all of the place about the Battery clear over beyond Castle Garden filled with a howling mob of men, women and children. The pier was covered, and the calls and yells of derision of this mob amused us. They cried, "Yez can't enforce yer draft if ye bring yer whole d---d Army of Potomac up here."

We made no reply but every once in a while some dirty Hoosier would take out a few cartridges carefully saved through a field campaign, and tossing a handful into the crowd would say, "Look at those, they are all loaded." They were 54 caliber and very heavy cartridges.

We formed a line of a Company across the pier, [and] fixing bayonets, marched off driving the crowd before us.

The Regiment was formed in line and finally the Brigade, and so in line with fixed bayonets, we cleared the Battery Park.

We camped there that night, and the crowds forced our sentinels in so often that we had them doubled until one man for every five yards surrounded our camp.

Next day about the 3rd of August, we were told off for various duties. I went with four companies to Gramercy Park.

As we marched up Broadway, we were a sight to behold. Unshaven, dirty, in old clothes with our bright guns and brilliant red patches we looked as we felt, like business.

Crowds followed us. A few police marched in front and rear.

Arriving at Gramercy Park I searched every gate and could not get in, but a man came with a key and into the Park we marched. In a few moments shelter tents, or dog tents as they were called, were pitched and there we were as comfortable as on any other Campaign.

Crowds filled the streets, and fences and windows were packed with human beings to watch our every action.

The proprietor of the Gramercy Park Hotel came over and asked the Officers to go to the Hotel. We did so and were amazed to find that he had picked out very convenient rooms for us to occupy. We were more amazed to see the Hotel. It was so large as to extend from street to street facing the Park, and it was filled with Spanish and Cuban people. None of us had ever seen such lovely women, or met more refined men.

We had to guard an Armory on 4th Avenue, and another on 6th Avenue, and our duties did not amount to much.

Genl. Canby lived at this Hotel, and he laughed at our first appearance in the dining room. He was in command of the troops in the city. We soon fitted ourselves and our men out to look decent, and enjoyed life very much. Our men caused us no trouble. The draft passed off all smoothly as the mere presence of so many men from the Army of the Potomac in the city maintained the peace.

But the order came for us to go after about three weeks stay at Gramercy Park.

We had lived at the top of the heap, had four meals a day, and the run of the Hotel, and had paid nothing or thought of paying, so when the order came to go to other duties, we were appalled to think of what our bills might be.

I got the Officers together, and told of the order and slowly broached the subject of the hotel bills. All had been thinking of that subject. On taking an invoice, we found about $50.00 in the party of ten Officers, and I was deputized to make terms with the hotel man. On approaching him he said he would meet us at Luncheon in the ordinary and say good-bye.

After the party was seated, he arose and announced that I had called for the bills of the party, and he had only to reply that in the glass of champagne, which he held aloft, the full bill of each and everyone of us was canceled.

So we left, and I went to Fort Schuyler with the Headquarters & Companies B, D, F, & G, while Lieut. Col. Mickel went to David's Island with Companies A, C, E, and H.

Fort Schuyler was under the command of Genl. Harvey Brown, and as both he and Col. Taylor were on other duties, I was left in command. In fact, I relieved the General one day, the last of his stay at Fort Schuyler. I can never forget my meeting with the old man.

I was only 23, and was long and thin and with a boyish face, and I never felt so small and out of place as when I walked off the boat at the Schuyler Landing and met old Genl. Harvey Brown. He was an old soldier quite gray and the personification of dignity. He turned over the command to me about the 24th of August. In a short time I was detailed on a board of examination for Officers. The Board was to meet at Fort Hamilton and composed of Regular Army Officers entirely, with the exception of Col. Edwards, 37th Massachusetts, and myself.

Capt. Royal I. Frank, 8th Infantry, now Colonel 1st Artillery, was on the Board, and there were four other Captains including D. D. Lynn, 6th Infantry, as Recorder.

Col. Edwards sent for me and said, "Major, have you ever served with Regulars?" I said, "No." "Well," he said, "This Board is composed of Regular Officers except you and me. Now we rank the crowd and will have to hold them down."

We went out to Hamilton, and met as pleasant a party of gentlemen as one could imagine. Finally, on the 13th of October, we were ordered to assemble at Governor's Island to return to the Army of the Potomac.

On the 16th we were taken by steamer to Amboy and thence by rail to the Army. We found them near Centerville, and went back into our old Brigade, the 2nd of the 1st Division, 3rd Corps.

The riot in New York thus gave us a delightful outing for two and a half months, and we entered on our field service again with a zest, even if the first march to Kelly's Ford was a little wearisome.

COMMENTARY: *From the outset of the war, volunteers filled the ranks of the Union Army. (The Confederacy implemented conscription in April 1862 for all white males.) The Union initiated conscription in early 1863. It provoked major riots; in New York City over 100 people died.*

CHAPTER 14

KELLY'S FORD & MINE RUN

1863-1864

I n the beginning of November 1863, the Federal Army occupied a line along Lickings Run about Catlett's Station and it was deemed desirable to advance beyond the Rappahannock to winter, if possible. Accordingly, an advance begun on the 7th of November. The 3rd Corps marched 17 miles in six hours, and went into position opposite Kelly's Ford at noon. The north bank of the river here was much higher than the south side and commanded the latter. From our position we were in plain view of the Rebel camps across the river. Our batteries were soon in position, and at 1:30 P.M. opened fire on the Rebels.

Several Regiments of DeTrobriand's 3rd Brigade, with the 20th Indiana and 99th Pennsylvania, were ordered to charge across the river and take possession of the Rebel earthwork on which our artillery was playing. The ford was about wide enough for a Company front, so we crossed in column of Companies. The water was about up to our waists, but into it we went and, on the run, up the bank.

The Rebels made a short resistance, and then fell back to Brandy Station. We had eight wounded in the Regiment. We captured their camps and found that they had prepared log huts in the hope of spending the winter there. We captured 400 prisoners, a large mail just in from the south and a good deal of camp equipage. The mail afforded us no end of amusement.

Maj. Genl. French had command not only of his own, the 3rd Corps, but of the 1st and 2nd Corps.

On the 8th of November we were ordered to advance on Brandy Station, eight miles from Kelly's Ford. The 3rd Corps advanced and, on nearing the Station, found some Rebel Infantry in position. The 3rd Division, 3rd Corps went forward and had quite a little skirmish, but the Rebels fell back beyond the Rapidan River.

We then began our preparation to stop all winter near Brandy Station, and the various Brigades were placed in position to enable them to easily erect huts to live in. The different regiments vied with each other in displaying skill in design and arrangement of their huts. The 17th Maine and our Regiment were rather ahead in the construction.

Our camp was about a mile from the house of John Minor Botts, an old Virginian who had protected his home by sort of a middle course. I suppose there is no doubt but he opposed secession and so went for a Union man. He had a fine large mansion, and we were compelled to protect it in every way. Men carried off his fences. We had to rebuild them, & etc. Our Camp was in the pine forest, and was very pleasant in every way.

It was believed by Union Officers of rank that Lee's Army was very much reduced in November 1863, because it was supposed that he had sent many of his troops to the west. Hence, on the 26th of November, the Army of the Potomac was ordered from its camps to cross the Rapidan and to attack Lee in his position about Mine Run. Eight days' rations were issued to the men, and only a few wagons crossed the Rapidan. The Army was to be concentrated about Robertson's Tavern. This was on the Orange Plank Road, which ran from Fredericksburg to Orange Courthouse and about 25 miles from Fredericksburg. The tavern was at about the beginning of the open country after the Wilderness had been passed going south from the Rappahannock.

The 3rd Corps crossed at Jacob's Ford, which is near the mouth of the Mine Run, just before dark on the 26th of November and camped ½ mile from the river. The Ford was a very difficult one as the bluffs, especially on the southern side, were so steep that all our ambulances and artillery had to be sent down the river to Germania Ford and joined with great difficulty during the night. The mud was fearful.

At 7 A.M. on the 27th we left the bivouac and started for Robertson's Tavern. At a mile or so from Jacob's Ford, as we passed up the road, I saw old Genl. French hastily studying a map and we changed our direction slightly soon after. Advancing to a ridge called Locust Grove, we walked into the flank of a Rebel Column marching toward Mine Run. The 3rd Corps deployed and we soon came under a strong fire losing from the Corps about 1,000 men, killed and wounded. This mistake of the road caused a failure of Meade's plan of campaign.

We drove the enemy off the field at Locust Grove and remained there overnight. At daylight on the 28th of November we were on the march again for Robertson's Tavern and went into position on the right of the 2nd Corps which was commanded by Genl. G. K. Warren.

Genl. Meade decided that he would attack Lee on the right, left and center at the same time. Genl. Warren was to give the signal by firing his artillery on our extreme left.

We were formed on the 30th in three lines of skirmishers. The first line was at 20 yards interval, the second at ten yards, and the third at 5 yards; then the columns were to follow. These lines of skirmishers were about 100 yards apart. We could see from our position that the dirt was flying from the shovels of the Rebels and that they were strengthening their position fast as possible. It was ¾ of a mile for our charge, and it looked awfully serious. The men showed that they too thought of the chance against them, and each man stuck his name on a piece of paper to some part of his clothing. They tucked up the skirts of their overcoats to have them out of the way in running up the hill.

The long line of skirmishers extended far as the eye could see to the right and left, and we were all ready and awaiting for the signal gun. That signal never came as Genl. Warren reported that it was not practicable to charge without very great loss. Genl. Meade then gave up the idea and at 6:30 P.M. December 1st, we begun our retreat by way of Culpepper Ford crossing at 5:30 A.M. on the 2nd of December. On the 3rd we went back into our old camps near Brandy Station. The Regiment lost fourteen men wounded on the expedition. We remained at this camp until January 9, 1864, when the camp was moved to the farm of M. Rixey, 3½ miles from Brandy Station, and 2½ miles from Culpepper Courthouse. We remained here in winter quarters. February 6th we left all baggage in camp and marched to Raccoon Ford and encamped near Pony Mountain for the night. On the 7th, we marched two miles closer to the Ford and then back to our camp at Mr. Rixey's Farm.

February 28th we marched with five days' rations to James City and encamped there, supporting the 6th Corps at Madison Courthouse. The time from our return to camp on the 3rd of December was occupied in picket duty and little other work. We amused ourselves the best we could.

Our Sutler had been a member of the fillibuster ring expedition of Walker the American to Costa Rica, and he had great resources of fun. We repaid him by helping him out when the Provost Marshalls got after him. The latter were very strict. We received a good many papers of all sorts and were amazed to find that our favorite newspaper man had been arrested, tried, found guilty and hung for a spy.

On the 9th of January 1864, we changed camp to the farm of Mr. Rixey, 3½ miles from Brandy Station and 2½ miles from Culpepper Courthouse. On our first arrival at this camp, we found the water not very good or plentiful. In searching about, I found a damp place which I sought to develop by digging out the soil. I was successful in discovering a fine spring, which I walled in and we had fine drinking water long as we remained there.

We occasionally had a review at Division or Corps Headquarters, and twice we were all turned out to see deserters shot. Each of these times the entire Corps was marched to the ground and formed into lines on three sides of a square. The doomed men were brought in a wagon, sitting on their coffins, the music playing the "Rogue's March." Arriving at the graves, the coffin was placed near it and each deserter placed sitting on his coffin. A firing party was drawn up and arms placed in their hands. These guns had been stacked on the grounds, one half being loaded and the other half having no balls in them, so that none of the firing party could know whether his gun was loaded or not. The Provost Marshall gave the commands, "READY," "AIM," "FIRE," and all the guns went off at once. The troups then marched off, all passing the graves. Our Corps had only two occasions of this kind, and only two men thus shot.

John Minor Botts, near whose place we were, was anxious to be on good terms with us, but he was not quite enough decided to please all of our Officers and men.

At a reception given by Genl. Birney, reference was made to the fact that Botts was a Union man always. An Officer named Nash in a boisterous way denied that this was true, and getting upon a chair said that his

Nash's was not like Botts' as the former spelled, if one counted the fingers both on the back and on the palm, U-N-I-O-N, while Botts could spell on one side of his, R-E-B-E-L.

We men discussed, amongst ourselves, one day on the subject of names of individuals; one side saying that a distinguished or pleasing cognomen would draw the attention of nicer people and a larger number of people, than one without those qualities, while the other side said it would not make any difference. At that day, the *Waverly Magazine* was quite a paper, especially for such boys as we were, and it contained numberless advertisements for correspondence. We thought it would be fun to test our argument by advertising for correspondents. Each put his name in a way to suit himself and these ranged from Reginald DeCourcey to plain Edward Murphy. The test was a good one in a way, as the names selected of a high sounding or distinguished character received letters from correspondents of evidently higher grade in the world than plain Edward Murphy. I might say that all of us got bushels of replies from all over the country, but I know of no lasting romance connected with this attempt at a little fun, nor do I know of any injury to anyone from the venture.

We lived high during this entire winter, as our Sutlers brought us everything we could desire from Washington. But in the Summer of 1864, we paid fully for all the good living and fun of the winter. On March 2nd we returned to camp. On March 10th Genl. Grant, having been promoted to be Lieutenant General, was assigned to [the] command of the Armies of the United States and made his Headquarters with those of the Army of the Potomac.

The three years' service of many regiments was soon to expire in 1864, and the Government decided to induce the men to re-enlist as veterans. To that end Genl. Meade offered in December 1863 to give a month's furlough to every man who promised to re-enlist at end of his term then going on. If three fourths of any organization re-enlisted, the whole could go to their homes with their Officers, flags, arms and entire equipment.

The 20th Indiana decided to veteranize, as it was called, and all but about twenty gave their promise to enlist again. The Regiment went in a body to Indianapolis in the beginning of April 1864, the route being to Washington, Baltimore, Harrisburg and so on.

Arriving at Indianapolis, the Regiment was given a great reception by the people. It was marched to the State House and expected to be received by the Governor, Oliver P. Morton. He had been compelled to be out of the city, and had asked Genl. Carrington to act in his place. This General had been of great service to the Governor in many ways, but he had never been at the front, or in any battle at all, hence was not popular with old soldiers. So as he stepped to the front in the uniform of a Brigadier General and said in a loud voice, "Fellow Soldiers," every man in the Regiment hissed as loudly as he could. Again he begun, "Friends & Comrades," and the hissing was louder than before. He finally turned about and asked the Colonel to say to the men that Governor Morton regretted that he could not be there to receive them.

We all got furloughs to go where we pleased, and had full thirty days at home when the Regiment again collected and, with not a man absent, left again for the front. The Regiment at this time numbered full 800 men, counting old men and new. When we got back to the Army of the Potomac, we found many changes. The Corps were consolidated and our dear old 3rd Corps as well as the 1st were no longer in existence. The 3rd Corps was consolidated into two Divisions, and we were assigned to be a part of the 2nd Corps to be commanded by Genl. W. S. Hancock.

We were still allowed to wear our 3rd Corps diamond badge and never adopted the trefoil of the 2nd Corps. The discontent at breaking [the] 3rd Corps up was very great, as we had toiled, marched, fought and many of us had bled and seen our Comrades die under the diamond badge, and in its glorious record we all rejoiced. It was the first adopted (by Genl. Kearney) and all the sorrow at losing it, as a sign of some distinct body, was very great. The feeling has not yet passed away, as the Veterans of the 3rd Corps Society still wear their old time badge and have a separate Society distinct from all the rest of the Corps Societies.

We feel that the glorious record made by the 3rd Corps, from Yorktown through Williamsburg in front of Richmond, the Seven Days, Bull Run, Fredericksburg, Chancellorsville and Gettysburg, to have been so filled with glorious deeds that no other body can absorb or appreciate their full brilliancy. The consolidation of the Army Corps took place on the 24th of March when Genl. Hancock took command of the 2nd Corps.

On our return from Veteran furlough, we found the old Division of the 3rd Corps camped at Cole's Hill near Brandy Station where we joined them.

Genl. Grant remained almost constantly with the Army of the Potomac after our return from Indiana, and his presence instilled the most absolute confidence that we would accomplish something at last. All seemed to feel that his best efforts would be called for, and high and low were mentally prepared for the coming campaign.

The Army now consisted of the 2nd Corps commanded by Hancock, 5th Corps by Warren, 6th Corps by Sedgewick, and the 9th Corps under Burnside joined after the march begun. In all, there were about 121,000 men under Meade's command on the 4th of May 1864, while Lee had about 75,000 present of 98,000 present and absent.

Before the '64 Campaign began, Genl. Meade was instructed that Lee's Army would be his objective, that wherever Lee went, he would go also. The two plans of campaign offering themselves were one by Lee's right flank and the other by his left. It was decided to cross the Rapidan below Lee, moving by his right flank on account of the facility with which a base of supplies could be changed from one point to another as we progressed, as well as the ease with which we could keep up the connection with Genl. B. F. Butler, who was ordered to go up the James River toward Richmond and Petersburg.

There were 4300 wagons with the Army on May 4th and 835 ambulances; 29,945 public horses, 4046 private [horses], and there were 22,528 mules.

The Campaign of 1864 was called the "Grand Campaign," and Genl. Meade divided it into five Epochs:

1ST EPOCH:	The crossing of the Rapidan, and the Battle of the Wilderness, to the 7th of May.
2ND EPOCH:	8th to 20th of May 1864, the march to Spotsylvania and the battle there with other operations.
3RD EPOCH:	The March to the North Anna, May 21st to May 28, 1864.
4TH EPOCH:	Totopotomoy, Cold Harbor; crossing the Pamunkey May 28th to June 11th.
5TH EPOCH:	The march across the Chickahominy and James including the mine explosion (July 30, 1864), from June 12th.

CHAPTER 15

The Wilderness

1864

The 2nd Corps, consisting of about 27,000 men, broke camp at Cole's Hill and marched at midnight on the 3rd of May 1864 toward Ely's Ford. We arrived there at 5:25 A.M. on the 4th of May, crossed at once, and formed to cover the crossing of the trains.

At 8:15 A.M. our head of the column marched for Chancellorsville, five miles further on, and arriving there at 10:00 A.M., the Corps camped on the same ground where we had fought in the battle of Chancellorsville on the May of 1863.

The orders for the entire Army were to proceed as rapidly as possible toward the Po River about Shady Grove Church. At the same time that we moved at midnight of the 3rd of May or beginning of the 4th of May, the 5th and 6th Corps left their camps at Culpepper Courthouse, crossing at Germania Ford about six miles from Ely's Ford where we crossed.

The 5th Corps bivouacked at old Wilderness Tavern supported by the 6th Corps at the same time that we of the 2nd Corps stopped at Chancellorsville. The old Wilderness Tavern was on the Orange Courthouse Pike, and at 6 A.M. of the 5th of May, the 5th Corps followed by the 6th set out for Parker's Store, which was about four miles from their camp and was on the Orange Plank Road.

About the same hour, 6:00 A.M., the 2nd Corps started for Todd's Tavern. Both Parker's Store and Todd's Tavern were on the direct line of march for the two columns going to their place of concentration about the Po River.

The Cavalry had preceded the Infantry in crossing the Rapidan, and in the advance and soon after the start of the 5th Corps, they found the Rebels in possession of the Orange Plank Road about Parker's Store.

The 2nd Corps marched in the meantime to Todd's Tavern, and had arrived at a point about 2 miles beyond that Tavern at 10 A.M. where Genl. Hancock's command was informed of the presence of the enemy in Warren's front, and he [Hancock] was directed to march back and into the Brock Road for the purpose of supporting Warren.

Early in the morning of the 5th of May, Generals Grant and Meade had ridden to the front near Parker's Store and had determined to attack the force opposing Warren on the Orange Plank Road; hence the change of direction for our Corps.

In order to make the story of this campaign more easily understood and interesting, I would like to give a short description of the country in which these operations occurred after the crossing of the Rapidan. Words are not adequate to convey a full description of the country as it was then. Only one who saw this terrain could understand what it was like.

There was nothing in my experience, either in the Army or out of it, to compare it to. It was located in Orange and Spotsylvania Counties and was the poorest part of Virginia. The clayey soil lacked fertility to such a degree that enterprise had been discouraged and the face of the country had been given over to nature.

A dense thicket of Black Jack Oak and pine covered most of the ground. There were none of the improvements found in more prosperous communities. There were two excellent roads leading from Chancellorsville to Orange Courthouse. One was macadamized and the other planked, and they ran in an irregular parallel about four to six miles apart.

The country from Chancellorsville west for 12 miles and south for 10 miles is so densely covered by the thicket mentioned that its local name is the Wilderness. It extends also north to the Rapidan about 7 or 8 miles.

Orange Courthouse had been Lee's Headquarters during the winter of 1863 and '64, and on all previous campaigns in this country, the two roads mentioned had been regarded of the greatest value; they were Lee's best lines of retreat.

It will be understood at once that the use of the Wilderness was of a great advantage to either one or the other of the forces holding it. No one can conceive of a more unfavorable field for the movements of a grand army than this presents from Germania or Ely's Ford south to Todd's Tavern about 15 miles or from Chancellorsville to Mine Run about the same distance. The road crossing at Germania passes through the Wilderness to the Pike, and another road, called the Brock Road, crossing the Orange Plank Road extends the route to Todd's Tavern.

It will also be understood that Grant and Meade wished to pass this Wilderness as soon as possible, while Lee was equally desirous of holding Grant's Army in the thicket, if he could. Grant and Meade had thus sent the 2nd Corps through by an exterior road, but the immense train of the Army was not to be moved so rapidly.

Lee, in furtherance of his object, demonstrated against Warren, and Grant in return determined to attack. Warren attacked at once with two Divisions impetuously and carried the works of the enemy, but was flanked on his right and fell back to his starting point along the Brock Road where it strikes the Pike. He was flanked because the 6th Corps could not get through the thicket quickly enough.

Hancock moved the 2nd Corps into the Brock Road and at 2 P.M. arrived at the Orange Plank Road with our Division [Birney's]. He then found that Genl. Getty of the 6th Corps and Wadsworth of the 5th had formed before him on the right of the Plank Road.

Our Brigade filed up the Plank Road to connect with Wadsworth and Getty. We had gotten into position along the Brock Road in two lines from right to left, Birney's Division with our Brigade on the right along the Plank Road, Mott's Division next to the left, and then Gobbon next to Mott.

At 4:15 P.M., May 6th, Getty moved forward and we with him, and had very severe musketry fire continuously from 4:15 P.M. until about 8 P.M.

We slept on the battlefield. At 5 A.M. the 2nd Corps assaulted the enemy on the left of the Plank Road and we drove him steadily for one and a half miles. Out of ammunition, we were driven slowly back to the Brock Road. At 8:50 A.M. our Division again advanced and the fighting was very severe and bloody. The official report shows that the 20th Indiana captured the Colors of the 55th Virginia and of the 8th Georgia and a large number of prisoners. The Colors of the 55th Virginia were taken by Sgt. William D. Thompson, and that of the 8th Georgia by Sgt. Joseph R.

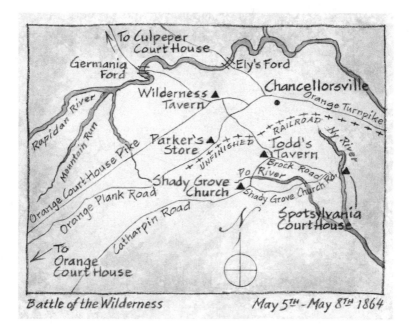

Battle of the Wilderness   May 5TH - May 8TH 1864

Barrett. The latter was captured as the Rebels charged our breastworks. The Major of the 8th Georgia, with the flag in his hand, came up on top of the log forming the work, and was killed by Sgt. Barrett and his flag taken. Both Sergeants have Medals of Honor given them by Congress.

During the fighting on the 6th of May, there were so many movements and changes in the way of advancing and retiring that I cannot take the time to follow all, but will mention only the most prominent.

In one advance we found that some of the enemy had massed and forced back the 40th New York and the 3rd Maine on our left. The 20th Indiana and 99th Pennsylvania were pushed forward to relieve the pressure, and the Brigade fell back to the Brock Road in good order. The thicket was so close that regiments acted without orders from Brigade Headquarters. In the afternoon of the 6th, Longstreet's Corps and Hill of the Rebel Army attacked our line and were finally repulsed. They halted 100 paces away and kept up a terrible fire of musketry. Our breastworks took fire, and we were literally roasted out of them. Seeing this, the Rebels attacked and took them, but we charged through the smoke and fire and took them again.

The official records say that the 20th Indiana and the 99th Pennsylvania did so well on the right of the Brigade as to be highly complimented and to receive the thanks on the field of Maj. Genl. Birney commanding the Division.

We remained in the breastworks all night and until 5 P.M. on the 7th of May, when we were moved back toward the trains about 2½ miles toward Chancellorsville, but we returned at once to the breastworks. We collected several thousand stand of arms which had been left by the enemy on the field.

Genl. Hancock reported that he was ordered to move his Corps during the night of the 7th of May, to the left, that he left a strong picket line in front of the breastworks under the command of Col. Thomas W. Egan, 40th New York Volunteers for the purpose of covering the withdrawal of the 2nd Corps.

I was in charge of the pickets in front of our Division extending from the Orange Plank Road for about a mile to the left towards Todd's Tavern. Col. Egan and I were ordered to be on the line all the time, and the work was very difficult. The Army was moving on the Brock Road, and the enemy kept pressing our pickets all night. We could not ride over our line, so I would go to the end of the line on the Plank Road and dismounting would walk along the line to the left when I would come out to the Brock Road, report to Col. Egan and then ride back to the right, and repeat this all night.

The enemy would slowly approach and open fire. All of our men would lie down and return the fire, when the enemy would fall back. As dawn began to appear, squads of Cavalry dashed down the road and then, being fired on, would fall back. I secreted about 30 men on the side of the road, and as a squad of Cavalry came on, waited till they got within about 30 yards when we let them have a volley which disposed of the crowd, and they did not interrupt us again. Our pickets were withdrawn about 10 A.M. on the 8th of May, and we had to join the rest of the Corps on the road beyond Todd's Tavern.

The Union loss in the Wilderness were 2246 killed, 12,037 wounded, 3383 missing or a total of 17,666.

The 2nd Corps lost 5092 in all, 500 being missing.

Of this loss, the Regiments of the old 3rd Corps lost 2941, of which our Division, Birney's 3rd Division, lost 2242.

The 20th Indiana lost 19 killed, and 105 wounded, 124 total.

Many missing returned within a day to their Regiments, but the majority missing were taken prisoners.

COMMENTARY: *Genl. Grant's long-anticipated push toward Richmond began at midnight on May 3-4 as the Army of the Potomac (including Hancock's II Corps) crossed the Rapidan River. On May 5, Warren's V Corps clashed with Genl. Ewell's forces on the Orange Turnpike and the Battle of the Wilderness was joined. A worse site for a major battle between large armies is difficult to imagine: Its miles of scrub oak and pine made maneuver, communications, cavalry and artillery operations, and even recognition of friend and foe nearly impossible. Worse, when it ignited during the battle, smoke cut visibility and flames killed many trapped wounded soldiers. Grant sought to flank Lee's right, but Lee seized the initiative and managed to confine Grant's army to the Wilderness, where in two days of fighting it took over 17,000 casualties. But this time, the Army of the Potomac—under Grant— did not retreat or stop fighting.*

CHAPTER 16

SPOTSYLVANIA

1864

I t is generally regarded as faulty to move an army by a flank in the presence of an enemy. The system adopted by Genl. Grant in all his movements after the battle of the Wilderness did not partake of the element of danger generally assigned to such an operation. He moved Corps at the time from his right to his left, thus extending in that direction, while the great mass of his army was still in position on familiar ground.

Genl. Hancock, commanding the 2nd Corps, was directed to move it during the night of the 7th of May following the 5th Corps, but the road was so crowded that we did not get started till after daylight on the 8th of May, and reached Todd's Tavern about 11 A.M. that morning. Line was formed and operations of various kinds [were] taken by the Corps during that day, and we camped for the night about a mile south of Todd's Tavern.

On the 9th of May we marched at about 3 P.M. toward Spotsylvania Courthouse, 2½ miles from Todd's Tavern. About 1½ mile from camp, the 20th Indiana and 124th New York were thrown out as skirmishers near the Hart House on the north bank of the Po River. The 99th Pennsylvania joined us, and we skirmished across the Po, capturing few prisoners. The Brigade crossed and camped about 8 P.M., the skirmishers being drawn into camp.

On the 10th of May, the 20th Indiana and the 99th Pennsylvania moved two miles to the north to cover a body of skirmishers of the Division which had crossed the Ny River. The Brigade crossed back to the north of the Po, and at 12 noon were all sent at double time back to the Po to help to cover the crossing of the Barlow Division which had been pressed by the enemy. After the Division had crossed, the 20th Indiana and 99th Pennsylvania, being in position, were subjected to a heavy artillery fire and were withdrawn.

About 3 P.M., the Brigade was moved to a position and massed in column of Regiments preparatory to an assault on the enemy's works. This column was as follows:

First:
86th New York
3rd Maine
124th New York
99th Pennsylvania
141st Pennsylvania
20th Indiana
110th Pennsylvania
40th New York

The bayonets of the entire command were fixed, and the order to charge was promptly obeyed. The 86th New York and the 3rd Maine lost heavily but planted their Colors on the enemy's works, but we were driven back at once.

The Rebel line was at the top of a steep hill about 150 feet high. This hill was covered with pines and cedars so that the formation was broken to a great extent as we went up. On falling back to the foot of the hill, we remained with only picket firing until the night of the 11th of May. It rained all the night of the 11th. At about 9 P.M., having built extensive camp fires all about where we had camped, we began our march for position to make an historic charge on the enemy's works from the extreme left of our line.

The night was dark, roads muddy, narrow and difficult, and the rain drizzled on us all the way. The marching was extremely fatiguing for all the men. About 12 o'clock at night, we arrived at the Brown House on the left of our line, going into position as the Regiments came up. The whole of the 2nd Corps was placed for an assault on the earthworks of the Rebels. We were about 1200 yards from their line. The ground ascended sharply from where we were formed to the enemy's position, and was thickly wooded with the exception of a space 400 yards wide close in front of the works about the Landrum House. We could not see the works we were to charge.

The information was taken promptly without noise or confusion, although it was an unusually dark and stormy night. Genl. Hancock says he fixed on the direction by the compass. The line was formed by placing Barlow's Division, 2nd Corps on the left in two lines; Birney's 3rd Division (in which we were) was formed in two deployed lines on Barlow's right. Mott's Division was in rear of Birney. In our front was a marshy place, and then a dense wood of low pines. The fog was too heavy as dawn came on, so Genl. Hancock delayed the orders for the assault until he could have light to see.

I remember the scene well. Genl. Hancock sent for the Colonels of Birney's Regiments in line. They collected in rear of the 20th Indiana. He sent word to Barlow on the left to move with our line in silence. Our Colonels were told to move forward, firing no shots, but in silence. The guide was to be our Regiment, on the left of which was the 99th Pennsylvania.

The advance was delayed until 4:35 A.M. when Genl. Hancock said, "Gentlemen, are you all ready now?" "Yes," was the reply. "Then join your regiments and move forward." We did so in silence, not returning the fire of the enemy's pickets when later we ran onto a picket reserve. Col. Biles of the 99th Pennsylvania, supposing he had received the fire of the main line, let forth a yell which woke people in Washington, I would think.

Immediately, the whole line set up a cheer, and on we dashed, 500 yards more, and over the Rebel works we bounded; the Birney Division first in, exactly on the point of the salient. Firing had begun on both sides, but it did not continue in force from the Rebels. The Barlow Division reached the works to our left.

The Corps captured 4000 prisoners of Johnson's Division, Ewell's Corps, 20 pieces of artillery with all their horses and material, several thousand stand of small arms and over thirty Colors. Genl. Johnson and Genl. Stewart were among those taken.

Those of the enemy not captured fled in great confusion. Our men were in spirit now, and they dashed forward after the flying foe toward Spotsylvania Courthouse. We soon reached the 2nd line of works.

The assault and pursuit had broken up the different organizations so that there were no leaders, hence the line fell back and halted at the Rebel trenches. We readily took the outer side and arranged to hold them. We were helped to do this, because the formation of the works was such as was natural to us. We always made our works with a ditch outside, throwing the dirt up to form a breastworks. The Rebels always made their work by throwing the dirt out making a trench inside.

As we returned to these works, they followed us closely and the firing was a perfect roar for a while. They charged works we held and occupied the ditch inside. We stuck to the outside, and there the fight went on for 26 hours from the time their first picket shots were fired.

The Rebel flag was stuck on one side of a parapet, and the 20th Indiana's flag stood up in the mud on the outer edge. Men fixed bayonets and cast gun and all over against their foes. Cheer and fire was all anyone did. Men tore off pieces of their clothing to wipe out their gun with and then went to work firing again.

A battery (Gillies' Battery C and I 5th Artillery) was run up close to the line where it fired canister. Its horses were killed and its men suffered so that it was withdrawn by hand. A tree was cut down by leaden bullets. The enemy continued his effort to recapture the works he had lost, constantly sending in fresh men for that purpose but without success. The battle raged without cessation. A cold drenching rain fell during most of the time.

On the morning of the 13th of May, it was discovered that the enemy had retired to his second line, about half a mile to the rear of the line we had carried, thus yielding to us the palm of victory. As soon as this was discovered, skirmishers were sent forward and a picket line established. We, for the first time, had a chance to breathe and eat.

The trench on the Rebels' side of the works was filled with their dead piled together in every way with their wounded. The night was terrible and ghastly. We helped off their wounded as well as we could, and searched for our own wounded in front. Capt. Corey was killed and never found. Capt. Thomas we found with 12 bullet wounds. He had fallen and then had been shot to pieces, possibly by his friends.

The horses of the regular battery were so shot that each was not over 10 to 12 inches thick. Genl. Ward, commanding the Brigade, was placed in arrest for cowardice on the 13th.

On the 13th and 14th of May we stayed in one place in the works taken. On the 15th our Brigade moved a few miles to the left and took a new position, the right resting on the Ta River. We skirmished with the enemy but put up breastworks and remained until the 17th inst. when the enemy attacked weakly and were repulsed. The 20th Indiana and 99th Pennsylvania were ordered to advance and take position in the works captured by our assault on the 12th. We were relieved on the same day, but on the morning of the 18th the entire Brigade was formed in the same works.

On the 19th of May we moved off and massed near Anderson's House. At 6 P.M. that day, we were doubled forward to support a Brigade of heavy artillery which was engaged with Ewell's Corps.

Ewell's Corps had come out of their works and, by a detour, had attempted to turn our right and capture some portion of our train. We formed line, advanced to the attack at daylight, and captured 500 prisoners; our loss being small. At 11 A.M., we returned to camp at Andersons. This ends the Spotsylvania Campaign.

The losses of the Union Army from the 8th of May are worthy of consideration here. Our total losses during the Campaign were:

At the Wilderness from May 3rd to May 7th:
Killed: 2246
Wounded: 12,037

At Spotsylvania from May 8th to May 21st:
Killed: 2725
Wounded: 13,416

Total killed: 4971; wounded: 25,453.

The 20th Indiana lost at Spotsylvania a total of 63 men, which added to those at the Wilderness, made 185 from May 3rd to May 21st.

The following Officers of the Regiment were killed or died of their wounds:

Capt. Lafayette Gordon,
Capt. Lorenzo D. Corey,
Capt. Henry Quigley,
Capt. John F. Thomas,
1st Lieut. Ed. C. Sutherland,
1st Lieut. J. C. Bartholomew,
2nd Lieut. William Dickason

The latter died of wounds in prison. It is impossible to procure the names of the enlisted men killed and wounded at this late date.

COMMENTARY: *Ignoring his costly setback in the Wilderness, Genl. Grant rallied the Army of the Potomac and continued to move southeast toward Spotsylvania Courthouse (and Richmond), once again seeking to turn Genl. Lee's flank. The two armies fought night and day without letup from May 8 to 21 spreading out around Spotsylvania and digging in for a spell of attrition warfare. The relentless combat claimed important leaders on both sides: Confederates Jeb Stuart and Genl. Longstreet (wounded) and Union Genl. John Sedgwick. Grant continued to sidle to his left, moving the whole battle to the south and east. And such fights as the 18-hour slugfest over the "bloody angle" caused casualties the Confederates could not replace. As the Spotsylvania fight waned and Grant moved to find a way around Lee, the two armies remained in constant contact and combat, as they moved closer to Richmond.*

CHAPTER 17

The March from the North Anna

1864

On the 19th of May, 1864, we were encamped about Anderson's Mill, near the Ny River. Genl. Early of the Rebel Army, in the movement referred to in previous chapters, had approached closely to Army Headquarters and had made his principal attack on a number of new regiments which had joined our Corps from Washington. These Regiments were Heavy Artillery Regiments and were very large, consisting of 24 Companies each. They had had no experience in war, but readily obeyed their Officers, and while they lost a good many men, stood their grounds well.

We acted as their support, and passed over the ground on which they had fought. We saw long rows of their killed and wounded. We remained in support all the 19th, and in the afternoon of the 20th, returned to Anderson's Mill. At 11 o'clock on the night of the 20th, we took up the march for Massaponax Church, and thence toward Guiney Station, which we reached at 8 A.M. May 21st. We halted for dinner on the farm of Col. Fauntleroy, having passed through Bowling Green at 10 A.M. This march was about 15 miles. Col. Fauntleroy had been a Colonel of the 2nd Dragoons in the Regular Army. He had served from 1836 and resigned from the Army May 13, 1861, on the breaking out of the war.

We marched through Milford Station and halted for the night two miles beyond the Mattapony River. Our total march since 11 P.M. of the night before being about 21 miles.

We built a splendid line of works near Coleman's House, and were soon strongly entrenched. We remained quiet all of the 22nd of May awaiting an attack of the enemy. Our object in so hurriedly occupying this position was to secure the crossing of the Mattapony before the enemy could form to resist us.

At 5: 30 A.M., May 23rd, we moved toward Chesterfield Station, our Division following the Cavalry at the head of the Infantry. We followed on the Telegraph Road toward the North Anna and about 12:45 reached Long Creek within one half mile of the crossing of the North Anna. We could see the enemy in their works on our side of the stream, and we were sent to charge them. A part of our Brigade was formed with the 3rd Maine on the right, and the 20th Indiana on the left, followed by the rest of the Brigade.

We charged about 500 yards over an open space, the ground ascending sharply toward the enemy's position. They kept up a rapid fire, but we were onto them before they thought, and we captured the works easily. The 2nd Corps lost about 150 men, the 20th Indiana loss being very small.

Genl. Hancock who was present describes what he saw by saying that this affair was very brilliant and spirited. We remained in position on the north bank of the North Anna that night, while the enemy occupied rifle pits along the south bank.

The bridge we were at was on the Telegraph Road leading to Hanover Junction. The regular bridge had been destroyed the year before, and in the meantime another had been put up in a very poor way. It was about 500 feet long, high from the water, and only wide enough for a wagon. Firing was kept up during the night to prevent the Rebels from burning it, and on the morning of the 24th of May, we arranged to cross.

This crossing was effected in this way: Lieut. Col. Meikel of the 20th Indiana took part of the Regiment down the steep bank to the water, and felling trees, soon crossed a man or two who cut trees to fall on those from the north bank, and crossing a few more men he soon had a skirmish line. We, in the meantime, keeping up such a firing as to hold back the Rebels. Capt. John C. Brown of Company K with about 20 men volunteered to cross the bridge. So when all was ready with the men below, the Captain made a dash at the head of his men for the other side of the bridge. About 10 feet from his objective he was shot, but his men ran on and soon their rifles began to bark and the Rebel pickets ran off or were killed or captured.

The command down by the water got over safely, and their skirmish line was joined with the others and pushed up the bank.

1st Sergeant Kirk, Company F, captured 13 prisoners whom he found in a demoralized state. They thought he had a large force, and as they were armed, when their surrender was demanded and given, they were chagrined to find after they had thrown down their arms that Kirk was alone. Kirk was given a Congressional Medal of Honor in December 1897 for this act in 1864. Capt. C. Brown mentioned above was shot in the face, the ball entering about one inch below his left eye, and passing out without much damage. He is still alive at the end of 1897.

On the same day of the 24th, the Regiment with the First Brigade moved out about 3 P.M., and constructed breastworks in front of the Fox House under severe Artillery fire.

On the 23rd, we could see the Rebel columns going into their works already built on the south side of the North Anna, and by the time we got our works done on the 24th, their position was too strong to attack. We recrossed the North Anna on the night of the 26th, and massed with the rest of the 2nd Corps about two miles from the river. We destroyed the bridges and the railroad.

At 10 A.M. on the 27th of May, the 2nd Corps marched in the direction of Hanovertown and at 10 P.M. camped about 3 miles north of the Pamunkey River about 20 miles by our route from last camp.

The fourth epoch of the campaign begins with the 28th of May. About noon on this day, we moved to the Pamunkey River and crossed at Nelson's Ford on a pontoon bridge. After advancing about 2 miles, we formed line of battle with the 9th Corps on the right, and 5th on the left. The operation of the regiment in this portion of the campaign consisted of much marching and fatiguing picket duty. We advanced across the Potopotomoy Creek and then withdrew. We did not have much fighting, and on May 31st attacked and drove the Rebels from their rifle pits, which we held. June 2nd, about 1 A.M., we marched with the Brigade to Cold Harbor about 10 miles by our way of going, and we there massed on the extreme left of the Army as a support for the 1st and 2nd Division of our Corps. On the 3rd of June, our Brigade was moved to the right to occupy a gap in the main line between the 5th & the 18th Corps.

On the 3rd of June, the 2nd Corps assaulted the enemy's position. Their entrenchments were very strong. The 1st Division under Barlow and the 2nd under Gibbon formed the assaulting line, and they were supported by the 3rd Division under Birney. The attack begun 4:45 A.M., and after a desperate and bloody fight, Barlow and Gibbon took the works of the Rebels, but before we of the 3rd Division could get to them, the Rebels reinforced and drove them out.

Our men did not run away but fell slowly back, and under a heavy fire, halted and threw up a breastwork using bayonets and tin cups for moving the soil. While covering themselves they were under a scathing fire of musketry from the Rebel line at from 30 to 75 yards away. Genl. Hancock said that the men showed a persistency seldom seen.

The skirmish fire along the front of the 2nd Corps was without cessation from the 1st to the 12th of June, and the nights were characterized by heavy Artillery firing and sometimes by heavy musketry, the close proximity of our lines causing unusual nervousness.

At 4 P.M. on the 4th of June, we were relieved and sent to our formed position on the left where we constructed breastworks along the road leading to Dispatch Station. We were now again on the Chickahominy opposite what was called Sumner's Bridge in the campaigns of 1862.

Genl. Hancock reports that the bearing of the troops composing the 2nd Corps, and the march from the North Anna, and during the operation on the Totopotomoy, and especially at the bloody battle of Cold Harbor was distinguished for bravery and good conduct.

The Corps lost from May 28th to June 12th 1864, 3164 men. And the 20th Indiana lost from May 22nd to June 12th, 28 men.

On the 12th of June the remnant of the 14th Indiana Regiment, consisting of 58 men, was assigned to the 20th Indiana. Our losses from hard fighting and hard marching, picket duty and general hard labor were so great that with the men of the 14th Indiana we scarcely numbered 250. Our total loss for the campaign of a little over a month had been 213 of which 40 were killed, 161 wounded and 12 were taken prisoners. There was no account of sick or other absentees. The spirit of those remaining in the Regiment was good and the material was of the best, and their feeling of devotion to the cause for which they were fighting was undaunted by their losses.

CHAPTER 18

THE RAPIDAN
TO THE CHICKAHOMINY

1864

I t may be of interest to record some features of this campaign from the Rapidan to the Chickahominy which are not generally discussed and of which little is known: The Army of the Potomac consisted of 115,000 men including the Cavalry on the 11th of June 1864. It had lost since crossing the Rapidan May 4th: Officers killed, 539; men killed, 6750; total 7289; and had 37,405 total wounded. There were missing 9856 in all, some of which were wounded, some prisoners and many stragglers or a grand total of 54,550 in 39 days.

We had captured 22 pieces of Artillery, 31 Colors in the 2nd Corps alone. We had lost one Color only in the 2nd Corps. We had marched and fought every day and night for 39 days, living only on the dry ration of hard bread, coffee, sugar, meat (either salted or fresh), and occasionally rice or beans. No fresh vegetables whatever had been issued to us. The men were required to carry 50 rounds of ammunition on their person, three days' full rations in their haversacks, three days' bread, and small rations in their knapsacks. The meat ration for these last three days being beef on the hoof. As the campaign progressed, we out marched the beef so far that we had salt meat for over one half the campaign.

The depots of supplies and for sending off the wounded were changed first to Aquia Creek, Bell Plain, Fredericksburg, Port Royal, White House and at last to City Point, as the Army fought its bloody way along and approached within striking distance of these points. Each Regiment of Infantry was allowed to have two wagons with six mule teams for all purposes and only three wall tents for Field and Staff. All others carried shelter tents.

The Signal Corps in 1864 was a very small affair, yet they did very efficient service. It only consisted of 21 Officers and 25 men for the Army.

The handling and treatment of the immense number of wounded, however, forms a subject of the greatest interest. Pope Leo VI declared, "If you desire that your soldiers go willingly to battle, the greatest care must be had for attending to the wounded," and as the Medical Director of the Army of the Potomac, I.A. McParlin says, "There is wisdom in the saying." No more devoted body of men could have been selected for service than the Medical Officers of that Army. The organization of the Ambulance Corps, as well as all connected with the Medical Department, was complete as could be desired.

Their labor in the Wilderness was especially hard. The wounded were collected as well as possible and sent to Hospitals for 1st treatment which were located near the line of battle, whence they were sent to the General Hospitals further to the rear. Army wagons as well as ambulances were used to carry off the wounded. Regular trains were formed after the bloodiest battles to take wounded to places for shipment. The Army wagons were filled with boughs of trees, and the unfortunate were as well cared for as possible. Blankets were gathered off the field and used for wounded.

In the Wilderness, many perished from the utter impossibility of finding them. The woods took fire and many, it is estimated 250, perished from that cause. As has been said, the battle of the Wilderness was one which no man saw or could see. The dense thick of undergrowth rendered the use of Artillery almost impossible and compelled the opposing lines to approach very near to each other in order to see their opponent. Only 250 Artillery wounds were found. It was a series of fierce attacks and repulses on either side, and the hostile lines swayed back and forth over a strip of ground from 200 yards to a mile in width. On this strip, the severely wounded from both sides were scattered. It is supposed that over 200 perished therein, 960 wounded men were left in the Hospital on the field at the Wilderness with ample supplies and Medical men for a short time.

There was no interval of importance in the 39 days following the crossing of the Rapidan between the cessation of hostilities and the march of the Army, so that Medical Officers had little opportunity to send off all the wounded.

The Sanitary Commission, an organized society of charitably disposed people, rendered great help to the sick and wounded at all times, but especially on this campaign.

The survivors all have their own accounts of narrow escapes and thrilling adventures, and it is not wise to cast them off as too much exaggerated, as anyone passing through fire of a battle, especially such battles as the Wilderness and Spotsylvania, cannot but wonder for the rest of his life how or why he did not go with the unfortunate instead of being a survivor of it all. When the fire is heavy, one forgets the danger and instinctively follows his call for duty. When he has time to think is the time of greatest danger of running away. Natural cowards slink away early in every action, and some even remain away through a campaign except to be present sufficiently to avoid a charge of desertion.

Still, in every campaign or rather every battle comes a time when the bravest may say I can do nothing more. A saying is that the bravest falls, but the equally brave who has touched elbows with him laid low, may be spared. At Spotsylvania three Officers were talking together while the two lines ten feet from us were firing as rapidly as possible. The center one was killed.

At Cold Harbor, it was desired that we advance our lines, and to do so necessitated the selection of the grounds beforehand. Lieut. Col. Meikel and I went out through the brush to select the ground. He was to the right and I, facing him about 300 yards, to the left. We had crossed a small run or wet place and were intent on searching out the ground when I heard a noise saying, "Yank, if you don't get into your lines pretty quick, you will go to Richmond." I ran for the works as did Meikel when he saw me getting over the ground so fast. The sight of the second now arose their ire and he got a volley from about 20 men, but fortunately escaped.

During this campaign, the Officers of the Regiment had to do the best they could and take care of themselves as best they may. All carried their tents, rations and blankets, although the Field Officers and Staff being mounted were not troubled much by this. Company Officers messed with their men as a rule and fared the same. Every man usually cooked his own ration. We had cooks only in a camp held a long time.

We never saw the wagons carrying our extra things from beginning to end of the campaign, and many of us never again saw the goods we had stored with the Quartermaster's wagons. They were thrown away to give room for more important things.

June 12th, 1864, the best estimate placed the strength of the Army at 115,000 men including the Cavalry, and the whole of the Command of Lee at Cold Harbor, Richmond and Petersburg at 80,000 men.

After the assault and the battles of Cold Harbor, Genl. Grant decided to move the Army under his immediate command to the south side of the James River. He had brought from Butler's Command at Bermuda Hundred the 18th Corps commanded by W. F. Smith, and they had joined us at Cold Harbor on our first arrival there. This Corps numbered 18,000 men and came to us by way of York River and White House.

The problem now before Genl. Grant was to so reinforce Butler as to enable him to resist the attack of any force Genl. Lee might send against Butler's isolated little army. There was danger of his being overwhelmed as soon as any relaxation of our efforts at Cold Harbor should indicate a change of base.

The distance to be marched from Cold Harbor to Petersburg across country was about 50 miles, and as there might most likely be detention on account of attacks from the Rebels holding interior lines, Genl. Grant thought the quickest way to strengthen Butler would be to send troops to him by water. He accordingly ordered Genl. Smith with his 18th Corps to go to White House, and taking boats there, to proceed by way of Pamunkey and York Rivers and Fortress Monroe into the James River and to Bermuda Hundred.

He at the same time informed Butler that the rest of the Army would be only one day behind Smith in reaching Petersburg by marching across the country. Thus to give one day, he sent 15,300 men by steamer on the long route given. This single day was of so much value because Grant wished to seize Petersburg at the earliest possible moment. On the afternoon of the 12th of June, we received orders to be ready to march. This order was very agreeable to all of us as there seemed no hope of breaking the enemy's lines here, they being so strong and powerfully garrisoned.

The order issued by Genl. Meade was a model for its clearness, conciseness and brevity: The Cavalry was ordered to cross the Chickahominy at Long Bridge to be followed by the 5th Corps, and that by the 2nd Corps. The 6th Corps was ordered to cross the James Bridge 9 miles from Long Bridge, and to be followed by the 9th Corps. The rest of the Cavalry was to follow the Army.

We began the march at 11 o'clock at night, marched all night and crossed the Chickahominy at 9:30 A.M. We stopped to cook breakfast after crossing and after that marched rapidly all day and reached the James River at Wilcox Landing at 5:30 P.M., June 13th, having covered 35 miles since 11 o'clock the night before.

We formed a line of battle and were a weary crowd. The country through which we passed from Cold Harbor had not been disturbed this year by armies to any great extent, so that it presented a beautiful and refreshing sight.

We began crossing the James at 11 A.M. on June 14th by transport vessels, landing at Wind Mill point, and our whole Corps was finally landed at 5 A.M. on the 15th of June. We waited until 10:30 A.M. for rations we did not get, and then started for Petersburg. We could hear the boom of artillery, so stepped out briskly, and at 6:30 A.M., we reached the Rebel's works at the Byrant House. It was a lively 18 mile march as we made something of a detour.

We found that Genl. Smith had taken a portion of the Rebel works, and 17 pieces of artillery.

I was sent off by Genl. D. B. Birney, commanding the 3rd Division, to explore a road. He said in a slow, cool way, stuttering a little, "Major, ride down that road a couple of miles and see what you can find, and go at once."

It was getting dark, I had no escort but had nothing to do but go. The horse I rode during this campaign was a little bay. I called him Sammy. He was possessed of great intelligence and of easy gate. He did not show alarm at firing of any kind of guns. At times when I was on him under fire, he would remain perfectly quiet except as a shell came shrieking over, when he would settle back on his haunches holding his breath till the thing passed, when he would straighten up and breathe as rapidly as after severe exercise.

On getting my orders, I turned Sammy's head to the left and off I went down the road. I came to obstructions so arranged that I had to pass around off the road. About a mile riding and Sammy's ears pricked up. I checked him to a walk, and seeing something move, I called, "Halt there, surrender or I shall fire." The object came toward me with a, "Fore God, boss, don't shoot." It was an old darkey, and on asking him where the road went, he said, "Down her to de Cote House and up dar to Petersburg."

I took my captive along and went back to Genl. Birney, and from him the General got a good deal of information. That darkey never was so tickled in his life.

We bivouacked behind the Rebel fortifications which had been built a long time and which had just been taken by the 18th Corps.

At daylight on the morning of the 16th of June, the enemy opened fire on us with batteries, killing and wounding a considerable number of the Brigade. It was at once formed and an assaulting column consisting of the 17th Maine and the 20th Indiana was ordered to charge and take the enemy's works in our front.

Our starting point for this charge was at our bivouac, and the direction was down in front of the rebel lines, extending to our left. The woods in front of this work had been cut to form an abatis, and we were ordered over this on the supposition that there were few men in the works on which we were advancing. The trees had fallen in every conceivable way, and our progress was very slow, but hurrying up as fast as we could, we got within a few hundred yards of the work which was occupied by only a skirmish line, when we saw a column of rebels running up from the rear and into the works. They opened fire and we tried to fall back, but we were too close to the Rebels, as every time we mounted a log, a good work was presented to their rifles so we simply laid down behind the trees and let them pop away.

The rest of the Brigade was formed, and they attacked inside the old rebel line. This let us out of our fix about 3 o'clock in the afternoon, and we joined the other in the charge against the same line.

The General commanding the Brigade, DeTrobriand, said that the gallantry of the charging parties was not equal to taking a position which a whole Division afterwards failed to carry. Another attack was made on the right that evening at 6 which we supported and assisted in. Genl. Meade reports on the 17th of June at 6 A.M., that there has been continuous fighting all along the line since the attack begun at 6 P.M., yesterday (of the 16th). Advantage was taken of the fine moonlight to press the enemy all night. Loss in the Army, 2000 killed and wounded.

He says, also in the same report, our men were tired and the attacks have [had] not been made with the vigor and force which characterized our fighting in the Wilderness. The operations after dark on the 16th of June resulted in the capture of two redoubts, four guns, 450 prisoners and 3 Colors by the 9th Corps.

Genl. Grant in his report dated the 17th of June 1864 says, "Our force drew out from within 50 yards of the enemy's entrenchments at Cold Harbor; made a flank movement of about 50 miles march crossing the Chickahominy and James Rivers, the latter 2,000 feet wide and 84 feet deep, and surprised the enemy's rear at Petersburg without the loss of a wagon or piece of artillery and only losing 150 stragglers."

He also says June 17th, "Too much credit cannot be given troops and their commanders for the energy and fortitude displayed during the last five days. Day and night have been all the same, no delay being allowed on any account."

At daylight on the 17th of June, we were placed within about 150 yards of a new rebel line. At this time I received the following order:

Headquarters, 3rd Division, 2nd Corps.
June 17th, 1864.
Special Orders,
No.
(Extract)

11th. Major Gilbreath, 20th Indiana Volunteers, is hereby assigned (temporarily) to the Command of the 17th Maine Volunteers. He will assume command at once.

By command of Major General Birney:
Sgd) C. Macmichael.
Captain A. D. C., and A. A. A. Gen.

Official:
M. M. Cannon,
Captain & A. A. A. G.

I felt this a very decided compliment as I was from a different state but was selected by the General commanding the Division to command this Maine Regiment.

As for the next month I was to remain their Chief, it will be of interest to see how they took my assignment.

The following is taken from the columns of the *Evening Courier* of Portland, Maine, June 27th, 1864:

> We are permitted to make the following extract from a letter from the 17th Regiment dated June 20th: "On the 17th, we were put in the front line of Rebel works. Captain Pennell was struck in the head by a sharpshooter's bullet and expired very quickly; he never spoke.
>
> On the same day Major Gilbreath of the 20th Indiana was put in command of the Regiment.
>
> He is a fine Officer and will lead the Regiment gallantly."

At daylight on the 18th, instant we advanced on the enemy's works and, finding them deserted, we pushed on about a mile and a half further toward Petersburg. We found ourselves within 200 yards of the enemy's new line, and we entrenched ourselves, but, at 1 P.M., we formed in column for an assault on the Rebel line. Our line was composed of nine brigades each in column of regiments.

The position of our Brigade was at the Hare House which was a fine large brick mansion, very roomy and surrounded by beautiful grounds. O. P. Hare, the owner, had kept a racing establishment and had 12 or 15 small stables for horses, jockeys, and for racing purposes.

Our Brigade, in its advance, passed through the yard in front of the house and dashed for the Rebel line. The 20th Indiana was formed as a skirmish line, and the other regiments were in column with the 40th New York, then the 17th Maine. We ran for it and got within about 20 steps of the line when the firing was too heavy for us to stand, so back we fell and rallied behind the stables referred to. They were no shelter from bullets, but they looked like it, so we halted and then fell back slowly behind the grounds. The little Color Bearer of the 17th Maine said, "Major, this Color goes where you say," and he stayed with me until the Regiment was formed. The loss of my Regiment, the 17th Maine, was one tenth of its strength; 3 killed and 17 wounded.

To show how indifferent men become to firing, an incident of this assault may be given. While we were collected behind the stables and shots from the Rebel line were passing through these frail structures, one Captain of the 17th Maine said, "We would have gotten up all right if the 40th New York hadn't been put in front." With that, a Captain of the 40th New York got mad, and they begun a regular fist fight while under Rebel fire.

At dark on the 18th, we pushed up as close as we could, and, working like beavers, we constructed a beautiful line of breastworks.

The Hare House was obliterated, and in 24 hours no man would have known that the house and other buildings had ever stood there from the appearance of the grounds. Fort Steadman was afterwards built on this spot.

When we advanced to the charge referred to, we saw staring us in the face the words in white chalk "Owner O. P. H.," which everyone knew meant "[Owner] off" instead of O. P. Hare. The people had left the place without removing anything from the house or buildings, apparently. My men brought me a beautiful blanket horse cover, bridle and bits, and I got a fine gray mare which I used for a good while and then sold for a fine price.

Our line was not more than 150 yards from that of the Rebels', and it was a hard place to hold. The Rebels afterwards captured Fort Steadman and held it for some time.

We gradually constructed bombproof holes in the ground to shelter us from Rebel fire, and those following us constructed other protections of like character so that the place was soon covered with their rat holes for us to hide in.

We brought up mortars and so did they, and each set their guns in their own works all along for miles. It was wonderful to see how accurate the mortar firing became on each side. The shot from a mortar is tossed into the air, and its accuracy in hitting an object in front depends on the angle at which the gun is set. Each side could drop a shot inside the other's work.

As the siege progressed and the number of mortars increased, they were kept firing all night long, and as many as thirty could be seen in the air at once, each forming a beautiful arc of a circle high in the air by the trail of fire from its fuse. These mortar shots too had a peculiar sound, made as the shot revolved, and when the fuse came to our side, it sounded like "wish, wish, wish, boom," slowly at first, but more rapidly just before the explosion. These never did much damage.

COMMENTARY: *Genl. Grant continued his Virginia campaign, moving south toward Richmond and Petersburg, holding the initiative and maintaining pressure on Genl. Lee, who had little choice but to stay on the defensive. But Lee anticipated many of Grant's objectives and moved parallel to Grant, quickly enough to fashion a succession of strongpoints that made each fight a costly one. After the bloodletting at the Wilderness and Spotsyvania, both armies brought in reinforcements to maintain their battlefield strength. Still, time and attrition were on the side of the Union. Late May was a time of extensive skirmishing and marching—toward Richmond.*

In reaction to the heavy losses at Wilderness and Spotsylvania, Grant was criticized as "a butcher" (though Lee was losing a higher percentage of his army), but at North Anna, Grant showed that he knew when not to press a major fight, judging the Rebel defenses there too strong. Instead, Grant moved again, around Lee's right.

Lee moved ahead, building strong defenses at Cold Harbor, just eight miles northeast of Richmond. Grant's initial attack at Cold Harbor in early June nearly broke the Confederate line but was followed by more costly and unsuccessful assaults. After a truce to tend the wounded and bury the dead, Grant pulled the 100,000-strong Army of the Potomac out of the trenches on a well-concealed march across the James River to Petersburg.

CHAPTER 19

The Siege of Petersburg

1864

I t is quite impossible for me to fully describe our manifold duties during the siege of Petersburg. We occupied various places in the line of battle, dug covered ways, threw up breastworks, marched from point to point, and fighting a little, were seldom a single day not under fire. On the evening of the 18th of June, after the charge described, we moved as closely to the front as possible and erected a new line of works. On the 21st of June, we were placed in position on the left of the Jerusalem Plank Road, well in rear of the picket line, and we moved almost every day to some new position.

About the last mentioned date, I was placed on duty which will illustrate the manner of performing some of the labor demanded of us. I was sent for to report to Corps Headquarters for fatigue. On my arrival there I found that I was to take charge of about 800 men to be detailed to construct a breastwork.

I went in the afternoon with an Engineer Officer to one of the roads leading to Petersburg, and dismounting in the woods, we walked toward the front until we could see the ground he wished me to work on. He pointed out the direction the works were to run from the road to certain trees to our left. I was to place the men on the grounds, and they were to cover themselves by throwing up the earth as soon as possible. I was directed to throw the earth toward the Rebel line, as the design was to make the trench I dug a cover way.

In front of me was a strong picket line, and I was to rely upon them for protection while a battalion in rear remained in line ready to reinforce the picket if necessary. Of course we were to be as silent as possible, as we were under easy rifle fire from the Rebel lines.

Returning to our horses, I went back to the Regiment and reported again at Corps Headquarters after dark. I took charge of a party and marched them near the ground and explained what we had to do. I fixed the place for the battalion in rear and then marched my men on to the ground in single file, directing the men to drop out in line to the right and about three feet apart. Each man was supplied with a shovel or spade, with every fifth man carrying a pick. I had no difficulty in placing the men, and they worked faithfully and had a good breastwork finished before four o'clock in the morning, about which hour the men returned to their Regiments and the line was occupied by armed men.

My line extended from the Plank Road to an elevation, and I found on my next visit that I got it fairly straight. The irregularities were corrected.

The day following the completion of this breastwork, we were ordered to occupy it with the Brigade, and here occurred one of the most foolhardy affairs I ever saw. Col. Egan formed the line well to the rear and then directed the regiments to march to the front, each to a place in the line directly before it. The Bands played and the Colors were flying. The Rebels saw us coming and the foolishness of so exposing ourselves so astonished them that their breastworks were lined or covered with Johnnies looking at the display.

The Regiments got well into the works before a shot was fired, but the firing on us then became so fierce that we were glad enough to hurry up and find cover. The work I had made was strengthened every day, and in rear of it was cut a covered road so that a battery of artillery might pass along it without being seen.

At the left of where our regiment was placed, a Fort for 11 heavy guns was built. It was so close to the Rebel line and firing about it was so heavy sometimes as to keep everything hot enough. The men named this place Fort Hell, and the name lasted throughout the siege in all reports. It had before been called Battery No. 10. Fort Hell was occupied by the 99th Pennsylvania Volunteers.

We had constructed bombproof shelters in rear of our works. These were simply holes in the ground, roofed over with a heavy covering of earth. Lieut. Col. Meikel and I occupied one which was all open to the rear and about 5 feet deep. Some of these bombproofs would hold a large number of men. Others only one man. In Fort Hell there was a large bombproof and a magazine, both heavily covered over with timbers and soil.

The Rebel pickets were about 30 feet from the muzzles of the guns in this fort, and our pickets were not over 10 or 15 feet from the Rebels. They had a system of signals so arranged that a man on our side touched one of the guns in the Fort and down would go all the Rebel pickets, and then their artillery would open from all along their line and, our guns replying, would make a regular pandemonium. The pickets here would not shoot at each other at all, but talked and chatted when they could in the most friendly manner.

Deserters came in here very often. One came in on our picket line one night, and the rule was to first question a deserter at the Picket, then at Division Headquarters, then at Corps Headquarters. By comparing each of these talks, it was thought the truth might be arrived at. At the time this particular deserter came in, Genl. Grant was fearful that Lee had gone toward Washington with a force and so was very anxious to find out Lee's whereabouts. I asked him the questions as I was Brigade Officer of the Day, and said to him: "When did you see Genl. Lee last?" He replied, "Yesterday 'sah." "How was he looking?" "Well 'sah, his head was mighty white, but his neck was powerful stiff." We found out that for about another year that neck was powerful stiff.

We were often visited by foreign Officers, especially the English Army Officers, and they bored us sometimes. Notice was usually sent around the line that so and so was coming to see the sights. One day, which had been unusually quiet, a lot of Officers were collected in the bombproof inside Fort Hell, when notice came that a large party of Englishmen would visit this Battery and to please show them some attention. Now the 99th Pennsylvania was commanded by Col. Biles, who, up to the breaking out of the war, had been a Sergeant in Battery K, 4th U. S. Artillery. He was Irish, and naturally disliked the English, so on receiving the message, Biles said, "I show 'em attention till they can't rest."

The English Officers came and, dismounting some distance away, came in and looked the place over. The senior said they would like to see some firing. The wish had no more been uttered than Biles yelled at the top of his voice, "Fire," when every gun went off and instantly probably 50 guns from the other side began to fire on Fort Hell. Everybody flew for the bombproofs, and we piled in without regards to any previous position or condition. All men kept under cover for one half hour or so when the firing ceased, and our guests went off without very many thanks for the amusement given them.

Our lines at this time were very close together, being not more than 500 yards in many places. Pickets, of course, were much closer. There was usually no firing between pickets on these close lines. Wherever the Colored troops were, however, the Rebels fired at everything they saw, and the popping of the guns could be heard at any time. Men on each side would come out and sleep on top of the breastworks or lay around in the sun. No advantage was taken of this exposure on either side, but if anyone called, "Look out," there was great tumbling off and getting under cover.

A ravine ran down to our right from in front of Fort Hell, and opposite the right of our Brigade there was quite a deep ravine between the two picket lines. As there was a fine spring there, men from each side would assemble there without arms and exchange papers & etc. or trade boots or shoes for tobacco. I, as Division Officer of the Day, was ordered to try and break up this sociability. It was a difficult thing to do, as if either party saw an Officer coming they hurried away. I fixed myself with a cartridge box, belt and bayonet, went down with an orderly and found a large crowd. An Officer from the other side happened to come on the scene and we arranged to each set a picket post to prevent their meetings.

Genl. DeTrobriand came to command our Brigade about the 24th of June, 1864. He was a queer old Frenchman. He was accustomed to wear a blouse with a star fixed on each shoulder to take the place of a shoulder strap.

On one day he inspected the line, and as he passed along, the Coehorn Mortars began playing. No one paid any attention to their shells except to glance up to see if they were coming toward us. These mortar shells are very slow moving. One pretty large one came over and struck a short distance behind the General, and as it buried itself in the earth, it threw up a good deal of soil and literally covered the old man with the earth. He got up and brushed himself off with many foreign oaths, and said, "By gar dey see my shoulder strap." It was regarded as a good joke that a Coe-horn Mortar, 500 yards away, should play at the General's star of ½ inch.

By the 10th of July, we had miles and miles of earthworks extending from north of the James across the Appomattox and away toward the South Side Railroad. The enemy's works were equally extended, and the redoubts were immense, all connected with curtains. Our line was from one-half to 2 miles closer to Petersburg than the old Rebel line of defenses was fixed, and the works formed each a labyrinth that only those that were in them daily were able to find their way to the front, or being there could not get out. Sign boards were put up to direct the men.

It was required of us to destroy the old Rebel breastworks lest we should at some time be compelled to fall back when the Rebels could find a work of defense already prepared for them. The leveling of these old works with the rest of it caused a terrible amount of fatigue. In our Corps, the 3 Divisions of 10,000 men each were detailed for fatigue in turn.

About July 12th, I was relieved from command of the 17th Maine and returned to my own Regiment, the Lieutenant Colonel of the 17th having reported for duty.

We were camped in rear of the main line for a rest from the activity of close contact with the enemy, and were there joined by the 73rd New York Volunteers. They camped alongside the 20th Indiana, and our Hoosier Officers and men found in them a new wonder. The 73rd was a Regiment raised amongst the old style firemen of New York and from the slummy classes.

On their first joining us, we were aroused by a cry, "No. 4 on Deck." On looking out of our tents, we found a Company engaged in a regular fist fight with another Company. Lieut. Col. Burns was a big burly fellow, and he walked into the crowd striking right and left. Captain, Lieutenant or Private was all the same to him and down they went. No one struck back and he soon had the field to himself.

The Officers and men of the 73rd always wore their red shirt collars outside of their coats. This made a singular addition to their appearance on parade, especially. They were glad to find a crowd like our men to tell stories to, and our men not being at all accustomed to city ways, listened to their sayings with open-eyed wonder.

I was greatly interested in Col. Burns, whom I had known for some time. One day, I was in his tent and he was telling me of his life in New York. He did not know anything apparently about his father and mother. He had been raised by chance and lived with a butcher, whose trade he had learned. He was telling me, with all the lingo of the slums, about driving cattle and sheep about the Bulls Head in New York, and mentioned that his employer's name was "Billy DeHart." I said that there was a man named DeHart in Company D, 20th Indiana who was a butcher and from New York. Burns said he did not know what had become of DeHart, and asked me to send for the man I knew. The orderly came up with DeHart who timidly knocked at the tent. I may say that the Officers of the 20th Indiana were all well aware of DeHart's gambling habits, and he was after corrected, admonished or punished for his efforts at "Chuck-a-luck," so he supposed that the old offense was to be brought up again. As he knocked, I said, "Come in." He looked at me without saying anything when Col. Burns got up and said, "Billy DeHart, you d---d old rascal, what you doing here?" DeHart replied, "You['re] Bill English, or his ghost," and they sat down and the Colonel and the Private talked in the most familiar way of the life of each. The 73rd New York and its unique Colonel were very good fighters.

On the 9th of July, Capt. Charles A. Bell of the 20th Indiana was on fatigue duty in charge of a working party on a redoubt in rear of the line.

The Rebels succeeded in locating the position of the work, and begun shelling the woods where they supposed it was. On[e] of the first shells exploded high in the air, and a piece was thrown so as to strike Capt. Bell on his right groin. He died almost at once. He was a good soldier, and a brave man.

On the 22nd of July, Col. W. C. L. Taylor left the Regiment for home with all the Officers and men who did not wish to remain as veterans, this date being the end of three years service. None of these Officers or men came back, and their absence reduced the strength of the Regiment very much. Those of us remaining were under command of Lieut. Col. G. W. Meikel from the 22nd of July to September 10, 1864.

COMMENTARY: *In fighting off Genl. Grant's relentless attacks approaching Richmond in the spring of 1864, Genl. Lee sought above all to avoid having his Army of Northern Virginia encircled. His prophetic observation that if he were besieged in Petersburg, then defeat would be "only a matter of time" would come true. That siege, marked by some of the most savage fighting of the war, lasted ten months, pitting some 125,000 Union soldiers against Lee's 65,000 Confederates, in a complex of earthworks and trenches that extended for over 35 miles. The combined casualties of the two armies topped 73,000.*

The siege ended on April 2, 1865, with the last rail line to the south cut by Union forces, and with Lee, his overextended line finally broken, withdrawing from Petersburg with just a handful of days left before the surrender at Appomattox.

The Explosion of the Mine

1864

The 9th Corps occupied the line of works to the left of the Hare House for a mile and over, and a portion of their line was along a ravine, the opposite side of which was crowned by the Rebel line. In front of this ravine was a Rebel redoubt, and Genl. Burnside decided to put a mine under this Fort and blow it up. The explosion of the mine was to be followed by an assault before the Rebels had gotten over their astonishment.

We of the 2nd Corps were to assist in this matter, first by a demonstration to the north side of the James, and after that by supporting the assaulting columns. Accordingly at 4:30 P.M., July 26, 1864, we left camp and crossed the Appomattox, and at 6:30 A.M. on the 27th, the last of the Corps was across the James River at Jones's Neck on a pontoon bridge. Sheridan's Cavalry crossed after us. The bridge had been covered thickly with hay to prevent the enemy from hearing the tramp of the horses' feet. The three divisions took position at once: Mott's 3rd Division, in which we were, on the right; Barlow in the center; [and] Gibbon on the left.

At 6:45 A.M. the skirmishers advanced, and in a few minutes after dashing up the slope, we were engaged with the enemy and were followed closely by our line of battle. At about 7 A.M., our whole line rushed into the enemy's works and they scattered in all directions. We captured four 20 pounder Parrott Guns. They opened on us from a field battery on our right, and our Brigade was sent to attempt its capture. We had a sharp fight, but the enemy got their guns away from the line and we did not get them.

The whole line advanced to Bailey's Creek, the Potteries and the New

Market and Long Bridge Road. The Gun Boats in the James River helped us by firing, throwing their immense shot and shell over our heads. We could see these 15 inch missiles strike in or about the Rebels' line, and could see the Rebs flying from them in all direction for shelter. We had sharp skirmishing all day and captured some prisoners.

On the 28th of July we occupied about the same line but extended it toward Malvern Hill and were busy all day. At 8 o'clock at night, Mott's Division took up the march to go back to our old position at the Hare House. We arrived in the rear of this house on the morning of the 29th of July and camped for the day. In the evening we marched into the line in front of the Hare House and to its left, and we held this position during the assault following the mine explosion on the morning of the 30th of July.

We had been notified that the mine would be exploded in the early morning of the 30th of July, and we were early on the qui vive to see all we could. Our instructions were also to charge the Rebel line in our front at once if we should see any great confusion amongst the enemy.

I got out of my bombproof early and thought I would take a wash. I had a darkey servant and no wash basin, so the servant poured the water on my hands from a canteen. We stood just at the corner of the bombproof, and I had gotten my hands full of water to apply to my face when "bing" a bullet struck the corner of the bombproof and into the latter went darkey, canteen, water and Major in a pile. A sharpshooter had taken a pop at me, and I don't think I was ever more frightened than when his bullet struck within six inches of my breast.

There was a good deal of delay in firing the mine, and we were all expectation and anxiety to see it. The ground occupied by the Regiment sloped down to a ravine, and the Rebel Fort was in plain view. We had an excellent place to view the scene. There were 10,000 pounds of powder in the mine, and it was directly under the Fort. Finally at 5 A.M. while we were looking and wondering, the powder exploded. From where we were, the earth seemed to rise in the air and was thrown to a great height. It then fell back and the whole redoubt had been destroyed with its men, guns and material. Many men must have been killed.

Immediately all of our artillery along the line for miles to the right and left of us opened, and it was a constant crashing roar of big guns which was sublime. All about the crater and in the valley in front of the Fort was covered by a cloud like a pall of black smoke which hung low above the earth. It was one of the most magnificent war pictures I ever beheld.

Genl. Burnside's 9th Corps, on whose line the works was, was to make the assault following the explosion with the 18th Corps in support, and the two Divisions, the 1st and 2nd of our Corps, in reserve. The 3rd Division, Mott's, was all in the works, and he saw the advance to attack.

Genl. Burnside had a Division of Colored Troops in his Corps. They had never had anything to do, and had been but little under fire, but then he trusted to them the leading of the assault. They were said to have been poorly formed and worse led, and they rushed in as far as the crater of the mine and huddled together.

The enemy's old troops soon recovered from the scare and disorder of the explosion, and they advanced on the run upon the Negroes in the crater and killed hundreds of them. The total loss of the 9th Corps at the crater was 4523 killed and wounded, and 1396 missing, or 5919 in all. The Rebels lost in the explosion 975 men. The effect of the firing of the mine on the rest of the Rebel line was singular. Heads popped up all along, and many men ran away from immediately about the crater.

All along our front there seemed to be a good deal of uneasiness. But it passed in a moment, and they rushed in the troops from all sides. Those near us went to work again pot hunting for Officers on our side. The heavy fighting closed at 10 A.M. as the Union troops had been withdrawn at that hour.

It was an inexcusable blunder to send the green troops of the Colored Division to lead the assault. The whole failure was chargeable to Genl. Burnside's mismanagement or incapacity.

COMMENTARY: *Genl. Grant was seeking a way to break through the static siege of Petersburg when Genl. Burnside suggested mining the Confederate strongpoint in front of his position. The Union plan was to tunnel under a South Carolina Regiment's artillery battery and mount a strong diversionary attack toward Richmond that included the II Corps and Gilbreath's regiment, for the purpose of drawing off some of Lee's forces defending Petersburg. In July, coalminers of the 48th Pennsylvania Regiment and others ingeniously drove a 500-foot tunnel and placed four tons of black powder beneath the rebel line.*

CHAPTER 21

OUR LAST BATTLES & MUSTERING OUT

1864

The Regiment with the 3rd Division moved out of the trenches July 31st and camped with the entire Corps about two or three miles in rear of the line. On the 5th of August, 1864, there were rumors and reports of deserters that a mine would be sprung on our line between the Appomattox and the James. Genl. Mott was ordered to take our Division across the former stream for a support of the 18th Corps. We returned to camp on the 8th or 9th.

On the 13th of August, it was decided to make a demonstration on the north of the James so that Genl. Warren could advance on the left of the Army. It was intended to give Lee the impression that we were going to Washington. Accordingly we marched on the 13th to City Point and embarked on a steam transport there. All being loaded, we steamed up the stream instead of down, and landed at Deep Bottom on the north of the James. Our Division was sent forward with one Brigade thrown out as skirmishers. It was our Brigade which advanced on the skirmish line, and the Rebels fell back as we advanced till they reached their entrenched line.

The 20th Indiana was on reserve near where some old potteries had stood. These potteries had been used to manufacture stoneware, jugs, crocks, & etc., and there were two large open cellars where the bad or broken pieces of ware had been thrown. We tried the enemy every way we could to find out whether they had any artillery in the works on the ridge beyond Bailey's Creek where the skirmish line between the potteries and the Rebel line was. The Rebs did not make any showing of artillery, no matter what we did.

Without thinking much about it, I proposed to use my red bandana handkerchief as a signal flag, and putting it on a stick began to wave it from side to side as if signaling. No more than three or four movements had been made with the bandana than there was a puff of smoke and a shell struck in one of the old cellars with a "bing" and threw pieces of that crockery all about us. The artillery was [thus] discovered, and the signal party suddenly discontinued operations. Genl. Chambless of the Rebel Army was killed at the potteries and buried there by us.

We remained about Bailey's Creek until the 18th when we went back and into the trenches in front of Petersburg. We remained in the trenches until the end of September, there being only one event of importance to the Regiment during the month. It had been explained that the pickets were very close in front of Fort Hell. It was very amazing to have the Rebel line so close to our work, so it was decided to attempt their capture or to force them then further away from us. I believe that the proposition to do this came from Lieut. Col. Meikel of the 20th Indiana. Genl. Mott directed Genl. DeTrobriand to carry out the idea, and the latter placed the 2nd U.S. Sharpshooters under the command of Lieut. Col. Meikel.

One o'clock in the morning of the 10th of September was fixed on for the operation. Col. Meikel was instructed to place the 2nd Sharpshooters and the 20th Indiana on some low ground near Fort Hell and then, by rushing down the Rebel picket line, to scoop in as many prisoners as possible. The Sharpshooters were to establish a picket line, and assisted by the 99th Pennsylvania, the picket was pushed well to the front.

Genl. Mott reports that the instructions were carried out most punctually and brilliantly by Lieut. Col. Meikel. The enemy was completely surprised and overpowered; [they] offered but feeble resistance and abandoned their lines in great haste, leaving in our hands one Lieutenant and 100 prisoners. We lost 37 men in all during the operation. The 99th Pennsylvania, in the darkness, advanced too far to the front, so that when daylight came on, they lost 2 Officers and 52 men in trying to draw back to a proper position.

The picket had for so long a time been resting in a quiet way along this line that they seemingly regarded this night attack of ours as treacherous, so that they were ready to fire at any and everything. It was unfortunately under this condition of affairs that Col. Meikel, after daylight on the 10th, exposed himself and was mortally wounded. He died that day. He was a brave man and a good soldier.

This left me the senior Officer present with the Regiment, and I fully expected promotion to the Lieut. Colonelcy to be followed by advancement to be Colonel when Col. Taylor should be mustered out. I had no one at home to press this advancement for me and in fact did not think that anything would occur to prevent my becoming the Colonel of the Regiment. But, it was decided to not send recruits to the old Regiments from Indiana, and to instead consolidate all the Regiments in the Army of the Potomac into one. The 14th Regiment had already joined us, the 7th had been transferred to the 19th, and now the latter was put into the 20th.

Col. [Taylor] was not mustered out until October 5th, and the 19th had Lieut. Col. Lindley present. Col. Lindley had the arrangement of the new Regiment, and he did it so as to protect his own old Regiment. The new Regiment retained the number, 20th Indiana, but aside from keeping their Chaplain, Surgeon, Quartermaster and a few line Officers, all of the Officers of the old 20th Indiana were mustered out and the other offices were given to men from the 7th, 14th and 19th Indiana Regiments. I was one of those mustered out; my discharge from service dating October 19, 1864, the date of consolidation being October 18, 1864.

The reorganized Regiment continued in the 2nd Corps till the close of the War and fought well in the battles of the 2nd Corps at Hatcher's Run, the Hickford Raid, Watkin's House and Amelia Springs. Its losses after consolidation being four men killed, 7 Officers and 37 men wounded; total 48. The Regiment's last engagement was at Clover Hill, April 9th, 1865.

After the surrender of Lee, the Regiment marched to Washington and from there it was moved to Louisville, Kentucky, where it arrived on the 21st of June. On the 12th of July it was mustered out at Louisville, there being with it present for duty from the 7th, 14th, 19th and 20th Regiments as consolidated, 23 Officers and 390 men.

From Louisville, the Regiment was sent in a body on the 12th of July 1865 to Indianapolis, Indiana, under command of Col. Albert S. Andrews, originally of the 14th Indiana. It was welcomed home by Governor Morton in an address at a public reception in the State House Grove where speeches were also made by Genl. Hovey, Surgeon Orpheus Everts and Chaplain W.C. Porter. A few days after this, the Regiment was finally discharged from service.

COMMENTARY: *Through August and September 1864 the siege of Petersburg continued with skirmishing, but no major actions, as hard fighting continued in other theaters, to the south, the Gulf coast, the west, and nearby in the Shenandoah valley, where Genl. Sheridan and Genl. Early clashed repeatedly.*

It took all winter and early spring of 1865 for Grant to stretch the Rebel lines around Petersburg to their breaking point. On April 2, as the defenses of Petersburg were broken by Union attacks, Lee announced that he would withdraw from the defense of both Richmond and Petersburg and move to save his army. Both cities were then evacuated.

The 20th Indiana Regiment fought through the entire war to the final day, April 9, 1865, when Genl. Lee surrendered at Appomattox.

In Closing, January 16, 1898

THE 20TH INDIANA HAD IN IT FROM FIRST to last 1403 men. Its killed amounted to 201; its wounded amounted to 570.

Total: 771

Died in Confederate Prisons: 25

Died of disease: 88

Total: 113

There were 144 captured. Percentage of killed to enrollment, 14.3.

Owing to the late date of this story of the Regiment written, it is impossible to obtain the names of those who were killed or the wounded.

Application has been made to the War Department for the names of these heroes, but was refused because the records of the War have become so much worn that it required the greatest of care to preserve them.

I have had in my possession for years, however, a list of the Officers killed, and who died of wounds. It is as follows:

1. 1st Lieut. John W. Andrews, White Oak Swamps, June 30, 1862
2. Capt. James W. Lytle, Orchards, August 19, 1862
3. Col. William L. Brown, Bull Run 2nd, August 29, 1862
4. 1st Lieut. Ezra Robbins, Gettysburg, July 2, 1863
5. Col. John Wheeler, Gettysburg, July 2, 1863
6. Capt. Henry Quigley, Wilderness, May 12, 1864
7. Capt. L. D. Corey, Spotsylvania, May 12, 1864
8. Capt. John F. Thomas, Spotsylvania, May 12, 1864
9. 1st Lieut. E. C. Sutherland, Spotsylvania, May 26, 1864
10. 1st Lieut. J. C. Bartholemew, Spotsylvania, May 28, 1864
11. Capt. Lafayette Gordon, Spotsylvania, June 6, 1864
12. Capt. Charles A. Bell, Petersburg, July 9, 1864

13. Lieut. Col. G. W. Meikel, Petersburg, September 10, 1864
14. Capt. William P. Thompson, Petersburg, October 7, 1864
15. 2nd Lieut. William Dickson, died in prison of wounds, July, 1864
16. 2nd Lieut. Johnathan Robart, died of wounds received at Bull Run

Our loss in killed and wounded was greater than from any other Regiment from Indiana during the war. We lost more Officers and more men in battle than any mustered into the service. It is a fact to be noted that notwithstanding all this loss and activity on the part of the 20th Indiana Regiment, there was never but one Officer brevetted for any action, and I never knew of but one who asked or tried to get a brevet.

In all of the Records of the Rebellion now published, there are only three reports made by the Officers commanding the Regiment, and, so far as Commanding Officers were concern[ed], there seems to have been no Officer or man found worthy of a word of written praise.

It has thus been found extremely difficult to compile even so meagre a history of the Regiment as the foregoing, which had been written or compiled solely for the benefit of my children and theirs, and is more of a story of my experience than of the Regiment.

I participated with the Regiment in the following battles and affairs, the names of which are borne on the flag of the Regiment:

Chickamicomico, N. C.
Merrimac, Congress & Cumberland Battles
Norfolk, Va.
Oak Grove: 7 days
Peach Orchard: 7 days
White Oak Swamp: 7 days
Charles City Cross Roads: 7 days
Malvern Hill
Kelly's Ford, Va.
Bull Run 2nd
Chantilly
Fredericksburg
Chancellorsville

Gettysburg

Wapping Heights

Kelly's Ford

Locust Grove

Mine Run

Wilderness

Spotsylvania

North Anna

Totopotomoy

Cold Harbor

Petersburg, from June 15th to October 19, 1864.

Deep Bottom

Strawberry Plains

At Indianapolis, the State had erected a monument as a memorial to the soldiers and sailors of the Union who fell during the War of the Rebellion. It is represented to be the greatest of soldiers' monuments, and cost over 300,000 dollars. It is 280 feet high and is a grand work. The only flag that was placed in the corner stone of that monument was the tattered flag of the 20th Indiana, selected because the losses of this Regiment was greatest of any from the State.

I may say in closing this paper, that after leaving the 20th Indiana I was appointed Lieutenant Colonel in Hancock's Corps, which was called the First Corps, and was to be composed of Veterans of the War. The Corps was to be raised by Hancock and commanded by him. My appointment dated February 14, 1865.

I had been appointed a Captain and Assistant Quartermaster of Volunteers, January 25, 1865, and had accepted of this appointment before the other reached me. I was mustered out of the Quartermaster position July 28th, 1865, and was appointed a 1st Lieutenant in the Regular Army of the United States on the 23rd of February 1866. These three positions were given me for my war service which ended when I was twenty-four years and five months of age.

Whipple Barracks, Arizona

January 16, 1898

PART TWO

POST–CIVIL WAR

1866-1898

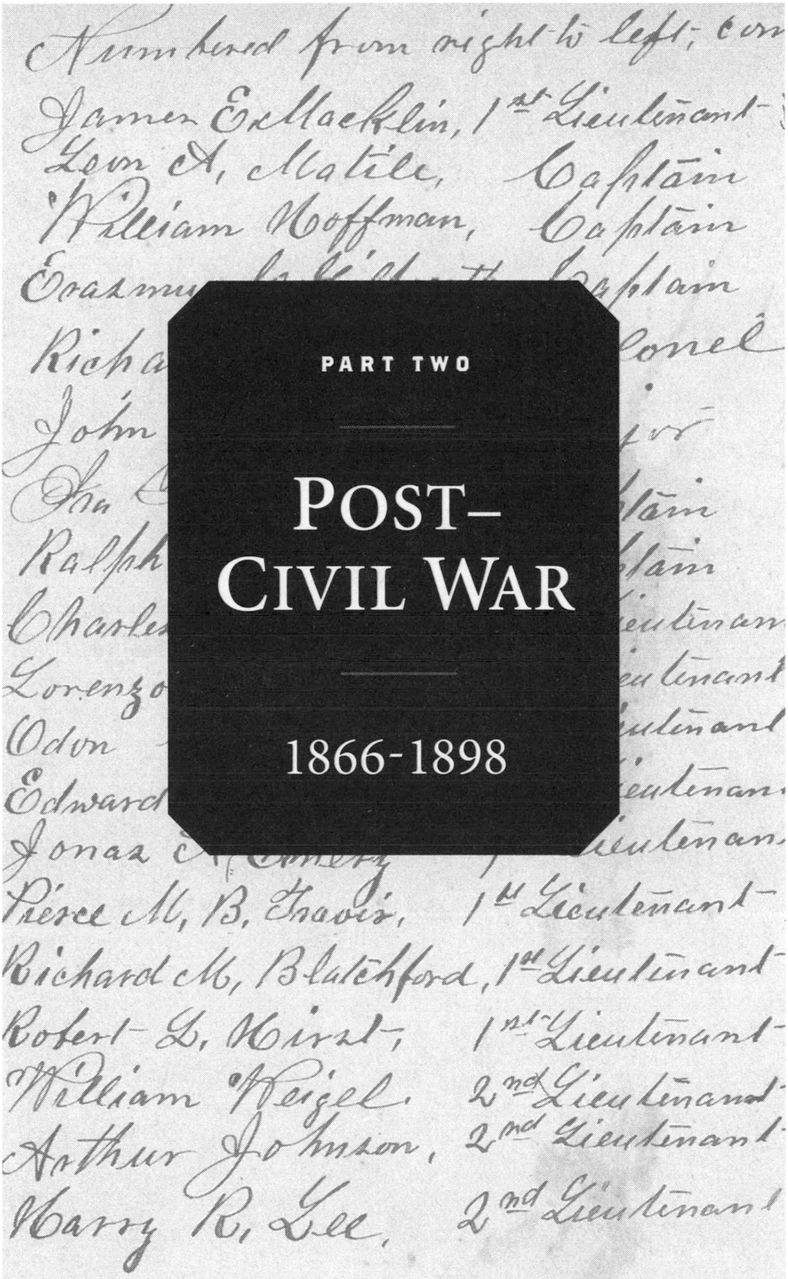

Marriage to Susan
& Arrival in Mississippi

1866

n 1866 I was commissioned a 2nd Lieut. and 1st Lieut. in the 15th U.S. Infantry, both commissions dating February 23rd, 1866. I was married to Susan Coale Corse April 24, 1866, at the house of Joseph Pancoast on Eastern St. above Madison Ave., Baltimore, Md., by the Rev. Mr. Barrett of the Baptist or Christian Church. We left Baltimore and arrived at Philadelphia, Pa., the same day and went on to Decatur, Ill., where my mother, brother, and sister were then living. At Decatur, I received my commission as above and accepted the same formally on the 2nd day of May 1866. I at the same time received orders to report at Carlisle Barracks, Pa. As we had journeyed west via the Pensa and Pan Handle Railroad, I thought it best to come east by way of Chicago and Canada, through Niagara Falls and Buffalo. We stopped for a day at the falls and then arrived at Carlisle Barracks on the 11th of May. The Barracks were under the command of Wm. N. Grier, a fine officer of the old school, familiarly called Billy and Commandant. I formed many pleasant acquaintances at Carlisle Barracks, some of which have lasted a lifetime almost. There were many newly appointed officers sent to the Barracks at the time, and all of the new ones had held commissions in the volunteer service, so that a saying at the Post as a newly appointed officer was seen to enter the gate, usually in a bright new uniform, was "What Brigadier General is that, I wonder?" or "Lieutenant, what brigade did you command?"

Many of these new officers were worthless, and still many proved to be valuable. Of the former class one Anderson was the most worthless

drunkard I ever saw. He was sent away under guard and to the 15th Infantry too, but did not stay long, having been dismissed for drunkenness
when he enlisted in the 10th Infantry.

After a couple of weeks' stay at Carlisle, 50 of us were sent off to our
Regiments. I was offered the choice of going west via Pittsburgh and
thence down the Mississippi to Mobile, but chose to go via New York and
by steamer to New Orleans. We thought a sea trip would be a grand thing
for us, and so with six or seven others, went to New York for the boat. I
first got a state room on the *Evening Star*, but as the rest wanted to go on
the *George Cromwell*, I changed to the latter ship.

We had headwinds every day, and the passage down was one series of
seasick spells. We left N.Y. at the same time as the *Evening Star*, 4 P.M., and
at sunset parted company with her outside Sandy Hook, but overtook
her again off the coast of Florida. To avoid the Gulf Stream, she sailed
closer to the shore than we and got in so close that she ran up on a coral
reef with which that coast abounds. I shall never forget how her masts,
smokestack, and the ship grew up out of the water as we approached her.

As we came near, our boat stopped about 4 miles off and their purser
came on board. The steamship (*Evening Star*) lay on the reef high out
of water so that her red water line showed from stem to stern distinctly
from our vessel. $50,000 was offered our Captain if he would pull her
off. But he refused as it would cancel his insurance. It was interesting to
see the wreckers collecting about the *Evening Star*. Before we reached her
vicinity, up and down the coast (as) far as the eye could see we beheld
numberless small sailing vessels skimming along the coast and all collecting around the steamer ready, when she should go to pieces, to pounce
upon the cargo and fittings. These pirates all desired to be merciless in
robbing any ill-fated vessel stranded near their homes, and they live almost wholly on their plunderings of unfortunate wrecks.

We lay off and on for some time but finally, after offering to take off
the passengers, we went on our way, the *Evening Star* fading into nothing
inversely as she had grown upon our vision. She was fortunate that no
storm came up and at a high tide she got off and went on her way south
without damage or loss. She arrived at New Orleans a couple of days
behind time. On her very next trip from New York, however, the *Evening*

Star was foundered off that same coast, losing some 100 lives, amongst which was one Army officer, a Lieut. of the 4th Cavalry.

We arrived at New Orleans one day behind time and stopped at the City Hotel, stayed a couple of days, and went to Mobile, Alabama, via Lake Ponchartrain and the route inside the Istaria. We stopped at the Battle House and found it a terrible place. Everything in the South was in a demoralized condition in 1866, as the entire country was still suffering from the effects of the war.

I reported to the Lieutenant Colonel of the 15th Infantry, Jas. Dawson, who was called "Black Jack." He was a disagreeable old martinet. I asked him for permission to stay at Mobile for a day or two as we were both tired from our sea trip. His reply was, "You will proceed to Vicksburg by the first train leaving the city, sir." The 2nd battalion of the 15th Infantry was at Vicksburg, and Company B, to which I belonged, was at Grenada, Miss. We traveled from Mobile on the Mobile and Ohio Railroad to Meridian and thence to Vicksburg on the V. and Vicksburg and Meridian Railroad. The railroads of the South were all broken up by the war and their rolling stock in a terrible condition so that we made slow progress. We were a long day in getting to Meridian and, on arrival there, stopped at the Globe House, but becoming dissatisfied with the surroundings, went round the block and stopped at the Logan House. It was dirty and uncomfortable. We had wet bedding and only a piece of a candle for our room. The food was very bad, so poor that Mrs. G. ate scarcely anything.

After we had been there a short time, we had a call from Capt. Norton, Company C, 2nd Battalion, 15th Infantry and Lieut. Hedberg of the 15th Infantry. At six o'clock the morning after our arrival, we started for Vicksburg in the most terrible train of cars I have ever seen. When I went to the Depot at Meridian, I thought I would run over to the camp of the troops to return the call of Capt. Norton and the others, and on knocking at the door, caused a commotion within. After being inspected through a crack, I was admitted and found a party seated around a table covered with a blanket and each had a pile of beads before him. They had been playing poker all night and were a sleepy looking crowd.

Norton was retired in 1870, and Hedberg was murdered by Lieut. Maney in 1893. Norton was a very absent-minded man, and it is said of him that he used to occasionally go out to roll call and walk up to the first company he came to and receive the report, neglecting his own company all together. He was fond of reciting "Bingen on the Rhine" and always did it with tears. It was his only piece for recitation. He was slightly deaf when we first knew him. It grew upon him and caused his retirement. He was a fast friend of mine.

OUR TRAIN TO VICKSBURG WAS VERY DIRTY, the windows were closed with boards, and the engine and cars were all so dilapidated that we did not reach Jackson until after noon and Vicksburg in the night. We stopped at the Prentiss House which was then the largest hotel. It was kept by an old man who was called "General" Jones. He wore a full dress uniform of Confederate gray with General stars and insignia. One of his peculiarities was that he had no bill of fare but stood in the dining room and called out the dishes. It was amusing to hear him call "Here's your lamb and your jelly and your jam." "Roast beef and fish and vegetables with every dish," and so on. He did his own carving and at intervals walked around the dining room and urged each guest in a polite way to have more of this dish or that. If the guest accepted or declined was all the same to him as he went on to the next and forgot all about the last one visited. He and his wife were unreconstructed rebels. He said that he got into the habit of calling his bill of fare while keeping hotel at Jackson, the capital of Mississippi, when he had so many members of the legislature stopping with him who could not read.

The Post at Vicksburg was some distance from the hotel. Some of the officers called upon us, among them Maj. N. A. U. Dudley, the Commanding Officer. When he came into the parlor with his Post Adjutant W. C. Beach, they created an impression. The General, as he wished to be called, and his Adjutant were dressed to kill: gauntlets, boots, and all. The former was dignified and cordial, while the latter wanted to be dignified.

The Adjutant assured me that he wished to be kind and on good terms with everyone when not on duty, but that in his office he was strictly military. He impressed Mrs. G. with his importance. She was not used to seeing such men, and asked who he was. I had to tell her he was a 1st

Lieutenant, only one file above me. We got into the Post soon as we could and began to live in very contracted quarters. We had only three very small rooms. The bedroom was just large enough to accommodate a bed and one trunk. Maj. Dudley was a good officer—at drill or for police or to command the Post, but he drank a great deal and had many eccentricities. He was called the Great North American Dudley.

Officers were few and I had command of two or three companies at a time. The companies were filled up in 1866 with the worst element I have ever seen, men from the war time, and we used to have 80 or 100 in the Guard House at a time. The General came for me one day and asked me to take a walk with him. We started for the Guard House. The sentinel called, "Turn out the Guard for the Commanding Officer." The prisoners all ran to the prison room window to see where the General was going. But he walked on past the Guard House and entered it unseen by the prisoners. We then quietly entered the prison room, and as the prisoners were all looking out the window, the General stepped up quietly and took the first prisoner by the ear and drew his head around. Soon as the prisoner's eyes fell on the General, he yelled at the top of his voice, "Attention." All the prisoners sprang back and took the position of a soldier in front of the bunk. The General then said to his prisoner, "Young man, you are too young to be here. Haven't you a mother?" The man said he had.

The General then gave him a lecture on love for his parents and asked him if he would remember his Mother and try to behave himself. The man whimpered by this time that he would do his best when the General told him to go. He then asked each one if he had a mother, and because he either had at the time such a relative or had had one at some period of his life, he let them go and so cleaned out the Guard House except, as he arrived at the last man, he found a character. It was Private Cuff of Company F, an old soldier who was usually drunk when off duty but fully sober on duty. He would be found vilely dirty at Reveille and apparently beastly drunk, but by nine o'clock he would go to Guard Mounting fully sober and carry off the prize of being Commanding Officer's orderly for being the cleanest man on the Guard. On this occasion Cuff was the last man in the prison room and he was not at attention, but lying back on the bunk with a stick of wood for a pillow, and he was laughing. The General stood in front of him and said, "Oh there you are, Old Cuff, you infernal old scoundrel. I won't release you from the Guard House, but I'll shoot you," and with that the General drew a big pistol he had hidden under his cloak, and extended it at arm's length high in air.

Cuff made one spring, landed at the foot of his bunk at attention and stiff as a ramrod. The General abused him a little while, and then left him alone in the prison room. These prisoners were all recent cases of men confined in what was called the General Prison Room, which was separate from the cells where harder cases were confined. The Quarters for the men, as well as for the officers in 1866 when we joined at Vicksburg, were what would now in 1894 be regarded as so terribly constructed as to be unfit for dumb animals to occupy. They had been built for Confederate troops during the war, and for each company consisted of one long low shed-like building 12 feet wide and 110 feet long. Bunks for the men were wooden affairs, double width and two stories high. The men had no bed sacks or mattress or pillows, and each bunk, accommodating four men, was supplied only with straw or hay to sleep on.

The Post was occupied by four companies, later increased to six companies of the 2nd Battalion, 15th Infantry. In 1866 each Infantry Regiment above the 10th consisted of 3 Battalions of eight companies each. Our 1st Battalion was at Mobile with Headquarters, 15th Infantry. The 3rd was at Mount Vernon Barracks and vicinity, while ours occupied Grenada 1 Company, Meridian 1 Company, Jackson 2 Companies, and Vicksburg 4 Companies. While we were at this Post, we had yellow fever, congestive chills and cholera at the Post. We often saw Jeff Davis, as this city was his home after his release from prison. His brother Joe Davis and a niece, Mrs. Porterfield, often visited the Post, and we were often at their house to attend social gatherings. Genl. Thos. J. Wood commanded the Department and gave frequent entertainments. His wife was a very delightful lady.

The first notice we had of the presence of cholera was when 5 men died one day. The men were placed in coffins on the parade ground and covered with flags. The Rev. Dr. Marshall of M. E. Church South preached the sermon over the bodies, and it was an eloquent one.

The troops were afterwards formed in a hollow square and the Doctor explained to them the symptoms of cholera and its treatment. This fuss was the last public demonstration, as afterwards all funerals were at night. I had a congestive chill which nearly carried me off.

———

IN THOSE DAYS THE COMMISSARY and Quartermaster Department supplied us with very little, so that we were compelled to pay war prices for everything down in the city. We boarded at first, but when we began to keep house, we paid 100 dollars for a stove and 25 dollars for a barrel of flour. We boarded for a time with a Mrs. McGregor just outside the Post and found it terribly dirty and tiresome. During the cholera scare one of our Captains, Brown, became very much frightened and left the Post and began to board at one of the highest points in the City. I had no permission and so we were surprised to see him turn up in the Post pale as a ghost on the second day after leaving us. A man had died at his "sky parlor," as it was called, in the next room to him and of yellow fever too.

A man escaped from the guard and ran off with a rifle. Several persons ran after him, amongst them Brown. It was not his business as he was not on duty. The fugitive ran through a cotton field near the Post, and Brown followed with the rest. A half mile away from the Post, Brown took a rifle from a Corporal of the Guard and fired at the prisoner who was about 700 yards off. He shot the man directly through the head, killing him instantly. The Captain was nearly insane over his accidental good shot and wouldn't sleep alone for some time. Brown had been wounded twice in the head during the war, and was called "Bullet Brown."

During the summer of 1866, all the companies of the 2nd Battalion, 15th Infantry came to Vicksburg except one at Grenada, B Company, and one at Jackson, Miss. Vicksburg was very interesting to all of us then, as there were about 12 or 15 old Confederate Forts about the city and the bluffs on which the city was built were filled with the caves and holes in which people lived during the firing of the United States fleet on the city during the war. The people were all hostile to us and we had no society with them except with the Porterfields (Davis's family). The P's were very kind and sent many things to our sick and to the well ones, and showed their kindness in various ways.

Very many funny things occurred, principally on account of our Commanding Officer's peculiarities. He bragged a great deal about his war service, was fond of speech making and of crying when in his cups.

In September or October, I was ordered to my own Company B at Grenada. We went by rail via Jackson, Miss., and when we got to Grenada, had a hard time to get a place to live. The Quarters at the Camp of the Company were not fit to live in, being merely log huts of the rudest construction. I applied at the Hotel, but they said they would not accommodate any Yankee, and I hardly knew what to do. Finally, however, the officer of the Freedman's Bureau, Capt. Sibley, took me to an old resident named Howard, and he consented to let us live in his house. He was a relative of Genl. O.O. Howard from Maine [who] had found his way to Virginia as a young man teaching school, had married a Virginia lady, and became a full Southern man. He had lost his wife and son and much property during the war, and lived alone in a good large old-fashioned house near our Camp. He took us in, or rather turned over the whole house to us. He had one old Aunty of a negro who had been his slave and who did cooking in an old open fireplace. All our meals were about alike: corn dodgers, bacon and coffee, but Mrs. G. improved a little on this bill of fare. The old man was thoroughly despondent and always asked just the same blessing in the same way. He would heave a great sigh, and as it began to weaken in coming out he said, "Oh Lord bless us in what we are about to receive." We became very fond of each other, and Howard came to see us after we had moved from Grenada. He was flooded with threatening letters and insults all the time we were at his house, but he paid no attention to them and kept us.

Men used to ride up in front of the house at night and fire off shotguns and pistols to scare us out. Howard was an educated gentleman and his stories of the war and his experience were graphic and entertaining. Grenada was taken time and again by both sides during the war, and Howard being one of the prominent citizens, had usually an active part. The Post consisted of Company B, 15th Infantry and (Solomon E. Woodward, Capt. 15th Infantry) was commanded by 2nd Lieut. Nye, 15 Infantry.

Soon after I arrived, I started in to get lumber for building men's quarters for my company. The first camp was on the banks of the Yellowbushy

River and very unhealthy. My Company was alone when I first got there, and was in a terrible physical state. The men lived like hogs, never had any drill and little military duty. The officer whom I relieved had tried to resign several times, but they would not let him go as there was no one to take his place. So he let everything go. I succeeded in getting off my estimate for lumber for one Company quarters, and then Wilson came with his troops, arriving about the 1st of December, 1866. He was nicknamed Duck Wilson and was a fool. I was Commissary Quartermaster and Adjutant, and he was Commanding Officer. I hurried up building and erected a good long house for Company quarters, one 14 x 26 for myself, a smaller one for Wilson. We moved in about the middle of December. The Cavalry Troop camped near where my company was, and the change began to show on the health and appearance of the men. I lived at Howard's after the men were moved into camp and Wilson was alone with them.

CHAPTER 2

Duties in Mississippi
& Our Son Is Born

1867-1868

About the first of January 1867, I moved into my house and then my son William Sydnor was born January 24th, 1867.

All the [local] people were very hostile to us except Col. Howard. They used to come into town and a crowd would get around, then ride out full tilt and shoot at our flag. Wilson went off on a court martial and left me alone and I stopped that shooting. I had been downtown during the day and expected something of the kind. So I told the 1st Sergeant that if they came by shooting at the flag, I wanted every man of the company to get out fast as he could and begin shooting and to hit if they could and to arrest the men. I was safe from causing any bloodshed as hardly a man in the Company could hit a "flock of barns" let alone men riding on horseback.

Sure enough, up a crowd of about 10 men came about 4 P.M. Every man fired at the flag and all galloped off. Out the 70 or 80 men of the Company came and begun shooting and chasing them on foot. The shots fell thick and fast, and the 10 flew about a quarter of a mile when they halted and held up their handkerchiefs or hats. My men went on and brought in the whole party. No one was hurt, but they were badly frightened. I lectured them and let them go, and we never had any more trouble.

Wilson had arranged his house for himself so he had a door in one [end] and a window on each side and a stovepipe hole in the end opposite the door. As the wind changed he had his stove moved so that the stovepipe ran out a different way with every change. Sometimes it ran out the door or one window, while if everything was calm and proper, it carried the smoke off though its proper opening. He would not cut the roof, as it might leak. He read his prayers or the service for the day by going outside so all could see him, and then as he walked very rapidly around his house he as rapidly read the book.

His house was about 12 by 14 feet square. He was very much afraid of his men and ordered me to put a guard from my company over his quarters. When I asked the reason, he said that his men were all Fenians and that he looked so much like an Englishman that he was afraid they would shoot him. Genl. Delos B. Sackett inspected us there, and we entertained him. He was wholesome and jolly as could be, and we liked him very much. After he went away, he reported that Wilson was not fit to command a company, much less a Post.

Grenada was the home of the Forrest family. One brother of the Genl. N. B. Forrest lived in the town and another was in hiding nearby, having been accused of assassinating a Freedman's Bureau officer in the town before I got there. We had many curious rides and excursions into the country to try and arrest John Forrest, but we never found him. The wife of Bill Forrest came and notified us that John would be in town on a certain night. We surrounded a square and searched it but did not find him.

I asked Col. Howard how he came to be called Colonel. He said that before the war they had a militia muster on a high hill, which he pointed out, and he was a candidate for Colonel of the 10th Mississippi Militia. The other candidate was chosen to be the Colonel of the 10th Regiment but Col. Howard had always been called Colonel since that election.

He said that after that Colonel was chosen, that officer wished to make a speech (to congratulate the men on their choice, I suppose). The new Colonel did not know anything about military commands but he rode out on the field and yelled, "Gentlemen of the 10th Mississippi Militia, form hollow square." The men moved about but all got confused and mixed up. So the Colonel again yelled once or twice, "Gentlemen, form hollow square." They only got more hopelessly confused as liquor had been free all day, so the new Colonel rose in his stirrups and said, "Gentlemen of the 10th Mississippi Militia, go to Hell every man of you." They all cheered and after some fun left the training ground for home.

The Regiment never assembled again. The Colonel's last speech broke up the 10th Mississippi Militia Regiment.

In May 1867 I was ordered to take my Company from Grenada to Brookhaven, Miss., on the arrival of Col. A. V. Kantz with the headquarters of his Regiment the 16th U.S. Infantry. He was a very courteous and polite gentleman of the old school and came about the 15th of May. I left at once by railroad for Brookhaven, and arriving there the same day found a very pleasant little town of 2500 people where no troops had been stationed since the war closed. I was made an officer of the Freedman's Bureau and was placed in charge of five counties of the state to reconstruct them. These counties were: Copiah, Lawrence, Liberty, Columbia and Amite, and before the war or in 1860 had in them 18,000 negroes.

There was not a civil officer in these counties, and all of them were to be reconstructed, and in all, the negroes had to be cared for by the Freedman's Bureau, so that I here began a new duty and an onerous one. Brookhaven was 128 miles from New Orleans and in a pine woods country and very pleasant to us all, although the people were always hostile to us and ostracized us. My first duty was to find a camping place "in or near the town" as my orders said, and I finally selected an abandoned place or one not occupied. It had a house of two rooms with a wide hall between them open at both ends and an attached kitchen. The place happened to be across the street from a Young Ladies Seminary of the M. E. South Church, and many protests were made to me against my selection. But I adhered to my choice and ultimately made a very attractive camp of it. The Young Ladies used to come out on the porch and sing Rebel songs. The men of my company replied every time by singing Union songs, and there were some very good voices in the Company. This was all the feeling between the two institutions, and I never had a complaint as to the conduct of my men.

There were 86 men in the Company, and they used to amuse lookers on by their dances in the Company street. I got a skilled man to build an oven for me and soon supplied the town with very excellent bread. In conversation with the President of the Seminary, I made him angry by speaking of the M. E. Church in the North in high terms. He said he could never forgive them for their preaching and action during the war and called them many names. I asked him if he had ever seen any Northern Methodists. He said yes he had been North once. I said how far North did you travel and how long did you stay. He said he had been up to Memphis once for a week. He had been no further.

I selected and recommended men for the civil officers of the Counties named. This was not always an easy matter to do, as all had to be appointed by the Military Commanding Officer of the district or State, and no one could hold office who had held office before the war and had afterwards engaged in rebellion, so that I could only select from young men or the few Union men who had dodged the war.

I had first seen something of the Ku Klux Klan. It consisted only of bodies of white men who paraded covered with white sheets and a fantastic cap. They used to parade at night and usually collected one at a time in some graveyard. They there covered their horses and themselves so that no one would recognize either horse or rider, and then they issued forth in a long string. Their object was to frighten negroes, and they did it effectively. They occasionally killed a negro or whipped one, and they kept all of the freedmen in a constant state of alarm. On starting out they usually fired a shotgun or two and then the colored folks would hide in short order. Their white covering was marked with red and black, and altogether they presented a hideous appearance. The negroes seldom made any resistance, and if they did, soon got the worst of it. My duties of Freedman's Bureau Commissioner required me to act as a sort of a Judge and to listen and inquire into all complaints made by freedmen against their employers. I had to settle their accounts and very often compelled the white employer to pay money to his help. It was difficult to get the white people to regard the freedmen as free, and so frequently a system of peonage was established. They would agree to give ⅛ of the cotton crop to a colored man, but as they supplied all the provisions, it was easy by charging $1.50 a pound for bacon and equally high for other things to not only eat up all the part of the crop belonging to the negro, but to keep him constantly in debt. These instances were not general, and while the desire to wrong the colored man extended to all classes, still a large majority of the whites treated their former slaves justly. It was a very difficult thing for the whites to get started after losing everything in the war, and still the majority tried and tried hard to do their best for the colored people.

The vicious class was in the minority, but they often compelled the entire community to act with them. The entire community approved of the Ku Klux Klan as the only means of keeping the negroes, who were in the greater numbers, in awe, and now in 1894 I look upon it as almost a necessity, situated as they were with their families and without law officers. The negro had no idea of liberty at that time and no just appreciation of his rights, and as then they were filled with brutal ideas, they were dangerous.

I had frequently to arrest horse thieves and murderers. The custom was to send such offenders under guard with the witnesses to Vicksburg for trial by a Military Commission. These arrests were almost always amongst white men. A Military Commission was a Court made up of Officers, the same as a Court Martial and was for the trial of civilians only. Horse thieves were usually sent to Little Rock Penitentiary for seven or ten years. Colored people used to come to me with all sorts of complaints of each other, and I was required to listen and record the matter. Some would come over 100 miles to see the "Beero" as they called it.

One effect of this was that they collected at Brookhaven, and having made their complaint and had it adjusted, were then either afraid to go back home or found it pleasanter at the town, so they squatted on the outskirts in the pine woods, and there soon sprung up quite a town of 1200 to 2500 colored people. They built a church and schoolhouse with the aid of Northern societies, and it was not an unusual thing to hear them singing all night long. This town was inoffensive, but the white people were always nervous about them. Once a complaint came to me that they [white people] were organizing for some purpose and were patrolling the roads. I did not believe it but rode out there after dark one night and sure enough they had guards out on the road about their church. I went in and broke up that meeting in short order and sent the white men out of town on the first train.

White teachers from the North were usually a very self-sacrificing lot of men and women and labored under very many disadvantages. The colored people were very ignorant and superstitious and hardly knew what freedom meant. They were anxious to learn, and old and young applied themselves closely to books and teachers. Many of these negroes still had confidence in their former masters, and could the latter have had more advantages or rather not have been so poor, they might at first have done much good for the negroes. As time advanced, the negroes became more suspicious of the whites, and as laws were passed making them equal as voters of the whites, the feeling of antipathy grew greater on both sides. The great mistake in the laws was the mistake of forcing suffrage on all indiscriminately. A line should have been drawn, allowing only those who could read and write understandingly to become voters. This should be the test for suffrage every place, but it applied with especial force to the released slaves of the South in 1867. Once in a while we had complaints of white men trying to force their former slaves to stay with them as virtual slaves, but in the majority of cases negroes could make new contracts with other white men than those they had formerly belonged to.

In 1867 the first election was held in Mississippi, and I was required to visit the 5 counties and select men to perform the duties of Judges of Election as well as to make the required registration of voters. I rode through the 5 counties accompanied only by a mounted orderly, and, while I was sometimes insulted, generally had no difficulty. At Hazelhurst, Copia County, I was challenged to fight a duel because I had not allowed a young man to go with an old negro to the polls. I paid no attention to the challenge or to the threats of the young man who brought the message. They collected about a dozen young men and waited until I was to leave town. I let them see me ride slowly out of town towards Brookhaven and after I had gone a mile or so I rode at a gallop around the town through the woods to the Liberty road and dashed off 15 miles very rapidly. Brookhaven was south and Liberty east. My "friends" rode on the Brookhaven road for some distance and searched the woods looking for me as I was afterwards told. As they were pretty drunk, I do not know what might have happened if they had come up with me.

On another occasion a crowd stopped a railroad train to see if either myself or another officer was on board. At Osaka I got into the house of a Mr. W., a Union man, by stealth and through the assistance of a negro, and so helped to protect his family from the attack of a wild young man. Mr. W. was in New Orleans, and his wife and five daughters were alone at the house. The friendship then formed was lasting, and Mr. W. was very grateful to me.

Lieut. Loot was sent to arrest a man for nearly killing a negro. He surrounded the house and knocked at the door. The man wouldn't open the door and, seeing he was caught, only exclaimed, "Where in h-l are my dogs?" He depended on his dogs to notify him of the approach of anyone.

The cholera and yellow fever were very bad in New Orleans in 1867, and I was required to establish a quarantine at Brookhaven for the railroad. I put up about 50 large tents out of town about 4 miles and established a beautiful camp near a large spring. Everything was controlled by the army in those days and all railroad trains were compelled to stop at our camp and allow a doctor to go through and examine passengers. We had cooks and attendants hired and took off several people, but not so very many. Yellow fever broke out in the town of Brookhaven, and 27 died of that disease. We did not have a case in our camp. In November, 1867, I was ordered to take my company to Vicksburg. We arrived about the last of the month and were again under Maj. Dudley's command. One of my Sergeants died of yellow fever soon after we got to Vicksburg. The Commanding Officer ordered that we go every day to the Hospital to see our sick. I saw my sergeant who told me while holding my hand that he was sure he was going to die. I tried to encourage him to think it was not so bad as that, and while I was talking to him he had a spasm of vomiting, and I saw that it was the black vomit or last stages of yellow fever. I left him and he died, and I was worried to distraction that I would take the disease home with me. I walked the Post until a late hour and consulted with doctors. Finally, I went home and told my wife. We had no sign of yellow fever and no evil effects from my contact with the Sergeant.

While at Vicksburg Capt. Brown afforded us amusement by his eccentric ways. He was officer of the day once and left the Post and city and went to New Orleans on a steamboat with a party of ladies not having anyone's permission. He was always making love to any girl that came in his way, and on this occasion he made impetuous love to a very pretty girl from Tennessee. He offered her as a sign of his devotion presents of a canary bird and a monkey. Both were declined, and that monkey was a thing of horror and wonder. Its only accomplishment was, when anyone came near, to utter a terrible squeak and skinny to the top of the pole to which he was fastened.

———

WHILE I WAS STATIONED AT BROOKHAVEN, MISS., in 1867, there was a great deal of distress throughout the whole state of Mississippi for want of food. The people had been completely broken up by the war. Crops had failed, as the new system of living and of free labor did not finance well. Levees of the Mississippi River had not been repaired, and there were great overflows from it which drowned out the crops in the lowlands. The people, or many of them, were almost starving, so that Congress made a large appropriation for the purchase of food for free distribution amongst the suffering. These supplies consisted of pork and corn principally, and they were sent to the officers of the Army in the various localities to be given out. I received five carloads of corn and 300 barrels of pork at Brookhaven, and gave it all away to needy applicants. It nearly all went to the suffering white population, although the colored people got food when they called for it. It was given out so as to allow each adult 2½ pounds of pork and a peck of corn each week. The people, white and black, flocked to my office, and I saw many very distressing cases.

The most affecting were the widows and orphans of Confederate soldiers who had been killed during the war. Ladies, many of them of refinement and education, were compelled to come for food as they were almost starving. These were all treated in the most liberal way possible and were saved all the humiliation possible. The entire supply was given out in three months. Although I was approached and my employees as well were offered $50 in gold per barrel for pork if we would sell it, yet I take pride in saying that I believe that not a pound was thus wickedly disposed of.

———

I WAS OFTEN SENT OUT OF THE POST on Reconstruction duty, most always went alone, and was called upon to do all sorts of work. Once I sold 500 bales of cotton, and once stopped the sale of 1000 bales.

I was sent up the Yazoo River to make an arrest of a desperate man named Gibson. He owned two beautiful plantations on the upper Yazoo, and from his house could see far down the river. His family were returning by boat from New Orleans before the war, and as the steamer rounded the bend, coming in sight of their house, it was found to be on fire. It was totally destroyed, and Dr. Gibson's family perished. He became a perfect demon from that time on, served in the Rebel army, and after the war, was one of the worst uncompromising Rebels in the state. I was ordered to go to Yazoo City, get a detachment of Sgt. and five men of the 5th Cavalry, then go to Greenwood at the head of navigation, and thence to Dr. Gibson's house and arrest him.

On arriving at Greenwood I found I had to go down the river about 12 miles and cross the Yazoo to get to his house. The waters were high, and I had difficulty in crossing side streams flowing into the Yazoo. We crossed that river in sight of Gibson's house and rode up to it. I called to the people, and a lady came to the door. When I inquired for Dr. Gibson, she said he had gone to Savais and then gave me an awful tongue lashing using all sorts of language. But I found a negro [woman], and on threatening her, found that he [Gibson] had watched us cross, and soon as I mounted my party, he mounted a fleet animal and left for his lower plantation six miles further down the river. I went to the barnyard gate and saw his tracks as he had mounted, and then we took up the gallop on his track. My party of course strung out and we flew through woods and cotton fields. I could see him occasionally going out at the farther side of a cotton field as I entered it. We kept up a gallop, and at a point on the river nearest his lower plantation as he turned short to ride away from the river, I saw that his horse had fallen. I spurred up livelier than ever and a mile or so back came to his barn. In it was his horse covered with foam and mud, and a negro said he had gone into a dugout and rowed into a Cypress swamp which came up within 50 feet of the barn. I gave up the chase and after resting, rode back to the river. When I got there I found about 50 men mounted and armed with double-barreled shotguns. They had come from plantations through which we had passed and were without doubt there to rescue Dr. Gibson if I had arrested him. One asked me if the war was over, and I asked him what they were hunting. He said, "Turkeys." They all rode up the river with me or behind me, and I guess it was just as well that I didn't catch my man.

I had made the trip up the Yazoo in the steamer *Countess* and had ordered her to wait for me and take my party back to Vicksburg, which she did, or at least part of the way. It was a wonderful sight to see the roustabouts on the boat load. Moon at night. The pine knots burning in their baskets gave a weird light, and the darkies all singing at the top of their voices as they marched to and from the deck of the boat. They also gave us a concert once in a while in the cabin of the boat, and we were regaled with plantation songs right from the source of such melodies, and the dancing too was from the original.

I got off the *Countess* below Yazoo City where I left my party and went back into the country to investigate a murder. Getting back to the bank of the Yazoo, I waited until 3 o'clock to catch another boat going down. I occupied the time catching channel catfish, "blue cat," and so took home a fine string.

When we were first at Vicksburg, my wife and another lady went downtown to do the marketing. They saw large coops of chickens, and on asking the price, were told $4.00 or so. They at once thought it a bargain and asked the man to send up one of the largest coops or crates. He obligingly did so and on looking at the bill I found it for $28. The man had meant his price to be $4.00 a dozen, while they had purchased them at $4 a crate or for 7 dozen. It cost me $1.00 to get the man to take them back and my wife was hidden under the bed during the whole time occupied in adjusting the matter.

———

IN 1868 I WAS SENT TO KEMPER COUNTY TO ARREST John W. Gully, one of the most prominent citizens there. I rode from the railroad to DeKalb, the county seat, and stopped with Judge Chisholm who was afterwards killed in a brutal murder in the courthouse.

I didn't find Gully and started for the railroad to catch a train going south at 12 o'clock at night. I left DeKalb at about 8 o'clock P.M. alone and when about 3 miles out, while riding through the woods, was surprised to see a white horse approaching from a side road on my right. My first thought was Ku Klux, but a cheery voice said, "Hello stranger hold on." The man rode up and asked if I was going to the railroad station, and said he was and wanted some company. About his first remark was, "I am John W. Gully, and hearing that you wanted me, thought I would catch up with you and go along to Vicksburg," and he did without any difficulty. I put him in the guard house where he stayed a day or so.

I saw much of the Yerger family while in Mississippi, and Ed Yerger saw me downtown one day shortly after my attempt to arrest Dr. Gibson. He stopped me and said I shall hold you personally accountable for chasing my friend Dr. Gibson from his home. He was dramatic and that was all there was of it. He was also counsel for Gully and asked if I arrested him. This same Ed Yerger in the spring of 1868 lived in Jackson, Miss.. Col. Craine, an officer of the Commissary Department, was acting as Mayor of Jackson. Yerger took offense at something Craine had done as Mayor, and one morning as the latter was going to his office, Yerger stopped him and threw his left arm about Craine. With his right he drew a Bowie knife, and as he held Craine up close to him with one hand he stabbed him in the back with the knife five or six times almost cutting him in two. Craine died at once. Yerger was arrested, but after a long trial, was released. He was tried by Military Commission; afterwards by Civil Court.

The cypress swamps along the Yazoo and Mississippi Rivers were peculiar hiding places for desperate men. They were peculiar as the cypress grows very large near the ground, sometimes six feet through, then it tapers as the tree goes up until at 20 feet the tree is slender and it grows very high. Cypress grows well in water so that a cypress swamp is a lake filled with trees.

In May 1868, I was again sent to Brookhaven with my company, and there my first Captain to serve with joined me. His name was Haller, and he was very much an old soldier. He used to tie men up by the thumbs over a well 80 feet deep or tie them by the thumbs to a tree leaving them a very long time. He suffered greatly from rheumatism and all of those in the Company suffered from his temper.

He was afterwards assassinated in Texas by a lot of white men whom he was going to investigate for a murder committed there. He was lost and not heard of for a long time, but finally a Mason in a Masonic lodge told an officer where to find the spot, and a search being made, Haller's bones were found. He had been tied to a tree and riddled with buckshot.

His bones were found with the rope around them, and the body was recognized by money and clothing still clinging to the remains.

My wife went home from Brookhaven for her first visit since our marriage, and I afterwards took a leave and went North. We returned to Brookhaven in September, and in October the Company was moved to Londernoll Springs where the Ku Klux Klan had become very offensive. The Post there was commanded by Capt. James Hearn of the 34th Infantry.

I should have said before, that in 1867 all the three Battalion Regiments were divided and each Battalion became a Regiment. Our second Battalion became the 24th Infantry. Capt. Hearn was promoted from the ranks and had all the ways of the old time Sergeant about him. His wife was a very kind woman, in and from the same standing, as she had married her husband while he was an enlisted man. We heard much of the Ku Klux, and once they rode past the camp at night in their regalia and on another occasion one was wounded and his horse killed when the party had attacked a negro in his house. I got the disguise the horse and man had on, and kept it as a trophy for a time.

COMMENTARY: *Early in 1866 following his transition to the regular U.S. Army, 1st Lieut. Erasmus C. Gilbreath was one of 200,000 army officers and soldiers assigned to occupation duty in the ex-Confederate states. Those states had been devastated economically, physically, socially, and politically by the war. A massive federal effort was mounted to reunite the nation and address challenges including shortages of food and shelter; shattered infrastructure, agriculture and civil government; and a breakdown of law and order. The toughest challenge lay in accommodating some 4 million newly liberated slaves. In this bitter time, many white southerners, not reconciled to the outcome of the Civil War, harbored a deep hatred for their northern conquerors.*

The burden of meeting those challenges landed on two organizations: the U.S. Army and the Freedman's Bureau. Army units filled many roles, including infrastructure reconstruction, law enforcement, administration of justice, and public health melioration. Their duties were carried out in a climate of hostility in a white populace that opposed Reconstruction by means that included extralegal lethal violence: By 1868, the Ku Klux Klan, once a small social club, had become a terrorist organization.

CHAPTER 3

ORDERED TO TEXAS

1869

In the early part of 1869, the Company was ordered to Vicksburg again, and then the 24th Infantry was ordered to go to Texas and to be united to the 29th Infantry. The Army was to be consolidated, and our new Regiment was to be called the 11th Infantry. Orders were that when the 24th Infantry left for Texas, all the men whose time would expire before the 31st of the following October should remain behind at Vicksburg and be discharged as their term of service ended. There were 175 of such men, and I was left in command of them at Vicksburg. I had Lieuts. Lott, Kingsbury, Warren, and Sunderland to assist me. We had a Post band at Vicksburg of 40 pieces, and they also were to be discharged. The Regiment with Maj. Dudley in command left by boat for New Orleans and Texas about the 1st of March, and after they had gone, the order was changed so that all of the men with me must follow.

I left Vicksburg after discharging the band about the last of March. Genl. Gillam with his staff and family went with us on the steamer *Frank Pargan*. Genl. Gillam was our Colonel and a very fine officer. The trip to New Orleans was a very pleasant one indeed. The *Frank Pargan* was a large steamer very richly fitted up and was plying between Memphis and New Orleans. She was arranged for carrying cotton, and the means adopted for entertaining passengers were very complete in every way. We had on board Genl. Gillam and his family, Lieuts. Quimby, Lott, Sunderland, and Warren, and at Memphis we took on Lieut. Kingsbury and some 20 men.

On arrival at New Orleans we went to call on Col. Buchanan, 1st Infantry, and then learned that when the principal part of the Regiment passed through New Orleans, Col. Buchanan, who had command of the 5th Military District, held in his care a telegram from Washington ordering the Regiment to go to the Department of the Lakes instead of Texas for a station. This telegram was not given to Maj. Dudley for the reason that he did not call and pay his respects to Col. Buchanan. It was a courtesy he should have shown, as the Colonel did not regard it as his duty to be on the lookout for our Regiment. His Regiment, the 1st Infantry, was ordered to the Lakes so that there may have been a little sharp practice. Genl. Gillam was a close friend of Col. Amos Beckwith of the Commissary Department, and we (Genl. G. and I) called on him. He took us out riding in his ambulance and, seeing a long pointed stick in the ambulance, Genl. G. asked its use. Beckwith said he never used a whip on a Yank mule as the animal soon forgot all about it, but he always punched his mules with the pointed stick and they would go like fury all day and never forget the prodding.

While we were at New Orleans, we derived much pleasure from visiting points of interest, one of the principal ones being the Old French Market which was more attractive in 1869 than it has ever been since. The quaintness of the people about the place was fascinating.

We were assigned to a wooden steamer for transportation to Texas. There were no railroad communications with Texas from New Orleans or in any direction in 1869, and the travel all went from N.O. by boat out of the mouth of the Mississippi River and thence to Galveston or other port. The steamer assigned to us was a small one, and as we had 125 horses and 175 men, not including the officers and other passengers, I thought it too small. So, after a vigorous protest, we were given a place on the iron steamer *Morgan* of the Morgan Line. It was a fortunate thing the change was made as we encountered bad weather soon as we got into the Gulf of Mexico and were delayed 36 hours in reaching Galveston. As it was when, during the storm when everything was battened down, there was lack of ventilation and the men suffered very much.

We arrived after being well tossed about at Galveston and went into the Post with the rest of the Regiment. This Post was in a very interesting spot about 200 yards from the surf of the Gulf of Mexico. The quarters were very small and, when we were all there, very crowded. We lived in two rooms in the Commissary Building and kept house. We found excellent servants and lived well.

Being so close to the beach, it was our custom to put on bathing suits and go from the house each morning for a plunge in the salt water. The quantities of fish we caught were a great addition to our living, and having a 300 foot seine, the men used to make great hauls of fish and have lots of sport.

The city is built on a low island, and often when a storm blew from the south or southwest, our parade ground was covered two feet deep with sea water. Everybody on the island depended on rainwater for cooking and drinking purposes. We had very large tanks at all of our buildings and used to get plenty of rainwater, but several times the quantity was alarmingly low. We got large amounts of fruits fresh from more tropical places, especially from islands off the coast of Mexico. The pineapples, bananas and oranges, having matured in a more congenial climate, were all delicious and luscious. These fruits sold for a song by the boat men, and their quality spoiled us for the enjoyment of such things in the North. Oysters were not very good. The Gulf beach at Galveston was the finest I ever saw, and being wide and level, one could go 16 or 18 miles from the Post without a break.

On the 19th of April, 1869, the order was issued consolidating the 24th and 29th Infantry Regiments into one and assigning officers to the new Regiment which was to be called the 11th Infantry. The Colonel was A. C. Gillam, Lieut. Col. Geo. P. Buell and Maj. Bissell. I was assigned as 1st Lieutenant of Company G. 11th Infantry with Capt. S. C. Green and 2nd Lieut. Daniel Taylor. The Post of Galveston was commanded by our Col. A. C. Gillam.

In the beginning of September 1869 Genl. Reynolds came to Galveston. He commanded the District of Texas including the entire state, and had charge of the reconstruction of the state and called upon Genl. Gillam to designate an officer to go to Montgomery County to attend to reconstruction matters there and to bring that county under some sort of control, to establish the municipal officers and get them into working order. Genl. Gillam designated me for the duty, and Genl. Reynolds sent for me. He was stopping in the city at the Exchange Hotel. Upon reporting to him, he told me that he was going to send me to one of the worst counties in the state, that there was not a single civil officer in the county, and he had never been able to find a man who would take the oath that he had held no office before the war and afterwards engaged in rebellion. Not a man would accept office under the military officers. He directed me to take 30 men with me and establish myself at the County seat and then to go into the work of finding officers for civil positions.

My wife went home in September 1869 to Baltimore with our son, and I left for Montgomery at once. I had 30 men of the 10th and 11th Regts. and took with me a complete outfit of baggage and plenty of ammunition. I went by rail to Houston and from there 48 miles north with wagons hired from citizens. The march was a pleasant one, and I was five days on the trip. I arrived at the town of Montgomery on the sixth day about 7 o'clock Sunday morning, and so slow going were the people, I camped Saturday night within four or five miles of Montgomery and yet got into the town and had stacked arms at the courthouse before anyone knew I was coming. It was not more than one half an hour, however, before every man, woman and child in town had gathered about my men. Many had never seen a Yankee before, and everyone was very much interested in our every movement. I found a lawless state of affairs at once.

Before I had established my camp, a man came in to report the assassination of another. The entire county recognized no officer and no law, and bloodshed and disorders of all kinds occurred in all parts of the County. It is hardly possible to describe the state of affairs in such a way as to make it clearly understood exactly how lawless and terrible the condition of affairs there was.

I selected a small grove 200 yards from the courthouse and put up my tents. I had some 15 for the men, two large hospital tents for myself, and with store tents, cooking tents, etc., soon had a quite a spread of canvas. Citizens did not receive me kindly, but, as one of my men was sick, I went to a physician named Ivons and asked him to attend the man. He seemed to hesitate but accepted and, as I saw him every day on his visits, soon came to know him well and he became quite friendly. Through him and my being a Mason, I soon came to know a large number of the most respectable men in the County. Men came from all over the County to see the Yanks.

It was the greatest place for gambling I ever saw. Men would bet on anything. Rolling ten pins was a favorite game, and it was amusing and interesting to see the gold and silver piled up on the table. They had never stopped specie payments then, and gold and silver were very plentiful. I could buy nothing for greenbacks, and had to sell them for eight or ten percent off for gold or silver and buy with that. Horse racing and shooting at a mark were also favorite ways of gambling and [they] even would flip at the crack all day with coin.

Churches had not been opened in the County for months, and schools were not in existence. Every man was armed with Bowie knife, Derringer shotgun, or revolver. Offenders against law or against public sentiment were summarily punished by anybody. The Sunday of my arrival, the colored people were trying to have a camp meeting near the town, and a party decided to break it up. They attacked the meeting and on looking down street from my camp, I saw crowds of white men and negroes shooting at each other, to kill too, and running back and forth.

In walking about the town with the citizens, they entertained me by showing me shot marks on doors or houses and trees saying, "So and so was killed at that tree, another man was stabbed and killed at this door and here a man was called out of his house and shot." There was no end seemingly to the list of horrors which had occurred. Negroes flocked to me with their stories of beatings and assassinations, and white men came to ask for protection. I saw I had no easy job, but began at once to straighten things out. I issued an order on Monday following my arrival saying that no man in the county would be allowed to carry arms at all except for hunting, and that all saloons or drinking and gambling places must close up at 10 o'clock on Saturday night and not open before 6 on Monday morning. I sent these first orders all over the County and was amazed to find everybody, without an exception almost, obeying. The following Sunday, church services were held in the town and in Danville, the next largest town, and Lodges soon opened all over. In a month after I arrived everything was quiet and orderly.

I had difficulty in filling the offices in the county. I did it in this way. I sent out a request that the most prominent men in the County meet me at the courthouse on the Saturday about two weeks after I got to the town. A great many came to the courthouse so that it was filled to overflowing. I took the Judges' or highest seat and told them I was an officer obeying orders. That these orders were to select and recommend men who could take the oath and would fill the places faithfully. There were many young men in the County who had been too young to take part in the war, and I was anxious to get some of this class for the offices. I told them I would only ask that the persons selected be of good character and that they would perform their duties faithfully under military orders. I was informed at once that no man would dare take the oath and occupy the offices.

I told them I could find a few Union men and that I would give them a week to think of it and so dismissed the crowd. No one met me at the end of a week, and then I caused it to be told that, as I was left to my own resources, I should have to select such men as I could, and that the only ones available so far as I could see were colored people. This brought them to town and I soon had plenty of names suggested so that I filled all of the offices in the County from Constable to Judge with as good a lot of men as I ever saw. I found that the custom had been for offices to run in families, as for example the County Clerk's family (named Gay) had held the office since the organization of the County, and other offices the same. This had as much to do with opposition to new men taking office, almost, as disloyal ideas.

After the new officials had been in place for a couple of months, an election was held and most of them were so popular as to be elected to the same offices to which they had been appointed. Appointments were made by the General commanding the department of the men recommended by me. The County Judge was named Yell, a Union man. He was a very good man in many ways and owned a large plantation near the town. He often invited me to his house. His parents had evidently thought to modify the harshness of the name of Yell as they had named him Pleasant N. Yell. During the months of April and May 1870 I had to get all the voting population registered. This was done in five precincts or divisions of the County by men selected by me. After Registration lists had been prepared, orders came for the Election in May 1870, I think, and instructions were given that, to insure the counting of a full vote, no threats or intimidation or crowding about the polls would be allowed. No soldiers were allowed about any of the polling places, but all the civil officers were ordered to carry out the instructions. All saloons and drinking places were closed on the day of election, and everyone voting had to walk 200 feet by himself to get to the ballot box.

The election day passed off quietly in every precinct in the County. There was not the least disturbance any place. The County gave, I think, 200 majority for the Republican candidates from Governor down.

After the election was over, I had under orders to carry the returns to Livingston, Texas, and turn them over to Maj. Whitesides, a Capt. of the 6th Cavalry who commanded the subdistrict in which Montgomery County was located. I hired an old-fashioned carriage and took two men with me as guards and had to drive across the country 90 miles. On the way I had no trouble at all except that at Sulphur Springs, where I had to stay all night. I thought I would be attacked. As I rode into the town, I saw a good many drunken men, but they treated me with seeming indifference and I went to the Hotel on the outskirts of the town. After nightfall, word was brought by a negro that they contemplated attacking me to drive me out of town. I got my men ready to defend ourselves, and as it grew dark, there was a good deal of yelling and shooting downtown. They came up close enough to fire off their guns and pistols over the house. As the shot from shotguns crashed through the tops of the trees around the house, they made a great racket. The men were informed by the people at the house that I was ready and would fire if the house was shot into, and coaxed off.

I delivered my returns to Capt. Whiteside and started back to Montgomery. Before arriving at Danville I found the whole country overflowed on account of heavy rains. In crossing a rough bridge my wagon broke down, and there was so much water ahead of me that I went to a nearby farmhouse to stay all night. I found the place filled with a rough crowd of citizens water bound. After staying all night and being guarded by a desperate character whom I had had in the guard house at Montgomery but who was now friendly, I started for Danville again. I was going with the mail rider on horseback. He carried the mail from Livingston to Montgomery twice a week, carrying it in old-time saddle bags. Just as we started, he was leading the way and about to cross a small branch when his horse plunged in head first. He came near drowning. The mail bags floated off, and his horse came back to my side of the stream and ran off to the farmhouse.

I went to the same place and got a man to come and cut down a large cottonwood tree to fell it across the stream. The citizens then helped me, and we had the horses swimming on the downstream side of the tree. The mail carrier had struggled out on the farther bank and had caught his mail bags lodged a short distance below but full of water.

On arriving at Danville I went to a man to hire another horse. He rather unwillingly let me have his favorite hunter. His hesitation arose from fear of the people around him, and I had to seemingly seize the horse. He was a flier. I never rode a horse that could go off on a long steady sweep so easily or for so long a time at once as that old speckled animal. The mail man and I were both wet, soaking, so we rode fast to keep warm and to get to some dry clothes as soon as possible. We arrived at Montgomery all right, but that mail was a sight to see. Both ends of the bag were filled with a mass of paper pulp which had been well churned as we rode. I sent my horse back next trip, and my men came in with the broken carriage in a few days.

My first incident with the desperado who guarded me at the farmhouse happened at Montgomery about a month after I had issued the order prohibiting the carrying of firearms. I was in my tent when I heard shots downtown, and looking that way, saw a big tall fellow with two pistols. He was cracking them together and calling to dare any Yankee to come to take them. He was cursing and swearing and raising a great noise. I took my Sergeant [to] one side and sent him with five men, ordering him to go around out of sight of the "bad man," and place himself so that he could see me. Then when I began to approach the man and his attention was fixed on my movements. I ordered the Sergeant to take all his men out, have them kneel, and aim their pieces at the man. It all worked well, and I walked toward him without any arms and alone. He kept on cursing me, and I stopped at about 100 yards.

I called to him, "Say, you lay down those pistols or those men will shoot you." At the same time I pointed to the men kneeling and aiming at him. He had his pistols over his head which he turned and got one look at the firing squad, when he bent over slowly and laid his guns on the ground. He had stopped swearing and came with me to camp as quiet as a mouse. I put him in the guard house and he broke out [shouted] again very violently and swore he would kill me if he ever got out.

I released him on a bond after a week's confinement and kept his pistols for a few months. I returned them to him after I saw him at the farmhouse as I was coming from Livingston. On that occasion as I rode up to the house, the first man I saw was this "bad man." I thought my goose was cooked, as I did not suppose he would ever become reconciled to being arrested. To my surprise, however, he came up, shook hands with me, and seeing I was alone, said I never ought to have stopped without a guard as there was a very bad crowd at the house and the owner was himself a hard case. But he said, "If any man here insults you, let me know and I will beef him," that is, kill him. He got a shotgun and became my guard in a very close way, insisted on sleeping with me, and announced to all in hearing that I was his especial protégé. He soon came to Montgomery and got his pistols, and after, used to come to my camp. I found he had a very bad reputation all through that part of Texas.

Quails were very plentiful in that part of Texas in '69 and '70, and one of my amusements was to go out with Doctor Ivons to net them. The net was made shaped like a long bag and was held in place with hoops. The mouth had two long wings which were stacked so that they stood on edge. The idea was, having found a covey of quail, to stake out the net and then, by slow movements on horseback, so herd the drove of quail as to make them run against one of the wings and into the round part of the net, when giving it a twist the birds were caught and killed. They were delicious eating.

I was joined soon after I got to Montgomery by a Doctor named Davis, a brother of Genl. Jeff C. Davis. He was a funny man in some ways, but a good fellow and doctor.

I asked Doctor Ivons one day if he had ever tasted beans. He had not, he said, so I got my detachment cook to bake a five gallon camp kettle full of them. The cook was a first-class one, and the beans were done up in fine style. Some of the citizens were invited in. It was Sunday and we had a feast of beans. And every Sunday after that I gave a free lunch of baked beans in my quarters.

Two Masons came in one lodge night and wanted to keep me from going out, but as I insisted, each took hold of an arm and so we went out of the house I then lived in. They pointed out a man sitting on a porch across the street and said he was a desperate character whom I had displeased, and they said they thought he was going to kill me, so they guarded me.

Two men there bet on their penmanship and left the matter to a schoolteacher to decide. One was old Judge Nat Hart Davis, and the other was called Judge Jones. Both wrote miserably. The teacher took Davis's paper and read it off at once. He then took Jones's paper, and after looking at it upside down, end ways and every way he could turn it, handed it back saying, "These are 'Spanish Brands' by George." One must see "Spanish Brands" on [a] mule or horse to fully appreciate the occasion, for brands of Mexicans on the rump of a horse are said to be like the divisions on the map of Mexico.

An odd old fellow in Montgomery in speaking of a lady he admired said, "She steps like a venison," meaning that she was graceful as a deer.

I was warned by negroes that a strong party was forming in Grimes County for the purpose of visiting Montgomery to shoot into my camp. After investigating the matter, I concluded it better to prepare for their coming, and I did so by moving my men out of their tents and into an old unoccupied Hotel in the thickest part of the town. I did this against the protest of the owner and very many of the citizens, but I told the latter they were to act as my picket guards. In case any attempt was made to shoot my men or drive us out of the building, I said I should resist by shooting from the building in any direction hostilities might come, and so the citizens would have to look out or somebody would get hurt. Citizens took steps to inform their friends in Grimes County of my situation and determination, and there was never any demonstration. In the same way, I protected my men in the beginning of my stay in Montgomery. Soon after I established my camp, a few desperate characters rode past my camp at night and fired two or three shots through my line of tents. No one was hurt, but I notified the citizens that if it happened again, my men would turn out and begin shooting in any direction they thought the assailants went. I was never troubled again.

CHAPTER 4

My Daughter Etta Was Born
& We Move to Galveston

1870

n the early part of 1870, I was ordered to go from Texas to Jackson, Miss., to appear as a witness before the U.S. Court. Capt. A. M. Brown, "Bullet Brown," was sent to take my place. I had to take a steamer from Galveston to New Orleans and thence by rail to Jackson. I was gone three weeks, and Capt. Brown left on my return.

In May 1870 I sent for my wife and children. My daughter Etta M. was born at Baltimore on the 9th of March.

I was ordered to leave Montgomery for Galveston and was informed that my Company G, 24th Infantry was to go to Fort Griffin, Texas, on the frontier. I arrived at Galveston about the 20th of May, 1870. On leaving Montgomery, I received a letter approving of my course there, signed by 300 citizens, and another of the same character, signed by fewer members who did not like the origination of the larger paper. I left the county folks organized with every officer in place. By advice and assistance, postal facilities were increased and express offices opened. All the churches and schools in the county were regularly carried on, and the entire county was almost free from disturbances.

On my arrival back at Galveston, I found Company G getting ready for the trip to Fort Griffin. The departure of the Company was delayed a little to allow my wife and children time to arrive from Baltimore, which they did about the 20th of May. In the meantime I bought an ambulance, hired a servant, and got ready as well as I could. We left Galveston on the 31st of May and went by railroad to Calvert, Texas, which was as far as the road was completed. From Calvert we were to march via Waco to Fort Griffin. The Captain of my Company was Theo. Schram who had been a friend ever since I first saw him. He was assigned to the Company from the 10th Infantry in place of Capt. Samuel C. Greene, the first Captain, who was retired. When I left Montgomery to go to Jackson, Miss., as a witness as above referred to, I found that I had company from Galveston in the persons of Captains Thos. H. Norton of our Regiment, Capt. S.C. Green of the same, also of Maj. Belger who had been a Quartermaster in the army and had been summarily discharged by Secretary Stanton. Norton was very deaf and quite eccentric, and Green had a brain trouble and was equally funny, while Belger was fond of liquor, which made him peculiar.

Going over to New Orleans by boat, all were seasick but me, and while Green and Norton went to their rooms and had it out, Belger sat in a big chair in the cabin and proposed to fight it out there. He said someone had told him that whiskey and pepper was good for seasickness and asked me to tell the steward to bring him some in a tin cup. When that was gone and he grew sicker, he said, "Gilbreath, tell the Steward to bring in some more whiskey and black pepper and if he hasn't the pepper, tell him to not mind it but bring the whiskey right away." I left Belger at New Orleans, and Norton and Green went on with me to Jackson. The latter, soon after the 11th Infantry was organized, married a young friendless girl and brought her to Galveston. Between their lovemaking and his jealousy of her, they amused the garrison. It finally ended by his whipping her on the porch of his quarters one day when she left.

On our way to the frontier, when we arrived at Calvert, we found Capt. Sanderson in command who had taken Norton's place as Captain of Company C. It was a typical frontier railroad town. Sanderson had built a guard house way up on some trees so that the floor was about 30 feet from the ground. It was for the purpose of confining citizen prisoners, and he supposed it to be very secure, as after the men were placed inside of the lockup, the ladder was removed. The Captain was surprised one day to find his sky parlor empty. He relied too much on the distance of the thing from the ground, and it was improperly guarded so that on a dark stormy night, some friends of the prisoners slipped in and, setting up the ladder, let the prisoners out.

We took contractors' teams from Calvert for our march and left there on the 1st of June 1870. The team furnished us was made up of Mexicans with very large freighting wagons. It was the first of the kind we had seen, and it interested us very much. They drove their mules four abreast, having two large mules at the tongue of the wagon. The mules were all very small, and they had a herd of extra mules which they drove along ahead of the train. This herd consisted of about 200 mules and was led by a white mare with a bell on her neck. The tinkle of this bell could be heard all day and all night, and the little mules always followed it. The train had with it numerous assistants who were not all the time at work, and several women. If the train stopped for any length of time, a crowd was sure to collect near some wagon to play monte, and at night they always had music—guitar and singing.

I was made Quartermaster of the expedition and had to be with the train all the time. The soldiers marched, except [for] a train guard, Capt. Schram and wife, and Mrs. Gilbreath. Our servant and children rode in their ambulances.

We were 30 days on the march, and all enjoyed it very much. We passed through a lonely country. One night our camp was fixed on the bank of a creek at a cut bluff or bank about 30 feet above the water. During the night it rained, and the waters of the little stream rose so that our camp was overflowed, and we found almost two feet of water over the ground. It was amusing to see the men get out in a hurry and the rest of us try to get our clothes on while standing in bed, on our trunks and bundles. We moved slowly to a hill something like a mile away and stayed a day to get dried out. As we camped in a grove of trees, we soon found ourselves covered with jiggers or wood ticks and had a time getting rid of them.

Our servant's name was Jane Pinchback and, being only a colored field hand, afforded us no end of amusement. She was a great tobacco chewer and would work the most of the day to indulge her habit, saying she only used it for a bad toothache.

On our arrival at Fort Griffin we found Capt. Claus, 24th Infantry, in command; and Capt. W. Davis of the 4th Cavalry; Capt. Chaffee, 6th; and Capt. Lees of the 4th Cavalry. The Post was a very peculiar one. Some of the officers' quarters were good and some were bad enough. The men occupied rows of huts made of pecan lumber. Each hut would hold 4 men sleeping in two-story bunks.

I took a log house which had been moved to the Post from outside by Genl. Sturgis. It consisted of two pens and a passage and a simple log house lined with canvas throughout. While I was getting this house in order, we occupied temporarily a set of quarters belonging to Maj. W. Davis, 4th Cavalry. It consisted of only one room. We put our things into this room and began unpacking. I was busily engaged unloading a small trunk which stood behind the door which was open. My head was down and my wife, who was on the opposite side of the room, exclaimed in a terrified tone, "Oh, Hubby, look." I looked first at her and then following the direction of her finger at the crack in the door. My face came up within about a foot of that of a hideously painted Indian. It was old Castio, the Chief of the Tonkawa Indians, a small friendly band who lived near the Post. It was our first sight at any painted Indian, and he looked hideous enough to impress his visit upon us. He had sneaked in noiselessly, in his moccasins, on purpose to see the effect. It was so startling as to please him I am sure. Thus began our first contact with Indians which has continued to the present time.

We moved into our house soon and began keeping house. Capt. Biddle, Company A. 11th Infantry joined us, and later F. Company of our regiment with Maj. Catlin. Capt. Biddle was transferred to Cavalry, and Capt. Choisey took his place. The Post was at first commanded by my Capt. Theo Schram, but later by Lieut. Col. Charles Whiting of the 6th Cavalry. I was made Post Quartermaster and Post Commissary, and placed in charge of the Tonkawa Indians, so was pretty busy.

COMMENTARY: *After his stint in Mississippi in the U.S. Army's occupation forces, 1st Lieut. Gilbreath was reassigned to Texas, then under Federal occupation. Assigned to Montgomery County, one of "the worst" in the state, he took charge of reconstruction and got a rude introduction to the "wild West" in a lawless community rife with gambling, gunplay, drinking, racial violence and vigilante "justice." Oddly, this was not the stereotypical cow town, but a land of cotton plantations once worked by slave labor; at the outbreak of the Civil War, half the population were slaves.*

FORT GRIFFIN, TEXAS

1871

J anuary 1, 1871, Col. Whiting was mustered out of service owing to consolidation of the Army, and Capt. Schram was again in command. The Colonel is a kindhearted old gentleman, and we were very sorry to lose him. In 1871 Col. W. H. Wood, 11th Infantry, came to the Post to command. He was our new Colonel in place of Col. A. C. Gillam who was transferred to the 1st Cavalry.

We found Col. Wood a very fine old gentleman, a great martinet but very kind in every way. There were a good many changes in the personnel of the garrison while we served at Fort Griffin. The Infantry remained about the same: A, F & G Cos. of 11th Infantry with Band and Headquarters of the Regiment, but the Cavalry changed.

During our two years and a half stay at Fort Griffin, we had great difficulty in getting vegetables so that we had few fresh things, and were compelled to use canned things instead of fresh. We had canned sweet potatoes, pumpkins and almost everything.

All our Commissary supplies were purchased at New Orleans and shipped by wagon train from San Antonio until 1873 when the Missouri, Kansas and Texas railroad was finished. Then purchases were made in Saint Louis, the first lot having been bought in 1872. These stores were sent to some point in the south of Missouri and thence the construction company of the M. K. & T. Railroad sent the stores in first-class wagons through the Indian Territory to us. The trains carrying these stores were made up of light two-horse wagons, each drawn by two fine mules, the intention being to sell the wagons and mules to farmers after the stores were delivered. Some of these trains got through all right, but many stopped in the Indian Territory and sold the wagons, etc. and simply piled up the stores on the prairie. The loss was great to the Government as many of the stores received were damaged and many lost all together.

I was assigned to various duties in addition to being Quartermaster and Commissary. I commanded H Troop, 4th Cavalry for awhile. I was sent out once to investigate the murder of a family by Indians. The Kiowas and Comanches were very bad indeed, and at a time when the streams were high, the former came quite close to the Post on the opposite side of the Clear Fork of the Brazos, and killed the father, mother and little daughter of a family, carrying off two older daughters. These were afterwards taken from the Kiowas at Fort Sill and had been treated brutally by the Indians. When I went to the house, I found that everything was covered with blood of the victims. The father and mother were scalped and cut up in various ways. The Indians were not caught.

We had two servants, Mahala and Ann, colored. The latter was fond of teasing the former. I heard a knock at the back door one day. Mahala, ironing, did not answer until the knock was repeated. She then said, "If that's a man, come in; if it's Ann, I'll knock you down." It was a man.

We were paid by Maj. Gould, and once he was anxious to go on a buffalo hunt. So we got a horse for him from a Cavalry Company and off we went. When about a mile from the Post, Maj. G. was afraid to go ahead with the rest of us because his horse was so rough a rider and he was afraid to go the mile back to the Post alone, so we had no escort to send and he was compelled to go on. That ride liked to have killed him. His clerk begged to be allowed to shoot the first buffalo. The plan was for the hunter to ride up beside the buffalo and then shoot. Mr. Isanco dashed ahead, and his horse ranged up alongside a large buffalo bull. Isanco shot his pistol, and the horse dashed ahead. The buffalo charged the horse, caught him in his horns between the hind legs and ripped open the flesh of both legs. Isanco was thrown, and the buffalo charged him and would have killed him, but a Tonkawa Indian shot the buffalo before it reached the man.

We saw a cloudburst (our first) at Fort Griffin. The rain poured down in the Post and about a mile away fell so rapidly as to be called a cloudburst. It filled the valley beside the Post which was a mile wide so that in one half hour the water was 30 feet deep.

All kinds of game were very plentiful about the Post: turkeys, deer, antelope, buffalo and quail. Wolves used to howl every night nearby, and once a big gray wolf came into an officer's tent.

In taking the census of 1870, as it was impossible for the enumerators to travel about in that part of Texas to collect the data for the census, an officer named Miller of the 4th Cavalry was sent to do it. He was some three months on the duty and said that during his trip he came to some, a good many, families where they had not named all their children, simply calling the two youngest either "Bub," or "Sis" as the case might be. He told the people they must give each child a name, and if there was any delay, he at once called each boy Joseph and each girl Josephine, so that his record showed a large number of these names. It amused us so much that we afterwards called him "Joe" all the time.

In Company A was a man named "Igo" who had been a quartermaster of volunteers during the war. He had never made any returns of property as required by law, so that when they stopped his pay for it, his papers were in a terrible muddle. He looked at the papers of all kind[s] for a while and finally sealed them all up in a nail keg and sent them to Washington, sending also a letter to say that, as they knew more about papers than he did, he would be glad if they would straighten his out for him. They mustered him out of service, and he finally enlisted as a private.

We had an officer named Hugo who had known this private before he enlisted. The first time they met was when we were fishing one day in the Clear Fork of the Brazos. They came face to face, and their mutual salutation was, "Hello Hugo, Hello Igo."

A citizen gave us a fawn when it was quite young. Mrs. G. raised it on a bottle of milk. It grew to be quite large and so fond of her that, if she slipped out of the house, the deer would find her track and follow her, hunt her up wherever she was, simply by the scent. I tied him up with a strap, and he never made friends with me again. I couldn't touch him.

We used to hunt turkeys a great deal. The way we did it was to go out in the daytime and find where they were in the habit of roosting. Then after night we went and shot them off the trees. Often many shots were wasted shooting at bunches of mistletoe which grew very plentiful there.

There was a store a mile from the Post at which cowboys used to collect on Saturday and Sunday, and almost every week some man was killed in their rows. Occasionally they would form two lines and shoot to kill at each other. A notorious family of cattle thieves was named James, but he called himself Old Man Jeems. He had six sons and they were always in some shooting scrape.

Each owner of cattle had his own peculiar brand, usually placed on the left flank of each steer or animal. Some of the brands were like this EV, OX, K, =, W, etc. These brands were recorded in the county where the owner lived. As cattle grazed about on the prairies, they drifted, as [it] was called, or wandered from home sometimes 300 or 400 miles. The general law was, amongst cattlemen, that it was sure death to steal cattle from each other, and they employed men called Inspectors who looked after the various brands. Every spring they had what they called a Rondo or roundup when cows with calves at the side were driven to huge pens, the calves caught or roped and branded with the same brand as the cow it followed. If a calf became a year old without branding, it was called a Maverick and any man could put his brand on it. Thieves used to brand as many oldish calves as they could find, or collect a band of marketable two- and three-year-olds and drive them off very rapidly to a market, usually through the Indian Territory to the Pacific Railroad. Cattle were worth 30 to 40 [dollars] each. Beef was furnished the post at six cents per pound.

A posse of citizens went to arrest the "Jeems" boys, and the latter defended themselves in their cabin, and several citizens of the posse were wounded. They called on the Post for troops, and Lieut. Turner, son of Admiral Turner, was sent out to make the arrest. After a battle, five of the crowd were arrested. On the way to the Post all 5, including 4 Jeems boys, were hung to the trees.

In August 1872 I was ordered to take 250 recruits to Fort Concho, Texas, from Fort Griffin, 125 miles. I had plenty of transportation and made a pleasure trip via Old Forts Phantom Hill and Fort Chadhorn which had not been occupied since the Civil War. Returning, I was held 6 days at the Colorado which was too high to cross.

Our mails were carried overland from Missouri by stages. The line extended from Little Rock, Arkansas, and Sedalia, Missouri, to California by way of El Paso.

Stages were often attacked by Indians, and we used to send a guard with each one. The drivers were always armed and, when attacked, used to fight. They drove the stage into the brush and then fought for their life. Many stages were captured. In consequence of the dangers of attack from Indians, they used to drive nothing but very wild mules. There were four to each stage, and they had to rope the mules to get the harness on, and they never stopped from one stage stand to another. These stations were about 16 or 18 miles apart, and those little mules used to go like sin all the way. To get in the mail and express, or passengers, the driver had enough control over his team to keep them moving in a circle in front of the post office. Mail and the passengers were put in behind or any way on the run. All stage stations or stands, as they were called, were built to be defended against Indians with high stockades, loop holes, etc. No horses were allowed to stay at a stage stand unless it might be one for a "bell mare" at a large station. This was because horses are always a great temptation to Indians, and will be stolen by them if such a thing is possible, while mules are not considered worth stealing.

COMMENTARY: *When 1st Lieut. Gilbreath relocated to Fort Griffin, Texas, during 1870, he was truly moving to the western frontier. Fort Griffin was beyond the reach of the railroads, and all transport was a matter of marching, wagon trains, and stage coaches. Fort Griffin, established in 1867, was one of many small forts constructed on the frontier. It was located near the Clear Fork of the Brazos River.*

Fort Griffin served as a supply center for buffalo hunters active in the area and protection for the nearby small settlements and for the Great Western Trail, an important cattle-drive route to Dodge City, Kansas. This region of Texas was subject to predatory raids by the much-feared nomadic Comanches and Kiowas, who often attacked stagecoaches and settlers, usually for horses. A rough-and-tumble settlement of buffalo hunters, cowboys, gamblers, cattle thieves and saloonkeepers—called The Flat—grew up adjacent to Fort Griffin.

CHAPTER 6

LEAVING FORT GRIFFIN

1872

I n the fall of 1872, I was detailed for General Recruiting Service and left Fort Griffin with my family on the 22nd day of December. My orders were to report in New York City, January 1, 1873. The only way to get out of the country was to go with an escort to Fort Richardson and on to the end of the M. Kansas and Texas Railroad at Dennison.

I had an ambulance and one wagon and an escort of a Corporal and six men. We expected to reach Fort Richardson on the 24th of December. A Norther began as we were about to leave the Post, and the Colonel [Wood] suggested that we wait until it was over. But we left on the day fixed and got as far as the "Nine Mile Water Holes," when we could go no further, so we camped. Just after getting into Camp, we saw a wagon coming through the snow and storm, and on their coming up to us we found them to be Lieut. Col. Buell and Lieut. Fred Grant, son of Genl. Grant. The latter had just come from the Military Academy and was a Lieutenant in Capt. Wirt Davis's Troop of the 4th Cavalry. They thought we would freeze, but we were very comfortable in a tent with lots of robes and wraps. The storm howled about, and it was very cold, but we had a small Sibley Stove and kept warm. We had in the tent my wife and myself, our two children, and Ann our black servant. It was 60 miles from Fort Griffin to Fort Richardson, and we expected to get through on the 3rd day out. The morning of the 23rd of December was still stormy so we could not get started early. But finally got off after heating stones to put in the wagon under our feet and we drove some 25 miles further and stopped at the only ranch on the way, Mrs. George's.

The next day we found it snowing very hard, and the Norther still continued. We did not start early. We had to cross what was known as "Salt Creek Prairie." This was a much used route for Indians going on thieving and murdering raids into Texas, and every month in the year someone had been killed on this prairie. About the center of it there was a high solitary mound or hill. This was a favorite place for Indians, and they could, and did, hide their war party behind the hill, while their lookouts could see from its top everything coming by the road from either the east toward Fort Richardson, or from the west from Fort Griffin. Small parties of citizens never used to cross this prairie in daylight. Indians seldom attack anything they cannot see that they have clearly the advantage of. Army officers had taught them a lesson too by filling up some covered wagons with as many men as they could crowd in to them. Then when no sign was shown of a guard and the Indians attacked, they found themselves outnumbered and whipped. So that a covered wagon at night was comparatively safe, and so small parties of citizens traveled at night. When we left Mrs. George's, she wished to go with us but said she was afraid to cross Salt Creek Prairie, even with us in the daytime. She waited until night, as we later found, and then drove alone to Jacksboro, the little town at Fort Richardson. It snowed so hard that we did not get off from Mrs. G's. until near noon when we started, expecting to reach Fort R. in the evening.

There was a lull in the storm when we reached the Brazos River and we passed through old Fort Belknap which had been abandoned. We passed this old Fort and descended to Salt Creek, and the storm began again, but we pushed on to cross the prairie which was about 14 miles wide. All were silent and nervous as we could only move slowly with the storm in our faces and through the deep snow. About halfway across, our mounted men saw figures of men moving about off the road. They appeared through the falling snow to be walking, and we had the wagon closed up and the men close about, and we moved slowly and examined the men as best we could. Once in a while we felt sure they were Indians but as we drew near we found them to be soldiers; the advance guard of a troop of Cavalry which we soon met. Lieut. Warrington, 4th Cavalry was in command and after halting and shaking hands and telling him of our fright, we continued on our way. After passing the mound or hill halfway across, we saw many graves of those killed by Indians, amongst them the recently erected crosses of the victims of their attack on a Mexican train. They made this attack about two months before and killed 16 Mexicans, roasting some over fires, and destroyed the train. By the time we had crossed to the timber, it began to grow dark and our drivers soon lost their way. We stumbled onto an open place in the woods and stopped, went into camp. I had a roaring big fire built of logs gathered about, and made all comfortable as possible. We slept on the ground and as the storm abated, slept well. Early in the morning we wished each other a Merry Christmas and soon finding the road, got off and reached Fort Richardson about 8 o'clock A.M.

We stopped with our old friends Capt. Jackson and wife, and passed Christmas with them. The ladies went into Jacksboro, a mile from the Post and got a few presents to exchange. On the 26th we started again for Dennison, 125 miles away. We passed through Gainsville, Decatur and Sherman, and traveled quite rapidly about 30 miles, and once, 40 miles. From Sherman the roads were frightfully muddy because the Norther having passed, the weather became mild and the ground thawed. From Sherman to Dennison we had to travel along the unfinished RR line. The pink eye had just reached Texas, and two of my mules and one Cavalry horse took the disease. I drove into Dennison with two spike teams.

This town was very decidedly new, and when we reached it after our journey of nearly 200 miles, we did not see a brown shingle in the place. We drove to the Palace Hotel which was as new as anything in town. The rooms were very small, so much so that we could not get our things inside. We at once began to fix for our journey to Saint Louis on the railroad. Mrs. G. first took our two children and as fast as she removed a garment she threw it out of the window. She then clothed herself casting away almost everything she took off and I followed the same course of action. We had been camping about eight days or nights and [the clothing] was anything but clean so that we were glad to get rid of all we had worn on our journey. There was only one train from Dennison north each day, and it was refreshing to get onto a sleeper after being away from the railroad for two years and seven months.

WE ARRIVED IN SAINT LOUIS ON THE 1ST DAY of January, 1873. We thought we were fixed up fairly well before we got to the Southern Hotel, but when we saw the people at dinner there, we all at once began to remember that for 2½ years we had not been in contact with fashions or fine garments.

While on the frontier we had no facilities like shopping by mail. We could not receive goods so shipped, and there were few fashion papers then to serve as guide for making clothing.

On the second of January, we left for Chicago where we stopped one day, and I left for New York while my wife went direct to Baltimore to her mother's home. I reported to the Superintendent of the Recruiting Service, Genl. John Gibbon, and was assigned to duty at Evansville, Indiana. My brother, Warren, came on to New York while I was there, and went with me to Baltimore and to Cincinnati and Evansville. I went before my wife so as to get a place to live when she should join me. This she did in a few weeks and I stayed on duty at Evansville for 15 months. We found it a very delightful place to live; had more society than we knew what to do with. Our son Willie went to the public school. We attended the Presbyterian Church and all in all had a very nice time indeed. I got my promotion to be a Captain in December 1873 and at once applied to be transferred to Chicago for duty. It was so ordered, and in March 1874, I went to Chicago for duty.

Duty in Chicago & Return to Texas

1874

This too we found to be very pleasant indeed as I was with my mother, brother, and sister. My wound received at Fredericksburg, December 13th, 1863, opened while I was in Chicago and troubled me very much. Surgeon W. C. Spencer, U.S.A., on duty at the Headquarters of Genl. Phil Sheridan which were in Chicago at the time, attended me, and although he succeeded in healing the wound up from time to time, still it opened again, and during the entire summer, troubled me a great deal. Lieut. Fred Grant was on duty in Chicago as Lieutenant Colonel, on Genl. Sherman's staff.

During our stay in Chicago we saw the second great fire which, although of not so great extent as that wherein so much of Chicago was destroyed, still 75 acres of buildings were burned. Everybody supposed the fire would extend as the Great Fire had to the north side, where we lived, at 220 Indiana St., but it did not come north of Jackson due to its present width. We crossed the Rush St. Bridge and went down to Marshall Field's establishment on State Street and watched the work of the firemen. This fire allowed the widening of State St. below Jackson to its present width. Before, that street was very narrow below that point. I attended the opening of the first cable line for street railroads in Chicago, and rode from 22nd St. to Madison on the first cable cars used in Chicago in September, I think, 1874. We visited my old home at Valparaiso, Indiana, during my service at Chicago. Mrs. G., and the children, Will and Etta, and I were very nicely received by my old friends there.

The tour of duty for officers on Recruiting Service was changed during my tour, so that the tour of each should begin October 1st instead of January 1st, so that my tour ended October 1st, 1874, and I was relieved.

We left Chicago on the 10th of October. Shortly before that, Mrs. Douglas, wife of Maj. Henry Douglas of our Regiment, came to Chicago to go with us to our Post at Fort Concho, Texas. So I had that lady, Mrs. G. and my two children as my party. We went to Saint Louis and thence by the M. K. and Texas Railroad to Austin, Texas. From there we were to go 210 miles in a stage to our Post. We remained in Austin a few days and then started with a stage full. It was very heavily loaded with mail bags and our party, and was drawn by four horses. The stage was of the old-fashioned monobrace style, and, after getting out on the road about six miles from Austin, the whole thing broke down and we had to unload. The mail and express and our trunks were put inside the fence at a log cabin, and our traps were all unloaded. I was to care for the mail, etc., while the driver went back to Austin for another stage. There was a rather weary wait of some hours. A crazy man in the cabin kept the ladies on the alert and in a constant state of alarm. The new stage soon arrived, and we loaded up and started again. That night we tried to sleep or to make ourselves comfortable, but it was a difficult thing to do as the road was rough and the stage rolled about at a terrible rate. About 12 o'clock that night, we arrived at a ranch which we should have reached, but for our breakdown, for supper.

The people were roused and had no doubt had that supper cooking or kept warm for several hours as it was about the worst I ever saw. It consisted of fat pork swimming in lard which had fried out of it some stony biscuits and weak flat lukewarm coffee. None of us could eat anything, but the driver seemed to relish what he saw. After paying 76 cents each for what we saw, and having horses changed, we started on our way. The ladies [tried] to make themselves as comfortable as possible, took off their bonnets and the switch of hair which was then the fashion to wear, and we tied the bonnets and things to the top of the stage. Our next stopping place was to be Blanco, for breakfast. On arrival there the ladies wanted to fix up a little after such an awful night. On examination of the stage both bonnets, hair, veils, etc., had disappeared. They had been shaken loose and had rolled out of the stage as it tumbled about during the night. The situation was horrible to them as to travel 200 miles more, even through Texas, without bonnet or back hair was calamity enough for a larger crowd than ours. The drivers of the "down" stage going to Austin promised to look for the things but we never heard anything of them.

All the drivers on the line kept the story going, telling it as they usually did every incident happening under their observation to all the people they carried, and for a long time it was common to be asked the question as to who the ladies were who had lost their hair.

We passed through Fredericksburg and Loyal Valley, so called because it was an awful nest of Rebels, I suppose. The former was a place where a very large number of Germans had settled direct from their country before the war. There we had a good meal. We passed Fort Mason, an abandoned fort surrounded by the worst community of desperate characters in the country, and Menardsville, worst of all. We also passed Kickapoo and Lepau Springs, and crossed many beautiful clear running streams.

The two springs above mentioned were peculiar, especially Kickapoo Springs. We crossed prairie country before reaching these springs, and there was no stream visible above them. On descending a small hill, we suddenly came upon a stream which burst out of a small bluff affording a stream of water some 200 feet wide of clear beautiful quality. No one knows the source of the stream above the springs, but it is simply some underground stream which here breaks forth. Lepau Springs are the same but not so large. An Army officer in traveling through that country long years before us, had carried with him a quantity of watercress and, distributing it in all the streams he came to, had very thoroughly stocked every stream with the delicious little salad. We found it every place.

Finally we arrived at Fort Concho and were glad enough to see the place after our wearisome stage ride of 3 days' and 3 nights' constant travel. We found Maj. Douglas in command and that my company was out on a scout against hostile Indians. It had been gone from the Post since August, 1874. We had no baggage yet from Chicago and had to sit around on bunks or boxes, but we got a bed and a servant and went to housekeeping. I was quite zealous then and so insisted on being sent out to join my company. Maj. Douglas did not want me to go but finally ordered me out. I soon got away and went by stage to Fort Griffin, Texas, 175 miles, in 175 hours, passing through old Forts Colorado and Phantom Hill. At Colorado I got a breakfast I can never forget. It consisted of Kid Hash and was the greasiest nastiest mess I ever undertook to eat. Arriving at Fort Griffin, I found it in command of my old Capt. Theo Schram. He fitted me out in a first-class way. I got a horse to ride, tent for myself and everything else I needed. I was to go from Fort Griffin, 150 miles west, to the supply camp of Genl. MacKenzie's scouting column where my company then was. I had to await the arrival of one of the wagon trains which periodically came into Fort Griffin for supplies. I got away from Fort Griffin with a train under the charge of Lieut. Lawtown, Regimental Quartermaster of the 4th U.S. Cavalry, and we traveled due west from Griffin, which was near what is now the town of Albany, Texas. On the way to the Supply Camp we crossed Otego Creek, California Creek, Double Mountain Fork, Duck Creek to Catfish on which the camp was located. On the trip from Fort Griffin, I was only a passenger as was Dr. Caldwell of the Army. I had no authority at all. The custom was, with all such trains, to hold the drivers responsible that nothing was removed from his wagon without the authority of the wagon master or the officer in charge. We had 40 six-mule wagons loaded to the bows, as they said, and when we camped at Duck Creek, we were joined by a train of about the same size going in empty to Fort Griffin for supplies. Of course the camp was large and all hands pitched in to have a good time. The officers in charge of our train on inspecting the lead wagon, which was one of Genl. McKenzie's Headquarter's wagons and drawn by eight mules, could not find a certain package. He got out of patience, accused the teamster, and would listen to no excuse. Riely, the driver, was a very excellent man and came to me as the officer had not only taken his team from him and discharged him, but had ordered him to go with the empty train to Fort Griffin.

The pride of a Government teamster is an unique characteristic. He disdains to accept help for himself or his team until every effort on his part has failed. His mules have pet names and often expensive and fanciful decorations bought by the drivers. His pride is to have everything about his wagon and team in the best of shape. He does not hesitate to supply himself either if he is not given what he thinks he needs to make his team and wagon perfect. He will steal extra open links for mending chains, extra wagon sheets, etc., so that he may be always ready with duplicates to repair damages. If a mule gets sick, he worries himself almost to the same condition, and his load is guarded with the most jealous care; no one can move a thing in the wagon but him, after the load is once made up. Riely was one of the best of men. His pride was injured by discharge, and in addition to his humiliation, he didn't want to go to Griffin to loaf until he could get his pay from Supply Camp by an irregular train.

I tried to persuade the officer to keep him, but it would not do, go he must. So I determined he should go with us if possible. I presented the proposition to Riely that he be my servant at $40 per month. He consented and put his things with mine. The officer was mad but could do nothing, as he could not refuse to carry my servant. He fumed and drank more and found fault. He wanted some revenge on somebody and in succession discharged some five or six other teamsters. Seeing he was not in his right mind exactly, I hired every man he discharged at once as a servant at $40 per month. He was paralyzed at the idea of my carrying six or seven grown men as servants, but knew he could not dare to refuse. Next morning both trains "pulled out," and a ride in the delightful prairie air did us all good. By the time Supply Camp was reached, I had no servants at all, and all the men had been returned to their teams.

So, fresh from Chicago on the 11th of November, I first took command of Company H, 11th Infantry at Supply Camp on Catfish Creek at the edge of the "Staked Plains" in Texas. My 2nd Lieut. who commanded the company was P. F. Kislingbury, who afterwards died while with Greeley in the Arctic regions. My 1st Sgt. was named Robert Joyce, who had been Captain of a New York Battery of Artillery at Port Schuyler, N. Y., at the same time I commanded it as Maj. of the 20th Indiana Volunteers. There was in the supply camp Companies A, B & C, 10th Infantry and my company, and our duties were to guard supplies and guard trains bringing supplies for the Cavalry scouting under Genl. MacKenzie.

The Staked Plains were so called because there was a very high level prairie of great extent whose boundaries were very clearly defined. The top of this level land was 1200 or 1500 feet above the surrounding country, and the grass was very heavy all over the level country.

Catfish Creek was simply a deep ravine or canyon running up into the Plain. Our tents were pitched on the sides of this ravine, and it was a pleasant camp. The Country all about us was filled with buffalo, deer, and antelope, etc. so that we had plenty of game. A few days after my arrival, the Cavalry came in from a scout and camped 3 miles away. We visited them and in returning to our camp, several of the party almost became lost as it was hard to find the camping place when we once came to cross a portion of the high plateau. It was decided to move our camp to the head of Duck Creek, and we changed to a better camping place by skirting the foothills of the Staked Plains. I was almost immediately sent from the new camp with a train of 35 wagons to Fort Griffin for supplies, and my orders were to exchange broken-down mules for new ones so that my train was supplied with all the poor broken-down mules at the camp. I had 17 men of the Company as guard and was not given any forage, the train being empty I was expected to graze the mules for their sustenance on the way. I lost 13 mules which died on the trip, and had great difficulty in crossing some of the streams.

At California Creek I had especially a hard time. The creek was high, and my mules were too weak to stand the trip in crossing. They could not stand the current, so I put the strongest across, and then had them drag the others over by hitching chains to their harness, carrying the chain back for them by a rope which those of us mounted [on horseback] carried through the swift running waters. At the crossing of the Clear Fork of the Brazos, which was very high, I came to a halt and had to wait until the water fell. On my arrival there I saw soldiers on the other bank and soon found that it was a scouting party under my old friend Maj. Schram. He had allowed his teams to drive into the ford, not knowing it was too high, and as the crossing was a diagonal one, the outcome being lower than where the teams had entered the water, his lead teams had drifted with the current and so ran into deep water below the ford. Two fine mules teams were drowned and the wagons carried away. As I was nearly out of provisions, I rigged up a rope at a favorable place, and Maj. Schram sent over some of his supplies when he went back to Fort Griffin. After four days waiting I crossed with difficulty and soon got into the Post 12 miles away.

In 1874 the War Department decided to make a vigorous effort to crush the Kiowas and Comanches. These Indians had always been the most bloodthirsty of wild Indians and were uncompromising enemies of the Texas people especially, and of all whites. They roved over the Staked Plains at will, knew all the watering places and the most fertile and secure valleys, and used to come and go from their secret camps in the most unexpected manner. They penetrated far into the settled parts of the frontier of Texas and returned ladened with scalps and booty to their temporary homes or to their permanent reservation near Fort Sill in the Indian Territory. Four columns were sent into the field against them in September 1874. One from the east under Genl. McKenzie, one from the northeast under Genl. Geo. P. Buell, one from the north under Genl. Miles, and one from Kansas under Maj. Price 8th Cavalry. The latter were united. They each campaigned on their own hook so far away from each other as to avoid falling in contact with each other. Genl. McKenzie's course was vigorous, and he did good work in hunting out the hiding places of the Indians. He killed many and captured 400 or 500, and the course taken broke up the Indian depredations. I did not come off recruiting service until too late to personally see much of the campaigning.

I began soon after my arrival in Fort Griffin in the beginning of December 1874 to outfit and load my train. Some 250 new young mules had been sent to Griffin for me in the various trains, and we had to put harness on all we used for the first time. They were fine large shave tail mules from Missouri, and it was great sport to see them caught and side lined. This was casting ropes about the animal and tying it up to the side of a wagon as closely as possible. The harness was then put on as best we could. I got the wild mules hitched to loaded wagons and mixed in with a few broken mules and then gradually got the team to working. I got some new wagons so that I had in all 45.

I was to load with a good deal of Commissary stock and then just as much forage as the wagons would hold. I was some two weeks in getting ready to start back. I established a camp six miles out of the Post and kept teams running all the time from the storehouses to the Camp with load after load of stores.

I did this because I heard that Genl. Buell's column had been ordered in to the Post, and it was necessary for me to get my load out of the Post before his arrival. About the 20th of December I got all ready to start when in came Genl. Buell and his Cavalry. I had taken every pound of grain at the Post, and he had none to feed his animals on. The weather was bad and roads heavy so that as he had no forage, he left his wagons out and drove his animals in a herd for forage. His disappointment was very great to find that I had it all, although the contractors were expected in to the Post every day with more. He tried every way to get some of my grain, and after I was all loaded and ready to string out on the road, he sent for me and said that being an officer of his regiment I ought to help him out, and that he could fix it so that all would be supplied if I would report myself to him for orders. I told him that I was under Genl. McKenzie's orders and that to do as he, Genl. Buell, wished would cost me my commission, so that I declined to do so.

I went to my camp and got ready to move when along came an ambulance with Genl. McKenzie in it. I camped again and went into the Post to see the latter as he directed. I found him at Maj. Schram's house and he and Genl. Buell had a violent quarrel, and I thought would come to blows. I tried to get away but could not. Next day I started from camp, and my wagons were loaded as heavily as they could be. The roads were muddy and the wagons cut deep, only traveled a mile a day for six days. On the sixth day out I had to cross Oteys Creek, and all of the journey to that place I had been compelled to double team it; that is get one wagon through to a certain distance, then put two sets of mules on the next, and so on. I had hard work crossing Oteys Creek, and as the first team crossed, I sent or took it to a little rise of ground and stopped it. The wagons cut in 10 or 12 inches. I sent all the wagons to stop at the same place and made a sort of an irregular camp in a kind of a circle with the teams inside. It was dark before I got the last wagon through the creek, and as I rode up to the camp I felt a little snow on my face. On looking around I saw we were going to have a Norther, and we got into our tents and fixed ourselves for a siege.

A Norther in Texas is a peculiar sort of a cold storm. It may be perfectly clear when, if you look off to the north, you will see a darkish sort of an appearance at the edge of the horizon. In an hour the storm will be on you and as the snow begins to fly and the wind to blow and whistle about, it cuts and chills one to the bone. On this occasion I was fearful that I would lose some of my mules as animals are often frozen to death by the sudden appearance of a Norther. I thought some of my new mules were to go sure, so ordered the wagon master to keep their feed boxes filled pretty well with corn so they could eat all night. They brayed, kicked and squealed as it grew colder, but next morning I found all alive. One mule had his legs go frozen, so I had him shot.

As the Norther began to blow I saw two figures coming from the direction of the Camp, which at first I thought were Indians, but as they approached discovered them to be two of the officers sent out to hurry me up as the Camp was short of supplies. The following morning I found the ground frozen as solid as a floor and as smooth almost. My wagons were fast in the frozen ground 10 or 12 inches each, and I set the men to work chopping the earth away. By 11 o'clock all were free and we started again. At Clear Fork of the Brazos, I was detained two days by high water but got across and succeeded in reaching the camp before there was any thaw.

LEFT:
Erasmus Corwin
Gilbreath in uniform,
in the 1860s

RIGHT:
Susan Corse
Gilbreath, 1869

BELOW:
Officers of the
11th U.S. Infantry.
Capt. Gilbreath is
seated, 5th from right.
(Others are identified
on page 321.)

LEFT:
Capt. Gilbreath, at Fort Lincoln, Dakota Territory, in the 1870s.

BELOW:
The only known photograph of the entire Gilbreath family together. Son William Sydnor, daughters Nan and Etta, and wife, Susan, seated.

RIGHT, TOP:
Capt. Gilbreath with wife and daughters in their dining room at Whipple Barracks, Arizona Territory, 1896.

ABOVE: *Fort Buford, Dakota Territory, in the 1870s.*

ABOVE: *Capt. Gilbreath with wife Susan and daughters Etta and Nan, on the porch at his quarters at Whipple Barracks, Arizona Territory, in 1896.*

TOP LEFT:
Capt. Gilbreath and
Oliver Edwards, third and
second from right. 1894,
Arizona Territory.

RIGHT:
Barracks at Fort Buford,
Dakota Territory.

BELOW:
Major Gilbreath with
son-in-law Oliver
Edwards, Florida, 1898.

ABOVE: Camp at Senaca, Arizona Territory, 1894.

BELOW: The 11th U.S. Infantry Regiment near Tampa, Florida, in the summer of 1898, before deploying to Puerto Rico for the war with Spain.

CHAPTER 8

I Must Have an Operation

1875

I passed the New Year's day of 1875 on the bank of the Brazos suffering from my wound and from being poisoned with poison ivy. I had to open my wound with my penknife several times on the journey and riding on horseback with the leg hanging down made me suffer a great deal. Soon as I got to the Supply Camp and unloaded I had to start right back to Griffin for the final supply to take us home. I performed this journey without incident and hastened again to Supply Camp. I thus rode 600 miles with my leg in bad shape all the time. In the beginning of February, 1875, we got orders to break camp after the 15th of that month and go directly to Fort Concho.

The distance from Supply Camp to Concho was about 200 miles, and we had a very delightful march of it. We traveled the whole distance through buffalo. It was one constant herd for the entire 200 miles. The country was black with them.

We arrived at Fort Concho about the last day of February, and I was about played out from my wound and was glad enough when the journey was ended. I found that Maj. Douglas was very sick from nervous prostration and that Genl. Grierson was ordered to come to the Post with Headquarters of the 10th Cavalry. Maj. Douglas left in April and Genl. G. came about the same time. Dr. Buchanan, the Post Surgeon, on examining my wound said I must have an operation performed on it to get well, and as he had no facilities for performing this operation, he thought I better go east. This I regretfully decided to do, and soon as Maj. Douglas's transportation got back, I took it and went over the same road, again to Austin and so on to Baltimore.

Concho was not a bad Post to serve at, but we had nothing like the amount of supplies then that are furnished now to Army Posts. The quarters were very good for those days, but they too have been improved. This Post was abandoned in 1884 or '85.

I never walked on my lame leg after coming in from the scout to the time of leaving the Post on sick leave, but was on crutches to get about.

WHEN I WENT TO BALTIMORE ON SICK LEAVE to have an operation performed on my old wound received at the battle of Fredericksburg, Va., Dec. 12, 1862, we travelled by ambulance from Fort Concho, Texas, to Austin. My wife, two children and myself at Austin took cars for the north. After going a short distance to Hempstead (we had but few people in our car) two sheriff deputies got into the car with a prisoner whom they were taking to some northern town in the state of Texas where he had committed an atrocious murder. The prisoner was shackled, his hands being handcuffed together and his feet shackled. This party occupied two seats in the front end of the car, and the deputy sheriffs were armed with revolvers.

Passengers got on and off at the various little towns, and we didn't pay much attention to them. At one place an oldish woman got on. She carried an old-fashioned carpet bag and wore a sun bonnet which concealed her face, almost. She took a seat, the first behind the prisoner. We went on to a station or two after her arrival and, stopping at a small town, were surprised to see a lot of armed men crowding into the car by the front and rear doors. Those entering the former went, with their double barreled shotguns all cocked and ready, direct towards the sheriff's party saying, "We've come for him." They all kept fooling with the hammers of their guns in a dangerous way. On the first appearance of the men close to the prisoner, the old woman with the sun bonnet got up and, opening her carpet bag, placed it wide open down by the prisoner. He at once seized a pistol in each of his handcuffed hands and got up. The old woman took out a third pistol and, closing her arsenal, took her carpet bag with her, and the prisoner then shuffled along toward the door, the crowd surrounding him. They got him out of the door of the car. The sheriffs did not dare to move and the passengers in the car were hiding under the seats. They put the prisoner on a horse and then, holding him, went off out of town, the old woman heading the procession. The party then fired off their guns in the air and went away howling and hooting.

WE WENT DIRECTLY TO BALTIMORE, and with the assistance of my wife's brother Dr. Geo. F. Corse, I rented for $10 per month a small house very near Dr. Corse's and about two miles out of the City. There I had an operation performed by Dr. Stevenson of Baltimore, and he took out a good deal of diseased bone. The place was a good long time in healing and I did not get into the city until late that fall. I was almost persuaded to apply for retirement and have always regretted that I did not. I stayed on sick leave 10 months and then left for my company. I went to Philadelphia on the way and in April saw the partially filled and completed Centennial Exposition buildings. I went on west and after stopping a short time in Chicago to St. Louis and San Antonio. At St. Louis I met Maj. Douglas who was just on his way to a new Regiment having just received his promotion to be Lieut. Col. of the 14th Infantry. Genl. Sherman then had his Headquarters in Saint Louis and I called there to register.

From San Antonio I went by stage to Concho the distance being the same as from Austin, 210 miles. I was the only passenger most of the way and was amused to hear the driver of the stage tell his adventures with various passengers. I arrived at Concho about the last of May, 1876, and having left my family at Baltimore, I began living in a mess kept by Lieut. M. M. Maxon 10th Cavalry. Our third child, who was named for me, had been born at Baltimore on 9th of November, 1875. In our mess we had about officers amongst them Lieut. Turner, 10th Cavalry, who was one of the most reckless individuals I ever saw. We had as a waiter at the mess, a colored man named Sam, who was an original genius. He could sing and play the banjo and had much wit. I said to him one morning, "Sam what's the news this morning." "Oh nothing sah cept there's a cision in the church." Upon asking how it happened he said, "Well sah we had two ministers in our church and Mr. Jonsing cused Mr. Brown of stealing a bushel of corn and dat's the cause of the cision." He had many amusing ways about him and afforded us a great deal of amusement. There were eight troops of the 10th Cavalry (colored) and Company H, 11th Infantry and Company A, 10th Infantry were the only white men at the Post.

The colored men made fair soldiers but were very prone to violent attacks on each other using razors or sling shots. I was officer of the day and in visiting sentinels at night approached a man on guard at the cavalry stables. As I drew near him he said, "Who' s dat?" "The officer of the day," was my reply. "Scuse me," he said. "I thought it was some of dem niggers from de guard house." I said, "What are your instructions here?" He said, "I dunno, aint got any." I said, "What are you here for?" "Oh, ise put yer to keep dem older niggers from stealing anything." The colored men put up a church for themselves outside the Post, and they used to sing and shout all night.

Across the river, or the north branch of the Concho, was a collection of houses called San Angelo. It was filled up with Mexicans and discharged soldiers and was not a safe place to go at night. Now it is a city at the end of a railroad.

After a time I changed my messing arrangements and went to live with Capt. P. H. Lee of the 10th Cavalry. He had a fine mess and we lived high. Everything was neat as a pin. Fish were very plentiful in both the north and south branches of the Concho. The Post was in the point between these two streams. My Company had a fine large library and reading society where they took a large number of papers.

The duties were very heavy because there were few clerks or artisans in the Cavalry troops. We had a military telegraph line built by the troops running from Fort Worth to El Paso, and to San Antonio from Concho. The officer in charge at Fort Worth used to send us the news from the papers he received every morning. This placed us a good deal nearer to civilization.

CHAPTER 9

Orders to Go to Dakota

1876

We heard promptly of the Custer massacre in June 1876, and on the 8th of August, I received telegraphic orders to go to Dakota. On the 11th day of August, I heard of the death of my little son and namesake who had died at Baltimore.

The same day I started on my march to Fort Worth, 240 miles away, where I was to take the cars. I marched a good part of the way on foot, but my game leg prevented my continuing to move that way. I reached Fort Worth in sixteen days having been delayed one day in crossing the Brazos River near Greenburg. The ford was too deep. I had one ambulance and three wagons for transportation. At Fort Worth we took cars and continued on to Yankton, Dakota, having to change cars (men and baggage) seven times. The men and all of us enjoyed the trip all the way from Concho very much.

At Yankton we went into camp to await the arrival of the other Companies of the 11th Infantry as the whole Regiment except the Headquarters were ordered to go to Dakota under the command of Lieut. Col. Geo. Buell.

This officer selected A Company, Capt. Choisey; B Company, Capt. Conrad; and H Company (mine) to go to what was then called Standing Rock agency and now Fort Yates, while the other companies were all kept at Fort Sultz and Fort Bennett lower down the Missouri. Several companies left Yankton on the *Nelly Peck* steamboat, and on arrival at Fort Bennett I was to be left alone on the *Nelly Peck* to continue on to Standing Rock. I was about ten days on the boat as she was heavily loaded and arrived at Standing Rock on the 11th of September 1876, just a month after leaving Fort Concho. I found the Post commanded by Lieut. Col. W. P. Carlin 17th Infantry, and there were six regiments of Infantry represented there by one or more Companies: 1st Infantry, 2 Companies; 6th Infantry, 1 Company; 11th Infantry, three Companies; three of the 17th Infantry; and one 20th Infantry. All the Captains were present. I messed with Lieut. Badger, 6th Infantry. The Post was strengthened because this agency was for the Sioux Indians who had sent many warriors to fight against Custer, and the entire tribe was in an unsettled condition. There were quarters for only two companies, so we had to go into the woods and cut timber to build houses for ourselves.

I sent for my family, and they arrived on the last boat up from Yankton. It was the custom in those days to send boats up the Missouri just before navigation closed, loaded with vegetables, and this boat was called the potato boat. The vegetables were to last until the following spring when boats began to run.

At the time of our first service at Galveston we were visited by a young officer named William French, 1st Lieut., 19th Infantry. He was son of Genl. French who had command of the 3rd Corps for a time during the war and who was called "Blinkey French" on account of the nervous affliction which caused him to be constantly snapping or blinking his eyes. The son called Billy came to visit Genl. Gillam, our Colonel who had served as a Lieutenant in French's Battery of Artillery before the war. Billy was peculiar. He had a drawling way of talking, and having no doubt observed his father's blinking, he as a boy probably feared he might be affected in the same way, so to avoid any blinking he had a habit of constantly raising his eyebrows. This, added to his drawl, was amusing. He went to Matamoros, Mexico, for a visit to see the place, etc., and on his return brought with him several pairs of game chickens which he bought in Mexico. [We] loaded and arrived at Standing Rock on the 11th of September 1876, a month after leaving Fort Concho.

I had several [pairs of game chickens] which I had picked up, and one Sunday morning as we were all in Commanding Officer's office, Billy was bragging on the fighting qualities of his "Gia." The name of the variety being as he said, "Gia Giena." Genl. Gillam said, "Billy, Gilbreath's fancy black can whip your Gia." Billy said, "Gilbreath will he fight the Gia?" "Oh yes," said I. Billy: "I'll bet you $20 he can't lick the Gia," and he laid down a $20 gold piece. I, for fun, put one down beside it when Genl. Gillam picked up both and said the bet is made and we will have the fight this afternoon.

About 12 o'clock he drove over to my house, and to get Mrs. G. out of the way as she would have put a quietus on a Sunday chicken fight, the General told her, "Mrs. Gillam would be glad to see her." Soon as the coast was clear by my wife's departure, I caught my black rooster, got into the ambulance and we drove to Col. Scully's house in the city where Billy and his chicken were stopping. B. said, "Gilbreath, he can't fight the Gia," but we all wanted the fight to go on although Billy offered to let me withdraw. Each was to let his own rooster go. So we stooped down each holding his own and at the word from Genl. Gillam let go the roosters. Mine was the larger. He made one dash at the Gia and that bird squawked, flew over the fence, and away he went. Billy looked at the fleeing chicken in perfect amazement while everybody else roared.

To return to Standing Rock, we all worked hard in getting out cottonwood logs for our temporary barracks as we had a great fear of a winter in Dakota, and we were 1200 miles about due north of Fort Concho. I got my Company into their house on Thanksgiving Day and later got a house for myself and my 1st Lieutenant, O. B. Read. The house for the men was one building 120 feet long of logs put up in panels and roofed with boards. At one end we had a storeroom and 1st Sgt's room, at the other was a dining room and kitchen.

Our own houses were built of logs and had two sets of quarters under one roof. They were lined with cottonwood boards behind which was packed sawdust. They were daubed with mud and roofed with shingles. Each house had only three rooms and a narrow hall from the front door. The bedroom was in front of the house, dining room next and the kitchen back. It was a right cozy little house, and in it we enjoyed the winter very much. The whole thing was built of green cottonwood, and as we put in very large stoves, the boards and logs soon became to season and shrink and there was an unceasing popping going on as a board would crack or split or a nail break off. And in the morning when the door was opened an immense volume of steam poured out.

The huts for six companies were built in a line with a short and narrow street between them and the officers' quarters. We called this street Sitting Bull Avenue. It was interesting to see the crowds of Sioux Indians which were collected from time to time at the agency. They wore blankets and all sorts of Indian finery and used to have some of the most picturesque gatherings it is possible to imagine. I can never forget a dance they had at the agency when the Commissioners came to treat with them for the giving up of the Black Hills country. It was held inside of a square, formed by agency buildings. A large fire of logs was built, and for several days and nights a crowd of young Indians danced, without stopping, dressed in very gorgeous costumes of feathers and paint. They had a great feast in connection with the dance. On the 22nd of September, 1876, we were notified that Big Eagle, one of the Sioux Chiefs, had returned to his camp having been absent from the reserve without permission and in the battle with Custer. We were ordered out at noon, and went on the jump to his camp, surrounded it and began to search for guns and ponies. We did not get many of either, but almost scared the Indians to death with such a sudden demonstration. Big Eagle and his men were arrested and disarmed, and their ponies were taken from them.

There were lots of buffalo in the country then as well as other game, and the trader's stores were packed full of skins of all kinds, and we had quantities of wild meat all of the time.

The herds of cattle for issue to the Indians were driven in about the agency in the fall, and soon as cold weather settled down, hundreds of cattle were killed, and the meat often being allowed to freeze was corded up in open storehouses to await the time for issue. This plan worked very well then, as the cattle would not lose flesh or weight so much as if kept alive on poor grass all winter. A beef issue day was another picturesque and very interesting sight. The Indians collected in bands from all directions, then as a lot of cattle was weighed out for them and driven into a separate pen, at once the shooting began and the cattle were slaughtered in short order and soon divided amongst the members of the band. Nothing was lost as all of the entrails were of some use to an Indian.

CHAPTER 10

Fort Custer, Where Nan Is Born in a Tent

1877

In May 1877, our companies were ordered to join those from Sultz and Bennett, and to rendezvous at Fort A. Lincoln near Bismarck to take transportation for the country about the Yellowstone River. We had a very good camp there, and Genl. Buell was in command. He was ordered to send two companies for field service against Indians to report to Genl. Miles at Fort Keough, to take the rest up the Yellowstone and Big Horn Rivers, and to build a post to be called Fort Custer.

Companies A and H were selected for the field service and left under the command of Maj. Bartlett. The Companies went off as steamboats were loaded for the upper country so that each boat would have a guard. My Company was left to the last with Maj. Schram, and I felt as did the other officers, that I was being left out in the cold. There were a great many steamboats in the Missouri then, as the amount of supplies to be taken up from Bismarck was very great. In addition we had about 500 mechanics for the Keough Post and for Custer, as well as all of our Regiment. The reasons for selecting A & H Companies for service under Genl. Miles was that we only had 60 men in the two companies and Genl. Buell wanted to take the strongest with him. They all got off, and finally Maj. Schram left me alone to go by myself on a boat. I was to take what I could get. I was disgusted, but in a day or two got notice that I was to go on the *Ashland* Steamer.

I went over to Bismarck on a ferryboat, expecting to see some little bit of an uncomfortable affair, and was surprised to find the *Ashland* the largest and finest boat of the season. She was a boat which had been used to transport cotton out of the Arkansas River to New Orleans and was a very finely outfitted boat. She was built very high to accommodate large quantities of cotton, and her cabin was handsome. I was very decidedly in luck to set my company on such a craft. Her build was such that she caught more wind than most boats and was consequently slow in her progress up the river. The distance from Bismarck to Fort Keough was over 700 miles by the river, and we arrived at the latter place on the 22nd of June, being almost a month on the boat. On the way up we passed many of the smaller boats especially in the Yellowstone River which was a very rapid stream and it required powerful machinery to stem the current. We overtook the *Dugan* which was carrying A and G Companies, 11th Infantry, and about 250 mechanics for Fort Custer. Maj. Bartlett was in command, and he was glad enough to bring Company A, Capt. Choisey and himself, and come aboard the *Ashland* arriving at Fort Keough. It was then called the Cantonment or Post No. 1, and was later named Fort Keough after Capt. Keough, 7th Cavalry, who was killed in the Custer massacre. We were placed in tents nearby, and our little battalion of 60 men expected to go into the field. It was a busy place with all of the: 5th Infantry, 10 Companies mounted on Oregon horses; 4 Troops, 2nd Cavalry; 4 Companies 22nd Infantry: 4 Companies 1st Infantry; and 2 Companies, 11th Infantry. We did not go into the field, but at this place I saw the last hostile shots fired against troops of the United States. It happened in this way. There was a stage station on the north side of the Yellowstone, our camp being on lower ground on the south side of that stream. There was a guard at the station to protect the men and animals against a possible raid from Indians. After sunset as we were strolling about, there were shots fired at the station and pretty soon a regular fusilade of firing from the top of the hills back of the stage station. The Indians rushed in and tried to drive off the herd at the station. They got a few animals, and then as they rode out, fired over 100 shots as they passed along the top of the bluff. The shots showed very distinctly in the darkness, and I have not seen a hostile shot since.

While we were at Fort Keough, Genl. Terry and Genl. Sherman came to the Post. The former was going to Fort Custer, and the latter to cross the continent to the Pacific coast. There was no railroad then west of

Bismarck, and these officers came up the river by boat, Genl. Sherman intending to take an ambulance and troop of Cavalry, and go west from the mouth of the Big Horn which was near Fort Custer.

After their visit at Fort Keough was over, it was decided that Maj. Bartlett and our two Companies should go up the river on the same steamboat with them and to Fort Custer for duty. We left on the boat *Rose Bud*, Capt. Grant Marsh. We made slow progress as the Big Horn was a regular mountain torrent, and we were compelled to do a great deal of corralling or warping to get over some of the rapids. This operation was done by carrying out from the bow of the boat a long cable, and after making it fast to trees or logs, the machinery was used to simply pull the boat over the difficulty. When the cable was not fastened to a tree, it was attached to what the boat men called a "dead man" which was a large log placed in a trench and held down by stakes driven in a slanting way over the log. The small engine used to draw in this rope, and thus pull the boat along, was called the "nigger," and we became accustomed to the cry "go ahead on the nigger," or "stop the nigger." The boatmen had many peculiar expressions. A Captain, asked if his boat could go upstream on a small amount of water, replied that all she needed was a little dew.

Grant Marsh was a character well known and liked by all Army officers. We had on board a Col. Broadwater who was the contractor for wagon transportation and the mark of his trains was R or Diamond "R." He used oxen principally and the frontier for ox train was bull train. On the occasion we got stuck in a bad place in the Big Horn, (and) when Capt. Marsh said, "Genl. Broadwater, we're stuck. How much will you charge to haul this freight up the Post with your bulls?" Broadwater said, "Oh not very much, Grant." Soon as the rope was fast and she began to move, Marsh said, "Col. Broadwater, I think I'll take your bulls to haul this freight." Broadwater, "All right." But soon as the boat was moving all smooth again, Marsh said, "Broddy, you shan't carry a pound of this freight if I have to take it all up in a yawlboat." It was General, when we were stuck fast; Colonel, when our prospects brightened; and when the boat was moving along serenely, it was simply "Broddy." The living on those boats was usually very good, and one could get a hot cup of coffee or a lunch at any hour by going to the pantry.

They usually supplied rice and hominy with every meal as the wharving men got their food after our people were through. The life of a roust-about, called for short Rooster, was anything but a happy one, and their fare was not good.

We used to have excellent appetites. Mrs. Gilbreath once said, "Capt. Marsh, I can't understand it, but I always have a fine appetite and enjoy the food you furnish." He said, "Well Mrs. Gilbreath, I don't understand it either, for I pledge you my word, I have been settin' down with them rice cakes and hominy balls in front of me for twenty years and have never put a tooth in one of them."

There were on our boat Genl. Sherman, who was at the time the General of the Army, and some members of his staff. His son, Tom Sherman, who afterwards became a Catholic priest, Genl. Terry and his staff, Genl. Miles and a good many other officers, and it was very interesting to hear them talk, Genl. Sherman especially, for he had such a fund to call upon. Tom Sherman was about 21. I think his birthday had not long passed, and he was very bright and attractive. On our leaving Fort Keough a trader there had given each of us a gallon of whiskey for snake bite, etc. Genl. S. had his put up in bottles, Maj. Bartlett the same. Mine was in a small gallon keg. When this goods was brought on board, it was stored in various places. A good deal was used up so that as we got up into the Big Horn, Maj. Bartlett proposed to open his case for the general benefit. After it was used up, Genl. Sherman sent to look for his gallon of whiskey, and it could not be found. A most extensive search was made and it was discovered that I had turned over for Maj. Bartlett's package that belonging to the General of the Army, and it was all gone. The General laughed good naturedly at the mistake and said that when he got back to Washington, he would mark opposite Maj. Bartlett's name and mine: these were the officers who stole the whiskey belonging to the General of the Army. I asked him to accept my gallon keg to take with him across the continent. He did so and placed it where it would not get lost.

He could not help showing great pride in his son Tom, and he was worthy of it. At Keough the General pinned the medals of honor on the coat of each of several men to whom it had been awarded.

On the way up the river Big Horn we met the steamboat *Silver City* coming downstream, and as she had Genl. Sheridan and a party on board, we tied up to the bank, both boats, and Genl. Sheridan came on board our boat for a talk with Genl. Sherman. It was a notable gathering. We had every grade in the Army represented except that of Major General. There were on board of the *Rose Bud* that day (July 23, 1877): Genl. Sherman; Lieut. Genl. Sheridan; Brig. Genl. Terry; Brig. Genl. Crook; Col. Poe of the Engineers; Col. Miles, 5th Infantry; Col. Bacon, 7th Cavalry; Col. South, Infantry; Maj. Bartlett; Capt. Gilbreath; Lieut. Macklin, Whitney, (and) Reva. After a long pow-wow, to which all of us were admitted, the boats separated and we went on our way.

Boats going up or down in the Big Horn or Yellowstone Rivers never ran at night on account of the current, so that we were six full days reaching Custer from Keough, a distance by river of 200 miles or more. I did not take my Company off the boat at Custer, as I was ordered by Genl. Buell to go back on the boat to the mouth of the Big Horn to find a place to land stores for Custer. It was not practicable to navigate the Big Horn, although I saw 15 boats at one time at the bank at Fort Custer. We started back on the afternoon of July 24th, 1877, and ran out of the river in a few hours and then up the Yellowstone River about two miles. Genl. Sherman went with us and left the boat to go with Capt. Norwood (troop L, 2nd. Cavalry), up the Yellowstone and on across the continent. After taking my men off the boat, we camped for the night in a cottonwood grove, and next day I rode up and down stream some distance, and finally selected a camping place where all stores could be landed. It was a beautiful spot, and we soon pitched our tents and got into good shape. In clearing off the beach for the camp, the men killed 16 rattlesnakes in one day. The sage brush was very heavy and thick. We framed our tents, that is, used the lumber at hand for a frame inside of each tent, and soon were very comfortable. I had for myself and for Lieut. Read three large hospital tents, and for the men for each two. Boats began to arrive, and I received millions of pounds of all kinds of stores: lumber, grain, hay, provisions and all sorts of material to be used to build the new Post. Fort Custer was to be a ten-company Post and was situated at the forks of the Little Horn and Big Horn, between the two.

It was on a high bluff overlooking both valleys and about ten miles from the Custer battlefield. All of the lumber for its construction, except the main timbers of cottonwood cut about the Post, was delivered at my camp and hauled thence by Diamond R trains 33 miles to the Post. I fixed on the name Terry's Landing for the camp. Lieut. Read and I sent for our wives who had remained at Port Yates or Standing Rock, and they joined us after a beautiful trip on the boats up the Yellowstone. We enjoyed the life of the camp very much. [We] had a much better life than the people did who came up the river first. The country was alive with game, and we used to have several different kinds in our larder at one time: elk, deer, buffalo and mountain sheep. Fish were very plentiful and delicious and so we had no end of sport. There were no settlements along the Yellowstone in 1877 so that our camp was a regular stopping place for all officers passing to and from Fort Custer. Everybody going off by boat came there, and so we were never without company.

We could see the road from camp as it passed from the ferry above us down on the other side of the river, so that we always had timely notice of the coming of strangers, on sight of whom, everything was got in shape for a lunch should they need it, which they usually did. We had all classes of visitors and thoroughly enjoyed having everybody. Occasionally they would think of us and bring us a surprise. Col. Broadwater once came covered with dust and getting out of his light wagon started, in a cheery way, to bring Mrs. Gilbreath a watermelon. As he reached the door his foot slipt, and away went the melon which he had carefully carried 120 miles, and being thoroughly ripe it broke into very small pieces. Another friend sent us a dozen chickens, the very first in that part of the country.

The ferry established for crossing the Yellowstone had been before we came up the river. The boat was of cottonwood cut down with an ax alone to a thickness or thinness of about nine inches. It was a heavy affair and was used, before we came, only occasionally. The mail used to cross only once in a while as Indians were too bad to trifle with. Our mail when we first went into the Yellowstone Country was sent to Bismarck first, then up the river on any boat which would carry it.

Often we would receive 20 or 30 sacks of mail without locks so that anybody thinking he might have a letter, could look the mail over. I used to take ours out and then send the bags on by trains to Custer. Soon a [railroad] line was established along the Yellowstone, and our mail came to Custer via Ogden, Utah, and Helena, Montana, and thence down the

Yellowstone. It was often 16 or 18 days hearing from New York. Letter mail was always packed alone so that in an emergency the papers could be thrown away. Later lines were extended to Rock Creek on the Union Pacific, south from Custer and from Keough, east to Bismarck across the country, and in a few months we received our mail regularly.

My daughter, Nan, was born in a tent at Terry's Landing, Montana, on the 31st of October, 1877, and I was worried enough that day. I had sent for a Doctor to the Post, and as none had arrived I could do nothing but walk up and down in front of the tent and look for him. He did not come, and we had to depend upon the services of our cook who happened to be a very skilled nurse. The second day after, the Doctor came and after staying a short time, left for the Post.

One day I saw a boat come down the river and tie up on the opposite bank near the ferry. Soon a tent went up so I went to see what it was. On crossing the Yellowstone I found that a Jew named Batzinski had put up a store tent. In it was everything imaginable except pianos. He had reading matter and fish hooks, grain and provisions, and calico and a big store. Instead of having one boat, he had three or four mackinaws which he had brought with his stock from Helena or Bozeman, and was on his way to start a store someplace. It was the beginning of a town called Junction City.

The mackinaws referred to were boats with flat bottoms and a square stern and, being wide, were available for carrying a large load. The potato and onion supply for the two Posts, Forts Keough and Custer, was purchased in Montana and sent by mackinaws down the Yellowstone.

I built a blockhouse for the protection of our families and men, as the Indians were very bad. The Sioux were always lounging about, and in August the Nez Perces had passed through the country about 12 miles above where I was. Genl. Howard had followed the latter for miles and Genl Sturgis of the 7th Cavalry had a fight with them at Clarks Fork Canyon about 40 miles above me.

At the time of this fight some men were coming down the Yellowstone in mackinaws loaded with chickens, bees, etc., on their way to Fort Keough or Miles City, a town started near that Post. Genl. Sturgis put his women and men on these boats and they came up to my landing. One man of L Troop, 7th Cavalry died before he got to the landing. I took him off the boat and buried him. The others I provided with canvas to cover them from the weather, and they continued on to Fort Keough.

The teams hauling stores from our landing to the Post were interesting. Oxen were generally used to draw the wagons, and the latter were placed with one large wagon in the lead and two smaller ones as trails, hitched onto the first with short tongues and chains. They used to have 18 or 20 oxen on one wagon with its trails, and they carried a very heavy load. The teamsters were a novelty and a study. Each teamster had his oxen named by himself. The man I remember had Harry Ward Beecher and Theodore Tilton on the tongue, and Hayes, Tilden, Webster, Lincoln, Douglas went paired in an amusing way. The oxen knew their names too. For to impress it upon the mind of each for all time, the driver would hurl out an oath and with a great swing of his whip he would crack it so loudly and so close, as to make the fur fly.

These teamsters or bull whackers, in their vernacular, were a queer lot from all walks of life previous to their present occupation. Many were well educated, one I remember had been a Superintendent of Education in the state of Kansas. All had drifted about from one thing to another on the frontier for years. Their pay was 40 gold dollars a month and rations. They used to amuse themselves in every way.

Once I went in the evening to the camp of a very large train. It, the camp, was always of corral form made by driving wagons in two parallel lines. At the place selected, the team heading each column was turned in so that the oxen were side by side. The teams next following drove their oxen inside the leading wagons so that the wagons almost touched. The rest drove in the same way while the two last wagons crossed each other's track and stopped (team inside) in a diagonal way. The corral was thus a pen of wagons with a small opening at either end into which oxen were driven in the morning to be yoked. Each team's yoke was dropped when they stopped. In the center the men did their cooking while they slept under the wagons. This form of corral was used by all trains, government and citizen, as a guard against Indians, as men could fight from the inside while the animals were protected by the wagons.

On the evening of my visit referred to, the herd was out grazing and the teamsters just finishing their supper. As each completed this repast, he rubbed off his tin plate [with] anything at hand.

As all finished, one very large man with beard all over his face and a very coarse voice got up from his seat on an ox yoke and said, "Who killed cock robin?" A very small man with a thin weak voice arose and said, "I, said the sparrow, with my bow and arrow," another followed with the next inquiry, and so on through the whole story of Cock Robin. Everything was carried out in somber earnest. One of these teamsters called himself "Calamity Bill," and never told what his name really was. He was educated to a certain degree, but had been followed, as he thought, by bad luck, so had dropped all his connection with the past and his name, and was trying to lose himself in Calamity Bill.

In 1877 the whole of the country about the Big Horn and Yellowstone Rivers was overrun by prospectors looking for gold. Most were on foot, but some came in with ponies. All were living on what they could kill or pick up. They used to come begging to Terry's Landing every day almost and were always cheerful and good humored. If food could not be furnished, they would borrow a fish line and go whistling off for something to eat or slip out and kill game of some kind. The surveyors of the Northern Pacific RR passed through the country fixing a line near Terry's Landing in 1877. I remained in command there until the 27th of December, '77 when I went with my company to Fort Custer. During the time I was at the landing, my Company cared for and shipped something near 6,000,000 pounds of freight. At Fort Custer, Lieut. Col. Geo. P. Buell was in command and there were Companies B, C, F and H of the 11th Infantry with Headquarters, 2nd Cavalry and four troops of the same Regt. The quarters were very good although not all completed, and the Post generally was in an unfinished state.

COMMENTARY: *The "Indian Wars" had been going on before and during the Civil War, but on the Great Plains, clashes between Sioux and Cheyenne and the U.S. Army escalated. The defeat of Lieut. Col. George A. Custer and units of the 7th Cavalry was a galvanizing event, and the army responded with shows of force on the Plains. Capt. Gilbreath's company's move to the Dakota territory and his important role in building the large post at Fort Custer, Montana, were emblematic of the burgeoning Indian Wars.*

CHAPTER 11

OUR BANNOCK & CROW CAMPAIGNS

1878-1879

I visited the Battlefield where Custer was massacred first, soon after the 1st of January, 1878, in company with Lieut. Chas F. Roe, 2nd Cavalry, who was with the Terry command and had gone over the ground two days after the massacre. My visit was 1½ years after, but the trail of the Indians, to the great camp where Custer found them, was still very plain, and the hill on which Custer and his men lost their lives was still covered with bones of horses and men. The latter had been buried but had been washed out or uncovered by animals. Lieut. Roe pointed out to me the places where the bodies of the officers were found, and the mutilation of each was described.

The winter of '77 and '78 at Fort Custer was a severe one, and snow was deep. Game was plentiful, and wagonloads of frozen trout, freshly caught, men brought to the Post. Of all the game I liked black tail deer the best with the back strop of the buffalo a close second. The "back strop" consisted of a long piece of flesh running above the backbone and along the spine. It was sometimes 3 feet long and of a diameter of 6 or 8 inches, and when cut across, furnished fine good sized steaks.

In the spring of '78, all of the quarters were completed and many of the walks. Trees were planted in front of our houses. In '78 the Post was a good deal broken up on account of a quarrel between several officers and the commanding officer. This resulted in a trial of the Juniors at Fort Keough, and to that trial all the officers were summoned and many of the men. I was left in command of the Post for a month and had only one officer with me, Lieut. Fowler, 2nd Cavalry. We got out the men and built a new road from the steamboat landing to the top of the bluff on which the Post stood.

In September, 1878, the Bannock Indians living on the west side of the Big Horn Mountains, having broken out with hostile intent, began to make their way through those mountains in an effort to follow about the same line of march as the Nez Percies had in 1877 and wanted, like the latter Indians, to get into British America. The Nez Percies got as far north as the Bear Paw Mountains above the Missouri, but the Bannocks were slower and not so well provisioned and only succeeded in reaching the north side of the Big Horn Mountains. Troops from Fort Custer were ordered out against the Bannocks, and at the same time Genl. Miles started up the Yellowstone to visit the Yellowstone Park having only the 5th Infantry Band as an escort, and several officers of the 5th Infantry accompanied him. The troops from Fort Custer were commanded by Genl. Geo. P. Buell and consisted of eight troops of Cavalry. I was ordered to accompany them with 50 Infantrymen of my own company and of others at the Post. I was at first ordered to go mounted on such horses as I could pick up for my men from the Quartermaster Dept., and from the extra Cavalry horses, but after a vigorous protest, got the order changed so that I could have my men march. I was ordered to take a pack train across the country to the mouth of Clark's Fork, there to meet the Cavalry and take charge of the wagon train. The Cavalry was to go to the Yellowstone and, crossing that stream, go up on the north side of it, cross again at Clark's Fork and then go up that stream. The object being to reach the mountains at Clark's Fork Canyon before the Bannocks came out of the mountains. I had 280 pack mules loaded with about 350 pounds each, and left the Post at the same time with the Cavalry on the 1st of September. We camped together at Fly Creek that night.

The Cavalry started out across the hills on the morning of the 8th of September and gave up the idea of crossing to the north of the Yellowstone. I was ordered to follow so as to camp with them that night. At noon I stopped for a lunch and coffee, and started on about 2 P.M., was delayed by Pvt. Keough, so that it was after dark, about 10 P.M., before I reached camp. At sunset we were passing through a notch in the hills. On our right was a steep bluff about 500 feet high and very steep. As I looked at this bluff, I saw on the top a very large mountain lion walking slowly alone. We fired at it but it ran off. The next day we reached the Clark's Fork near where it empties into the Yellowstone. I had had a good deal of difficulty with the pack mules as they were frisky all the way out and their loads became unfixed often.

Genl. Buell took the Cavalry and the packs and marched up Clark's Fork. I was to follow with the wagons of which I had about 40. It rained terribly and was slow going. I had to cross Clark's Fork 16 times with my train but finally reached the camp of the Cavalry near the canyon where Clark's Fork comes out of the Big Horn Mountains. I was soon filled up with mountain trout which Lieut. Read had caught and cooked beside the stream.

I found that Genl. Miles had gotten in ahead of Genl. Buell and had killed and captured all of the Bannocks before the arrival of Genl. Buell. Genl. M. had arrived at the mouth of the Stillwater with his party on the way to the Park, when a half breed, called Little Rock, who had been with the Bannocks, had come to him and reported that the Indians would come out of the mountains on a certain day. Miles took his band who were armed and some Crow Indians, and marching in the night, surrounded the Bannocks in their camp at daylight and had attacked them killing 15 and capturing 30 or 40. Capt. Bennett, 5th Infantry, was killed, being shot through the heart, and a few of the soldiers were wounded. The man, Little Rock, who betrayed the Bannocks, was one of the first killed by them. He had lived with them for years and had taken his wife from amongst them, had left their homes with them and, after coming through the mountains with them, had become displeased about something, had slipped off and reported their coming at the Crow agency, just as Genl. Miles arrived in the vicinity of it. Genl. M. took his band and the few officers who were with him, and had crept around the mountain in time to surprise them in their first camp after getting through. Little Rock was buried on top of a solitary conical hill which stood out in the valley of Clark's Fork. Capt. Bennett's body was taken to Fort Keough.

We went into camp in a park in the edge of the mountains and feasted on the most beautiful scenery I have yet seen. The park in which we were camped was 7000 feet above the sea and of about 1200 acres in extent with mountain spurs all around it. The stream running through it we called Bennett's Creek. We had no end of trout and game and so, very thoroughly, enjoyed our stay. After remaining in camp a week, we moved off for the Fort Custer, and went back by a different route, one which took us around the northeast end of the Big Horn Mountains through Pryor Gap and to old Fort C. F. Smith, which was built near where the Big Horn came through the mountains. On the way in, as we crossed the plain, we ran into a drove of winged ants which were migrating. These little pests were simply large red ants with wings which they shed later in their lives. They lodged on and crept down our necks, and on being pinched, would sting in a very disagreeable manner.

We had a wealthy man with us, Mr. Booth, who was from Boston, a tenderfoot as such people are called, and when we got in amongst the ants he rode hard as he could in a great wide circle to try to get rid of them, but as he simply rode around in the line of their movement, he only caught more ants, while we old stagers only quickened our pace and passed through the line on which the ants were moving. Booth wore a fancy leather suit of English make of which he was very proud. This suit got very wet and we had to peel it off of him and keep it wet so he could get into it for the rest of his trip. The officers in wearing buckskin or any leather garments usually wore outside of it other clothing to prevent its getting wet and stiff. We got back to the Fort from our Bannock Campaign about the 20th of September, 1878, after about as pleasant a Campaign as I ever was in. Capt. Conrad's Company B, 11th Infantry was at Terry's Landing during this summer. In 1878 my 1st Lieut., O. B. Read was promoted to be Captain of Company F, 11th Infantry and was sent with his Company F in 1879 to the Landing.

———

WHILE STATIONED AT FORT CUSTER, MONTANA, from 1877 to 1882, one of our favorite amusements consisted of a trip each fall to the Big Horn Mountains about 45 or 50 miles away. In 1878 we got up a party consisting of my family, two young ladies, daughters of Genl. D. the commanding officer, with Lieut. H. and Dr. Terry. We went up the Big Horn River to old Fort C. F. Smith, which had been abandoned at the demand of the Sioux Indians. It was 45 miles from the Post at the foot of the Big

Horn Mountains. From there the ascent was gradual and easy to the top of the mountain and there was a fine camping place near a spring which came out in a small ravine. The river comes through the mountain in a canyon about 65 miles long. West of the mountain the river is called the Wind River, but it becomes the Big Horn at the mountains, and the gorge through which it comes is a square cut narrow and deep one. On the east side of the mountains, and entering the Big Horn Canyon from the south is another canyon called Black Canyon. We could drive up to within two or three feet of the bluff at the junction of these canyons and, from an ambulance, look down to the river some 2000 feet below.

The Big Horn Canyon was entirely devoid of verdure, and the different colors of the various strata of rock was always interesting. Black Canyon was filled with all sorts of wild growth, and the little stream at the bottom gave good fishing as fine trout were there in plenty. Our camp was on the side of Black Canyon, and an easy path led to the bottom. We camped there a few days, then went along a trail on the east side of the mountains, and camped as the fancy suited us as there were numerous small streams running out of the mountains. Our road finally led us to the Little Horn down which we went to the Post. Our course formed a large triangle, and we sometimes went up one side and sometimes the other to the mountains. We made the trip mostly every year.

———

IN 1879 I WAS APPOINTED INSPECTOR OF SUPPLIES for the Crow agency and had to inspect and receive all of the supplies for the Crow tribe of Indians. The Crow agency was then situated about 140 miles by the road and about 100 miles west of the Post of Fort Custer. I had to go north to the Yellowstone River and crossing that, up the north side or left bank to the mouth of the Stillwater (River), and thence south 13 miles up the Stillwater to the agency. I continued to act as Inspector for about 3 years, and as during the first year I had to go to the agency once every month, I saw a great deal of the Crows. My duties required that I weigh all cattle and flour and other things received on contract, as well as examine all goods received.

I superintended the issue of annuities each year and counted the entire tribe, and also superintended the making of a treaty with the Crows by which they sold 3,000,000 acres of their reservation to the Government. The part so bought was the southwest and west end of their old reservation, and included all that part west of the Boulair and south of a line drawn along the foot hills of the mountains south of the agency. The treaty was made out in Washington, but the Indians would not agree to it. So I rewrote it making some modifications which they wanted, and after a month of hard labor got the treaty adopted by three quarters of the men of the tribe. The agent of the Crows was a man from Ohio, and they did not have much confidence in him, so he could not have gotten the treaty adopted without my help. We held the council in one of the buildings at the agency and, after a good many speeches, succeeded.

It was then proposed for the Department at Washington that a delegation go to Washington to see the President. The intention was to let some of the men, who had no idea of how many white people there were in the United States, see some of the cities and towns in the east to impress them with the white man's numbers and progress. We selected those inclined to be discontented amongst whom was one called Crazy Head. I asked him to go, and he slowly got up on a bench made a short speech, declining by saying as interpreted, that he had seen Indians who had been to Washington and all of them said that the Great Father lived in a beautiful White House, a house on top of a house (that is two storied), and that whenever anyone wanted to see the Great Father, they went to his house to see him. Crazy Head did not want anything from the Great Father but to be left alone, and his lodge was right down there by the creek. If the Great Father wanted to see him, he could easily find his lodge and must come to see him there.

They all were very superstitious. One of them once said in a speech to a crowd that the night before, he had stepped out of his lodge when he heard a dead Crow on the hill call to one by the stream and say, "Hello Crow, you tell Bear in the Water he must move his camp six miles away as where he is bad medicine and his people will die." Bear in the Water moved at once in a storm, although we tried to prevent him from doing so.

In passing to and from Fort Custer to the agency, I sometimes went by government transportation and sometimes on the stage. If with the former, I camped out at favorable points while, if I went by stage, I took meals at the various stopping places of the stage. In such cases the fare was anything but good, and I rode day and night having transportation sent from the agency to Stillwater to meet me. At Stillwater I sometimes had to stay all night and stopped with an old man named Countryman who kept the stage station. He and his two sons were the greatest liars it has ever been my fortune to see. He lived in the rudest way. All of his guests, himself and his sons slept on the floor of the common reception room of his log house. A bar was at one end of the room and a fireplace in one corner. For me he fixed up a sort of a bunk raised about 3 feet from the floor, but all the rest of the men slept on the floor with their heads to the wall. Countryman himself slept in the center of the room with his head against a fine large post which supported the dirt roof of the house. He changed his position as the notion struck him and sometimes his feet pointed south or north, east or west as his fancy at the moment dictated. It was a motley crowd which assembled there sometimes, consisting of cowboys, stage drivers, and Indians, and on the arrival of anyone during the night, the old man always got up and, after stirring up the fire, he swept the floor. He seemed to be always sweeping the floor, and so the place was filled with dust. I never saw the likes of the bed bugs; the walls of logs were filled with them.

A winter trip in the stage was anything but agreeable. On one occasion, I came down the Yellowstone in the stage to Huntley where I was to cross the Yellowstone to go to Custer. It was 12 o'clock at night when we arrived, and the only thing I could get to eat was some stale bread and pickled Beaver tail. The latter did not taste badly, resembling pigs feet to a certain extent, but being much more oily. I ate a good deal of it. On going to the river we found that the ice had been broken up and had formed a great ice gorge right where the ferry wire was stretched across the stream which was about 400 feet across. The mail had to cross, and I decided to go on as I was anxious to get to the Post to be present at the wedding of Lieut. Hoppin of the 2nd Cavalry. They rigged up a common hayrack, attaching it to two iron wheels or travelers, which ran on the wire, it being fixed by ropes so that a wheel was at each end of the rack. Then a board was placed on the rack in the center and the mail and express was piled on the board. The mail driver sat on the board at one end, I at the back end. Men on the ground then, when we were all ready, gave a strong pull at a rope attached under the rack and ran as hard as they could down the bank to the edge of the stream. The idea being to send us down the slack of the wire with such force that the impetus would carry us well up on the slope of the wire on the other side of the stream. I shall never forget that ride. The water was roaring and foaming about the ice gorge and we rushed down within two feet of the top of the gorge. The moon was shining dimly, and the situation was trying to one's nerves.

On reaching the end of the slope, as soon as we began to go up the slack from the other side, we both seized hold of the cable and began pulling for dear life. The weight was heavy and, we sitting down with the wire passing close over our shoulders, had all the strain on the muscles of the upper parts of our bodies alone. The thing almost stopped, but we kept tugging away at it, and crawling up at the last, inch by inch, finally reached the post and made fast to it. We threw off the mail and then climbed down the post. I think I was never so tired and so near exhausted as at the end of that trip. I then had 40 miles to go before I could get to the Fort and had to ride on the high seat of a common dead axle wagon such as farmers use for light hauling. I sat up by the driver and in spite of singing, smoking, telling stories, etc. to keep awake, I would go to sleep. The driver would grab me as I nodded to keep me from falling off. He had four good horses, however, and we got home early in the morning.

COMMENTARY: *By the late 1870s, the conflicts between Plains Indian tribes and the U.S. Army had escalated to all-out war. Hostile tribes were considered "the enemy" and were treated accordingly. Fort Custer, which had originally been called the Big Horn Post, grew into a major fort, in which Capt. Gilbreath's Quartermaster duties were extensive. The presence there of many important army officers—Generals Sherman, Sheridan, Terry, Crook and Col. Nelson Miles (soon to be a general)—underscored the gravity of the campaigns against combative Indian tribes.*

Not every tribe engaged in warfare with the army. Some, like the Crow, sold off much of their land in treaty agreements with the United States, and settled more or less peaceably on large reservations.

CHAPTER 12

On a Court Martial

1880

I n the summer of 1880, I was sent to survey a road from Fort Custer to Fort Keough on the south side of the Yellowstone. I went out with a Sgt and five Cavalry privates and a pack train of six mules, crossed the Little Horn about 2½ miles from the Post, and then across the hills to Tullocks Fork and on to Rose Bud, a stream which emptied into the Yellowstone about 40 miles above Fort Keough. I then went back, cutting off distance wherever I could from my first trail, and reported that the route was not practicable on account of the lack of water. The route was next year gone over and staked out for a road where I had been, but it was never used by a single train.

The same year I was ordered to Poplar River, Montana, on a Court Martial and went to the place via Glendive. The Northern Pacific Railroad was completed to a place called Forsythe, and this was a typical frontier railroad town, mostly composed of canvas houses and tents, and the gambling and drinking was something terrible. Of 89 houses, 69 were gambling places. I took cars at Forsythe and rode to Glendive and from there crossing to the north side of the Yellowstone. I was to ride in a buckboard to Fort Buford at the mouth of the Yellowstone, thence I was to go up on the north side of the Missouri River 60 miles to Poplar River. I stayed all night with the Glendive Hotel, and found the place of much the same character as Forsythe. There was no ferry so I was rowed across the Yellowstone by the mail carrier. He did not know I was an army officer, but left me in charge of his packages while he went back for another passenger and more mail. I was in citizens clothes and was seated in the shade of a cottonwood tree, when a man came out of an old shack nearby which I did not know was inhabited. He said, "Good morning stranger," which salutation I returned. He, "Are you going down on the stage?" I said I was. He, "Armed, I 'spose." "No," I said, "Never carry any." He, "My God man you better get a gun before you go. It's awful danger-ous right here now, not mentioning down the road. Stage was chased by Indians yesterday and they killed six, 14 miles below." I said, "I will take my chances without arms. It's too much trouble to carry arms." He went on and tried to frighten me telling me of the killing of men, women and children in the most cordial and bloodthirsty detail, and giving me particulars of how to look out for Indians and how to fight them, and finally said, "Whar you from?" I said, "Glendive." "Did you come in from the East?" "Yes, sometime ago," but I told him I got in from up the river on last night's train. He said, "How far up you been anyhow travellin' without arms." "Oh," I said, "up about the Big Horn." He said, "You're taking lots of chances. How long was you up thar?" I said, "3 years." He said, "What's your business stranger, ranchin'?" I said, "No, I am an Army officer." On that, he slapped his hands on his leg and said, "By G--d, I took you for a tenderfoot from the East, have a seegar."

The driver came back with his other passenger who was drunk as a lord. We loaded up the mail, and the driver and his two passengers got on to the seats as best we could and off we started. The other passenger at once began to tell me his history which was one of many similar cases we occasionally came across in the West. He was from New York City, and his father was wealthy. This son had gotten into bad company and drinking habits, and the father had brought him out to Montana, bought him a ranch, and stocked it and placed the son in charge to reform him. The young man showed me letters from his girl in which she begged him to reform and return to New York. As we stopped at his ranch he said, "Now, I'm reforming and you can bet I shall get out of this soon." He in-vited me in, and I was amazed to see the lavish waste of money in such a place. He was good picking for all the wild fellows about. His horses, cat-tle, china and tools had been stolen time and again. He showed me about and said, "Now here in the storehouse, I have my ice chest." He raised the lid and in it was brandy, whiskey, beer, champagne and every kind of intoxicating liquor one could mention. I thought he was reforming fast.

On this ride from Glendive to Fort Buford in 1880, I saw the last herd of buffalo. They had all been killed off by skin hunters, and, where formerly the hills had been black with herds of them, we now saw only one small band of six or eight. There was still some other game in the country, and we saw large bands of antelope. One of the mules of our team was always aroused at the sight of them, and she could see them before we could. She would at once throw up her head and dash off at great speed and would keep up a rattling pace as long as antelope were in sight no matter how far off they were.

On my arrival at Fort Buford, I found the Post commanded by Lieut. Col. H. R. Chipman of the 7th Infantry who was formerly a Captain in the 15th and 11th Infantry Regts. He received me with an old time courtesy which was very pleasant. He sent a fine ambulance out for me to meet and bring me into the Post and kept me at his house. After being called upon by all of the officers, Col. Chipman went with me in full uniform to call on everybody and he made me enjoy myself. Resting a day, Col. C. sent me on to Poplar River in his ambulance. I then found my old 1st Lieutenant, now Capt. O. B. Read, in command and the Post a rather pretty one situated near an Indian agency for the Assinaboins. The Court was not of long duration, and I returned to Fort Custer by the same route I had come over.

We had an officer at Fort Custer named C. who was a genial whole souled sort of a man and always getting into funny situations. He drank a great deal and one night had stayed until very late at the Post Tender's store, drinking. He had placed a light in his window so that he could steer for that when he should leave the store. He started home, the night was dark, and he was near sighted. A pit had been dug near his path, and as he was straggling along in the direction of his light, he fell into the hole. He struggled out and, facing his house, started again when in he tumbled again. He got out on the other side, but on straightening up he caught sight of the lights at the store and supposing them his own, he promptly fell into the hole again on taking the first step. This time he lost his glasses, so he sat down on the side of the excavation and began to call for help. The Sgt. of the Guard ran over to him and got him home all right.

On another occasion he was showing a stranger about the Post on a winter day. The Post was on top of a steep bluff on the Big Horn side, the edge of which was 145 feet above the ice on the stream. In trying to point out something to the stranger, C. got too close to the edge, his foot slipped and away he went sliding, rolling, and tumbling to the bottom where soon found himself sitting on the ice. Fortunately, the bluff was not very steep and enough snow was lodged on it to break his fall so that he was not seriously injured. His glasses were lost, of course, so that he had again to be led home. He once came to see me at Terry's Landing having been down the river with six large wagons to get nails for the Post. Each wagon was filled with a course of nail kegs so that not being heavily loaded he could travel fast. He rode up to my tent and was covered with dust and in a terrible hurry. He had ridden for miles sitting on a bag of straw on top of the nail kegs, and as he had to drive at a trot, it was a most uncomfortable position. He wanted a lunch and Mrs. G. gave him, as he would not wait, a hot blackberry pie with other things. It was amusing to see him go off with a rush in a cloud of dust with a hot pie in his hand.

CHAPTER 13

TERRY'S LANDING &
BACK TO MY COMPANY

1881-1882

I n the Spring of 1881, I was again sent with my Company to Terry's Landing and after being there until September, receiving stores and shipping them, I took a leave of absence and went east. My wife went east before me in July and went down the river on the boat which carried "Rain in the Face" and his band of Sioux who had surrendered that summer. The regular passenger trains only ran west then as far as Glendive, Montana, so that I had to go by boat as far as that place. Boats then ran regularly between Glendive and Terry's Landing, but the number was very much reduced. I had thought of being retired and not going back to the Army. We rented a house on Townsend Street in Baltimore and lived very comfortably and nicely enjoying ourselves all the winter. We sent the children, Will and Etta, to school and they made good progress.

AS I FOUND NOTHING TO DO, I GOT TIRED OF MY LEAVE and went back to my Company in the month of May, 1882. The Company was still at Fort Custer, having come up from Terry's Landing in the fall after I left in 1881. The landing was considered a part or a sub-post of Custer. In July, 1882, I was ordered to go to Fort Buford, Dakota, for a station. My family remained in the East.

We left Fort Custer on the 31st day of July, 1882, after serving at that place five years and one week. It was a delightful station, and I have never served any place which I remember with more pleasure than Fort Custer.

On going out of the Post, the band was turned out to escort us, and all of the ladies, officers and men came out to see us off. The band played "Auld Lang Syne," and with many good wishes and regrets, we got away. I was in command of H and C Companies of my Regiment and was to take boats for station at Fort Buford and to relieve the companies of the 7th Infantry which were there. We boarded the *Karo* at Forsythe to which place we marched, and we disembarked at Glendive. We crossed the Yellowstone and camped until the contractor furnished us with wagons for transportation. After waiting three days, we got off and in six days more reached Buford.

My old friend Col. Chipman was still in command and I relieved him. He was very dignified and formal in everything and turned over the Post in the most precise way. He asked me to accompany him to the office at a few minutes before 12 o'clock noon. At exactly 12 o'clock, he sat down at his desk and signed some final papers including an order announcing that he "hereby surrendered the command of Fort Buford, Dakota." I had been seated away from the desk. He arose after signing the order, shook hands with me, and giving me the commanding officer's chair, took the seat I had occupied. I signed an order "hereby assuming command of Fort Buford, Dakota," and after a social chat of a moment or two, I sent out the order to be read by each officer and we withdrew for the day. Col. C. with the 7th Infantry left on a boat for Fort Pembina the same night, and I was left with two companies, 11th Infantry and Lieutenants Mansfield and Wheeler.

I ran my own mess, and although the other officers wanted to come in with me, I was alone. My cook was named Mrs. Butler, and even at this distance of time, it still makes me sick to think of the messes she used to give me.

The last day of September, 1882, Lieut. Col. E. F. Townsend, 11th Infantry, came and took command of the Post and remained in command until in April, 1883, when he went for a leave of absence. As my family was still in Baltimore, the winter passed very slowly and I found it difficult to fill in the time. I used to, however, go often to Col. Townsend's and play picquet with Mrs. T., or whist with the family. I found Dr. Crampton, the Post Surgeon, on my arrival at Buford, and he only remained until the beginning of November when he was succeeded by Dr. Johnson. For both of these gentlemen, I formed a very strong friendship as well as for Mrs. Crampton. During the winter of 1882, the Companies at Fort Buford were increased by the arrival of Troops F and L, 7th Cavalry, and for several of the officers of these troops, we had several balls or hops and, as we had no military band, we had to hunt up such as we could get. The Quartermaster had instructions to employ any man who might show the least sign of being able to play on any instrument. So it happened that we got four fine players whose time during the day was fully occupied driving mules and who gave us dance music evenings when we wanted to dance.

The leader of this motley band was named Drake, and he was never without tobacco. He played the leading violin and with his ill fitting shirt—he bought one for our benefit—his tobacco, his attempt at blacking cowhide boots with which he kept time, and his manner of leading his band, he was a most absurd memory. He played along deeply interested, would suddenly jerk his head to one side and yell "C" to the man on his right, or jerk to the left and announce "B" to the player to the player to his left. He worked faithfully though and afforded for us no little amusement during a dreary winter.

CHAPTER 14

I Am Anxious to Get
My Family Out

1883

I n the spring, or as spring approached, I became anxious to get my family out. I was especially desirous of having them come before the rivers broke up as they could thus cross the Yellowstone and Missouri on the ice. It was always a bad time in the spring on the Missouri when the ice began to go out, as the dangers in crossing were great and the delays were annoying. One could usually cross on the ice up to the 1st of March, but after that time it was very uncertain. I telegraphed to my wife to hurry up as the appearance was that we were to have an early spring, or early break up of the rivers. After the ice goes out, the weather in that country is always more moderate. All of the streams of any importance which empty into the Missouri above the Platte, head well south of that stream, so that I suppose has its influence in the atmosphere about Buford.

My family started and got to Chicago about March 1st when, at Buford, the river rose very rapidly and I, supposing the ice would be all out in a few days, wired my wife to wait at Chicago. The ice still hung on at the crossing of the Missouri and at Glendive, where we had to cross the Yellowstone. The end of March came and still the ice held, but I heard that the Yellowstone ice was moving so I telegraphed Mrs. Gilbreath to come on to Glendive and started to meet her.

On going to the crossing of the Missouri with my transportation, which consisted of a wagon and an ambulance both having ten mules, I found that the river had risen some 20 feet. Thus the ice which had covered the stream when it was low did not reach the bank on either side by about 30 feet, and in that 30 feet the muddy water was running like a mill race. I took the Post yawl, however, and crossed some of my Company onto the solid ice. Then taking wagons apart, we carried the pieces to the ice and so on to the other edge of the great sheet of ice in the central portion of the stream. This ice was four feet thick and was still solid. After getting the wagons over all right, I then put ropes around the head of each mule and pushing them into the water the men on the ice simply pulled the mule onto the ice. This was easily done as the ice had frozen to the bank when the river was low, so that when high water came, there was an inclined piece of ice from the central sheet to the old bank under water. We got the wagons and animals all safely across the river without any accident and I started on toward Glendive.

Ranches were few but I stopped 25 miles from Buford for the night, and again 40 miles further on the next night, and on the third day reached the bank of the Yellowstone opposite Glendive, 80 miles from Buford. There was no one living on my side of the river at this time, and I had no place to stop.

I found that an ice gorge had formed the day before my arrival at a point a couple of miles below the crossing, that the river had been dammed up and was filled with broken ice under and, for a long distance, above the ferry wire. The ice was almost up to the slack of the wire. This was a situation. I knew my wife was at the Hotel at Glendive and I did not know what to do.

Finally the mail carrier came across the river pulling himself over in what he called a basket, rigged on traveling wheels, which ran on the cable. He said I could cross well enough, so calling for a volunteer from amongst the men, I prepared to make the attempt. Having in mind my former experience at Huntley in crossing on the cable, I left my overcoat and everything I could spare with my wagons. I was heavy weighing 230 pounds, and wanted to be as light as possible. The cable for use of the ferry boat was fully 800 feet from post to post, and passed over a low post on the farther bank which was high. While the post on my side of the river was fully 30 feet high, and was simply a cottonwood tree planted there for the purpose. The "basket" consisted of a box about six feet long, a foot deep and 30 inches wide. It was tied to the post on top of which was fastened a block and tackle to draw up anything which it was desired to take across the stream. I went up first by placing a rope around [and] under my arms and fastening it to the tackle block. The men then pulled away, and up I went. Having gotten my head on a level with the box, it took a series of gymnastics for me to get into it, which were of such a straining nature as to not be of much benefit in the struggle. The man was pulled up in the same way, and I helped him in. We sat down then. He with his back to the river, and I facing him. As we were seated, the wire rope passed over our shoulders about 10 inches above them. All being ready, I let go the fastenings and away we sped down the slack of the cable with a rush.

On reaching the lowest point, we found that the ice had risen a good deal since the mail carrier had crossed so that our box struck it with force. It was awful to see the great mass of broken ice crunching and crowding and looking so angry as it seemingly boiled and surged together. Luckily no large pieces were near us, although we saw them further away rolling over and over slowly like the tumbling of a porpoise. Had we been struck by such a piece, our box would have been crushed, but we went to work with a will, and now it was a steady constant pull. That hill up the incline was the longest and steepest, seemingly, we had ever seen. We gained foot by foot and at first made fair progress. We got clear of the ice and tugged and strained. Our position sitting down, as on the previous occasion, allowed us to only use the muscles of the upper part of our bodies. On the upper part of the slack, we could only gain by [an] inch at a time. On reaching 30 feet away from the pole, we had to rest often and then struggle on again as I gave the word to pull together. Reaching the post at last, we had to rest before we could tie fast. But fastening at last, we climbed down on the post and were both never so glad before to end a journey.

I found Mrs. Gilbreath at the Hotel called the Merrill House, and we had to stop of course until the gorge broke. I sent the man back in a day or two with salt, flour and coffee, also with money for the men to buy beef. We waited there six days for the ice to leave the river clear, and finally on the sixth night, the day having been warm, the gorge broke and with a roar and a crash, the ice plunged downstream.

The next morning we prepared to cross. I had now my wife, 3 children, a servant, and seven trunks to get over.

After looking around, the only person I could get was a Canada

French-man who agreed to take us over in a mackinaw for five dollars. The ice had left the central part of the river clear and open, but the banks were piled high with great blocks, stranded when the water fell. The top of these blocks were fully 15 feet above the water, and square cut on the face toward it. We put planks down on top of these cakes of ice and then dragged our trunks to the edge and lowered them into the boat, then we went in one at a time. This boat was a peculiar one. Either end was shaped like the bow of a boat, and it was about 30 feet long, by 5 feet wide in its broadest part. The Frenchman proposed to row it himself. We had for a load 7 trunks and 9 passengers, and he cast off, and very slowly our brave little rower began to struggle with the current. From the point where we got into the boat, we had to row upstream an eighth of a mile to round the head of an island, and as he worked up inch by inch, as it seemed, I was fearful he would crash into the ice wall on the island and cause it to tumble into our boat and sink us. But no such calamity happened, for our skillful boatman only asked that we keep in the center of the boat and sit still. He got us over all right, and we loaded up and began our journey.

It was late at night when we reached the first ranch 17 miles away. The roads were heavy with mud so the going was very slow. I roused up the ranch man, and told him we wanted something to eat and a place to sleep. He said he couldn't give us much to eat but we could sleep on the floor. We got out our robes and ranged ourselves on the floor, heads to the wall in one row and slept well.

After a very plain breakfast, we started on and stopped two other nights on the way, the last one being at O'Brien's, 25 miles from Buford. There was quite a collection of houses there on each side of a clear little stream. I asked O'Brien what they called the place, he said, "Hard Scrabble." As to why, he said that none of the lands hereabouts had been surveyed yet, and all the people were simply squatters, so they would have a hard scrabble to keep a house for themselves if the surveyors did come around. O'Brien, a discharged soldier, kept a saloon, store, and a gambling place for cowboys and the usual frontier tough[s]. His wife was a first-class cook, and we enjoyed our supper and breakfast there very much.

On getting out in the morning, I found that thieves had stolen two carbines from the men and two complete sets of mule harness[es]. So I had to patch up my team and drive on with a spike team, that is, only three animals to each wagon.

On arriving at the crossing of the Missouri, I found the ice, which I had supposed would all be out, still holding on. It had moved down, and the edge nearest me was shoved up to the bank. This made it easy to go onto the ice, but the ice itself made my hair stand on edge to look at. It was seamed into irregular squares and cracked in every direction. After walking over, consulting with my wife and the ferryman, we decided to try and cross. First, we sent onto the ice the trunks one at a time, and to avoid having too much weight in one spot, a man fastened a rope about 20 feet long to the trunk and then pulled it after him over the smooth ice. Each trunk was placed in the boat referred to at the edge of the ice. Then the family went on one at a time 20 feet or so apart, and I carried Nannie, our youngest child, over in my arms. When I got into that boat and finally got to the shore, my head was aching as if it would split from the anxiety. We drove up to the Post and were soon settled at home.

———

IN THE MONTH OF APRIL, 1883, Col. Townsend, 11th Infantry, went away, and I was left in command. The Headquarters and two Companies of the 13th Infantry were ordered to the Post. The Colonel of that Regiment J.N.G. Whistler came to the Post in June, and then at once went off on a four months' leave. I was in command four months when Maj. Tilford, 7th Cavalry, came and took command. Then Col. Whistler came back and took command. After the arrival of the Headquarters, and Band of the 15th Infantry, the Post was very much gayer and pleasanter.

During the winter in January 1883, the people at Poplar River, which was 60 miles from Fort Buford, wished to have a party to celebrate an anniversary. Their garrison was small so they invited the people at Buford to go up to the party. We thought it would be great fun and so arranged to take a party in two sleighs. Each had four fine government mules attached, and we started off in good spirits. The snow was deep, but the party was merry and we got along all right, notwithstanding the cold. At a point about one-half way, one of the sleighs was overturned in the snow and so broken that we all piled into one. With the fresh teams sent out from Poplar River to meet us, we got through the second night. A part of the road was so banked up with heavy drifts, that all of the officers had to get out and shovel snow to make a path for our teams, and we were compelled to stay all night at a small ranch house about one-half way. It was very much crowded when we all got inside, but they gave us lots of venison and potatoes and fair frontier grub, so that we enjoyed the delay.

On our arrival at Poplar River we found our old friend Capt. O.B. Read, Capt. Rose and several others, and by nighttime had prepared ourselves for a good hop. The dancing people enjoyed that very much, although sliding downhill and running around in many ways for fun, had tired them somewhat. It was about 25 below zero, that night and more snow fell the next day, so that we were compelled to stay a second night. Capt. Read sent out a relay of mules for us, 15 miles and another 30 miles from the Post, and then we had two relays between the 30 mile point and Buford because the snow was heavier on that portion of the road. Having so many mules, we rushed through and made the entire 60 miles in less than 6 hours. The thermometer indicated the cold as less than zero all the way, but we did not suffer.

My son, Will, became very anxious to see a Sun Dance which was to occur at Poplar River in the summer of 1883, and he proposed going with Frank Tompkins. A Sun Dance is a ceremony of the Indians by which they imagined they displayed their fitness to be full fledged warriors, and in former times all the young men had to undergo its tortures and thus show their endurance.

It consisted of a series of tortures which they inflicted on themselves, as cutting the flesh or skin so that loops could be made to which they used to hang Buffalo skulls and then dance until the skulls dropped off by tearing out the skin. There were many other tortures to which they submitted themselves, but this will show the character of the ceremony. Will and Tompkins got a pony each and a carbine from the Cavalry, and rode to Poplar and stayed all the days devoted to the dance. This was the last Sun Dance I ever heard of, as agents and officers all exerted every means in their power to stop or break up the repetition of such affairs.

The boys then started back, and on arriving at the halfway place, had intended to stay all night, but the place was crowded so they pushed on after getting something to eat, and then there was no stopping place until they got to the Post. Night overtook them, and they then thought of the fact that they would have to pass a cabin where a crazy man lived with his brother.

It was only 12 miles from Buford, but the boys would not leave the telegraph poles for fear of getting lost, in which they showed their good sense. So they tied their ponies to a telegraph pole and laid down to sleep until daylight. They had no bedding but their saddle blankets, but I imagine they slept soundly after a 48 mile ride in one day. Next morning they came in to the Post early, and Will was about as tired as anyone I ever saw.

There was one family at Fort Buford who amused us a good deal, Maj. W. and his wife. The Major was very eccentric about some things, and one of his anxieties was to buy things cheaply. He sent for catalogues all over the United States and to England, and always had a pile of them about two feet high. In looking these catalogues over, if he saw anything he fancied, he sent for it no matter what his supply on hand might be. If shirts were cheap in New York or Chicago, he ordered a half dozen and neckties, all alike. He would get a dozen of them at a time. He never knew, and nobody else did either, how many shirts he had on hand at a time. Once in a while his idea would change to pistols, or to folding bunks, of the latter he had six or seven, which would shut up in any way. Once he had no tailor in his Company for a long time. Finally one was sent to him. The Major then ordered him to first of all make eight pairs of pants or trousers for him. The uniform was changed before he had worn out the first pair. He always ate baked beans on Saturday and never drank anything but a miserable concoction made from cocoa shells. This stuff he used to buy by the quantity, and, as it was light in weight, he had a pile of it on hand. He once read of the sleeping bags used by Arctic explorers and decided to have one made of canvas and lined with a blanket. When it was complete, he tried it and got his man, or striker, to tie the string about his neck after the Major had gotten himself fixed inside. The man tied the string and begun to laugh. The Major asked what he was laughing about. But the man only laughed more, and left the room and house with the Major tied up helpless on the floor.

He was in command of a Post on the 4th of July once, and the men were having their usual sports, amongst which was to be a blindfold wheelbarrow race. Two of the men had arranged a little conspiracy by which they could win the ten dollar prize offered for the winner in the race. The man blindfolded was to listen for his partner to scrape the gravel with his foot when the one blindfolded was to start his wheelbarrow toward the sound. When the one who could see was to run away making signs and passing beyond the goal, would thus lead the blindfolded man to the winning point. Just at the signal for starting, the Major came along, head down thinking about something. He stubbed his toe and scratched the gravel. It was the signal, and the wheelbarrow started with a jump for the sound. Major quickened his pace and so did the wheelbarrow man. The Major finally ran, and the wheelbarrow man ran after him fast as he could go, chased the Commanding Officer onto a porch.

Col. W. and his family were amusing also, and they had the greatest faculty of telling harmless little lies on anyone I ever saw. A peculiarity of the family was that one member might tell what, on its face, would be without doubt a whopper, clear and undeniable. The other would listen respectfully and then with seeming joy, repeat the story as a true incident. In this they always reminded me of Indians, as these people, when gathered at one of their story-telling pow-wows, will sit around in a circle, while some copper colored liar gets up and tells how he stole so many horses on one occasion, on another counted a certain number of cows, or killed so many enemies who were carried off. There is no question or thought of denial on the part of his listeners. His speech finished, and his numbers emphasized by the little things he placed before his hearers, they simply look stolid and wise and say, "How, How" all around, when another member of the party gets up and just simply lays the first liar out cold by the size and number of his exploits. All the stories of my friend's were inoffensive ones, as if one killed a deer [and] the same shot almost invariably went through another which got away. If one saw ten antelope, [the] story fixed 100 as the number, etc. The old gentleman was courtly and kind-hearted, and I never heard either his wife or himself say a wrongful word of anyone. Only on one occasion did I ever hear any resentment from one of them for what another said, and that was when the old lady told once of going from Fort Keough on a boat to Bismarck, Dakota, in 24 hours having stopped for a few hours at Fort Buford on the way. The old gentleman listened respectfully, but as she finished, protested that the time was too short as it usually took four to six days. She insisted hotly that her trip was only 24 hours. He finally said, "But you couldn't have done it, my dear, unless you had been shot out of a cannon."

About the same time that Col. Whistler came to the post, Maj. Tilford, 7th Cavalry received his promotion to be Lieutenant Colonel of the same regiment and, of course, wanted to give some sort of an entertainment to celebrate the event. Mrs. Tilford was a very fine lady, and prepared a hop and supper for every officer at the Post, and the ladies. The hop was in a building separate from the quarters, and we all enjoyed it very much. Mrs. T. had given instructions about arranging tables about her rooms for the accommodation of her guests, and supposed everything would be prepared as she directed. Her husband wanted to be of use, so without the knowledge of his wife, went off and hired a colored man who said he understood things to assist the regular help at his quarters.

The man proved to be a regular bull in a china shop. He went to work with vigor and taking out the small tables Mrs. T. had ordered, put in one long table and crowded onto it all the dishes he could lay hold of and placed about it all the chairs he could find, so that it looked like a long crowded hotel table. Mrs. T. went home a little before the hop was to break up, and was horrified to see the new man and his wreck of all her plan, but she went to work and, putting the things off of the table in a hurry, soon got her small tables in place again. We saw nothing wrong on leaving the hop and arriving at the Colonel's house, but it was soon discovered that everything ran short. The supply of salads and cake and almost everything but coffee was very scant. Mrs. T. was much annoyed and could not understand it. Next morning, however, she discovered the cause, on cleaning out the rooms, as she found behind a curtain here, a fine bowl of delicious salad, or in a corner there, a tempting dish of something else. It appeared that in the hasty removal of dishes from the big table, dishes had been placed hastily in any space found. They had been forgotten, and so the guests of the evening were deprived of much which had been prepared for them.

Game was very plentiful all about Buford. We used to have our companies well supplied during the winter with deer, geese and ducks. A favorite hunting place was at the Muddy, 25 miles below Buford. It was called Little Muddy to distinguish it from the Big Muddy which emptied into the Missouri 30 miles above the Post.

On one occasion four of us went on a hunting trip to the Muddy. We had an open spring wagon. I never was much of a hunter myself, but my friend, the Doctor, was first class in every way.

None of us had ever seen the stream to which we were going, so that as we approached it over the prairie, we did not know we were so close to it. As we rode down into the valley, the Doctor got out to follow up a flock of prairie chickens which had dropped in the grass a short distance away. He approached cautiously, and as the birds arose, he fired both barrels and brought down two birds, while from nearby, and for miles above and below us, the ducks and geese and brant and crane arose by the thousands from the waters of the stream. They had been hidden from sight by the banks of the stream, and as they arose with much squawking and flapping of wings, we were all too much astonished to do anything but look in amazement.

The Doctor gathered up his two prairie chickens finally, and we began beating downstream towards Mathew's house at the mouth of it where we were to stop. We got several mallard and some small ducks, that is, the Doctor did, and we started along in the wagon. We came in sight of an oat field near his house on which we saw numberless geese feeding. I, in sport, asked the Doctor if he wanted a goose. He told me it was no use for *me* to try, but I got out of the wagon and setting my sights on my army rifle at 800 yards, fired into the flock. They all arose but one. I had winged a fine large gander, the first killed by our party. The next morning Capt. M. and Mr. Hedderick went up the creek very early while the doctor and I went out to the oat field and hid in the straw which had been recently thrashed. It was beautiful to see the geese come sailing around a little after daylight, with their peculiar honk honk, and light on the ground to feed, but too far away to shoot at. But the numbers increased, and they began to fly closer over head. We killed several and had all we could carry to the house. The other party did not do so well. Next morning Doctor and I went across the creek, and he left me while he went upstream alone. The idea was if either fired we might drive game to the other. I was possibly the laziest too, and let my more active friend go the longest distance. I laid down on the bank of the creek behind a sort of a bluff and did not notice that I was directly between two cut oat fields separated about 2½ miles, until I thought I heard a distant honk. I peered over the bank and, far off, saw a great flock coming directly toward me and flying low. I got ready, although I was excited at the sight. As they came close enough, I fired both barrels and down came two. No sound from the doctor. After a time, and several times, I got good shots and succeeded in killing seven. By this time I heard the doctor's gun far off, and shortly he appeared with four little Teal ducks. I had placed my game up on the bank in a row and then had hidden myself. The Doctor approached and came suddenly on my string of geese. He said, "Well by thunder, you have been raising H haven't you." We sent as many ducks and geese to the Post as we could by the mail carrier and in four days from our arrival, went home ourselves. We had 180 ducks and 75 geese.

BUFORD WAS, IN 1883, WELL OUT OF CIVILIZATION, and we used to do a good deal of shopping by mail, but from the last boat in October to the end of April we seldom saw many strangers and had to rely upon ourselves for amusement and entertainment. In the winter we had hops regularly every week, and almost every night had had something going on. We had a reading circle and card parties. Our ladies were not always up in fashion, but most dressed well. One lady sent home for a fine bonnet or hat. It came and was the envy of every beholder. She wore it during the entire winter and in the spring visited her friends in Chicago. They greeted her with laughter which, she discovered, was at the pride of her life, the hat. On inquiry, she discovered that she had been wearing it all the time hind part before.

We played whist a great deal, and our neighbor J.F. Bell and ourselves used to meet very often for that purpose.

Long before the country about the upper Missouri was occupied by United States forces, trading posts were established on many of the streams and they were always called Forts, although only occupied by traders and their employees. One near the mouth of the Big Horn on Tullocks Fork, to which it gave the name, was called Tullocks Fort. One lower down the Yellowstone was called Fort Alexander, another Fort Gilbert, and at Buford, exactly on the 105th degree of longitude, was one called Fort Union. All of these places were in ruins at the time we were at Buford, but they had undoubtedly been built very strong and substantial to resist attack.

Fort Union was about a mile and a half from the flagstaff at Buford, and all about it the Gros Ventre (pronounced Gro Von) Indians had an extensive camp, and they raised a good deal of corn and garden stuff. Their Chief was named "Crow Flies High," and they had built for themselves quite comfortable tents. They were very filthy and lived mostly on their pickings about the Post. In the center of their camp, or collection of houses, they had put up an enclosed Council House. It was about 100 feet in diameter and was nearly round and covered with earth as were all their huts. A hole was left in the top to let out smoke, and around the walls lived a good many families. In the center of the room was a fire for their cooking. They used to dance almost without ceasing in the Council House, and, if any of the officers went to the camp for any official purpose, they were always received in this Council House. The smell of the place, when filled up with a crowd of men, women and children, a howling lot of wretches, was indescribable and well nigh unbearable. We all used to go there occasionally to see their performances.

Once the Crees came down from toward the northern boundary for the purpose of stealing horses from the Gros Ventres or to kill any stray Indian found away from camp. The latter turned out on mules and went after the Crees, squaws and children came into the Post for protection. The Gros Ventres caught up with one lone Cree and killed him, and there was great show of brag and talk of brave deeds. The squaws cut off the hands of the victim, and putting them on sticks, went howling and singing all about their camp. The scalp and hands were displayed before every house and gifts begged from the occupants.

One of these Indians had been taken, when a boy, by some well meaning person to Amherst, Mass., where he had been educated and given the trades of painter and tinner. He was sent back to this band for his home in the hope, no doubt, that he would teach the whole party with at least a little of the good he had been taught. But he was too lazy to profit by his education and, when we knew him, was about the most worthless of the disgusting lot. This is the outcome in the majority of such cases, and it seems almost a cruelty to take Indians, as [in] is this case, and after giving them a chance to see the benefits and comforts of civilized life, then to turn them back to their tribe to grovel again in the ignorance and filth of their fellows. They return there, and no matter what their teaching may have been, are forced by those with whom they live to be like the rest. They have no opportunities for keeping up the good habits taught them. They are ridiculed as squaws if they do not paint and dance with the rest, and are easily tempted to marry two or three squaws, as often as they like, and either at once or gradually out-Herod Herod in their ways. An Indian cannot stand it to be ridiculed.

―――

WHILE STATIONED AT FORT BUFORD IN 1883, the Post was aroused by a report of the robbery of the paymaster, Maj. Whipple. He came into the Post and had a wonderful tale of his adventure to tell. He had received his money by express at Glendive, Montana. It came to him in small compact boxes which he put into his ambulance under the seat as he took it from the express office, while the small iron safe he usually carried was placed in a escort wagon where his guard rode. He had for transportation one ambulance and an escort wagon and his guard consisted of a sergeant and 16 men. The sergeant rode with the paymaster and his clerk in the ambulance. They came to a long hill where the ascent was steep and the escort wagon was at the foot of the hill while the Major went up it. As he reached the top and his lead mules in a four mules team got to the top, without any warning whatever the robbers, masked, began to fire at the mules and the people in the ambulance. The sergeant was killed. The paymaster clerk jumped out, and the driver fell out as he was shot. The mules started to run as they were startled by the shooting, and the Major got hold of the reins and whipped up for all he could.

In the meantime one mule was shot in the ambulance team and another party of robbers attacked the escort wagon. Taking the soldiers unprepared, they had them at their mercy, soon disarmed them. The robbers supposing the money was in the safe did not pursue the Major in the ambulance. He had the money with him, and they got nothing from the safe. The Paymaster had a long ride of ten or twelve miles by himself before he could get to a ranch. But he finally got away, and reached it in safety. He sent a man on a mule to the Post. A troop of Cavalry went out, but could not arrest any of the robbers, and they were never caught. This was the last time such careless escort duty was performed.

———

IN 1883, 1884, 1885 AND 1886 WE HAD a great deal of target practice and as then conducted, it was hard work. We used to go out before breakfast and stay all day at the work of firing on the target. It was a great strain on the eyes, and I now feel the effects of it. The system has changed a good deal since those days.

CHAPTER 15

Fort Yates & to New York

1886-1887

I n the spring of 1886, our Companies C and H, 11th Infantry, and the two at Poplar River, B and F, were ordered to Fort Yates, Dakota, for station. We thus returned to Standing Rock agency, after being away since 1877, and having served at Fort Custer, Buford, and on duties detaching us along the Yellowstone River.

Yates was now commanded by Maj. I. H. Page of our Regiment and, in addition to our companies, we had two troops of the 7th Cavalry, McDougal's and Godfrey's. This Post was much improved since we left it, and some of the quarters were very fine indeed for the frontier. Life in this garrison was very pleasant as we had a fine lot of people there, some with very decided theatrical talent, so that we had a round of parties, musicales and theatricals, and spent a very pleasant winter.

I was in charge of target practice and Inspector of Supplies for the Sioux Indians, their agency called Standing Rock being just outside our Post. These Indians were very much advanced in civilization. Many of them were farming, and whereas in 1877, when we left this Post, none at all of them wore citizens' clothing, but all were blanket Indians and wild as one could imagine, now in 1886 they were all clothed like white men, and many had cut their hair and had advanced in many ways towards civilization. There were many schools on the reserve and a few churches.

Standing Rock was called by that name because of a stone found near the agency. It was about four feet high and had been carried by some natural cause to a point on the open ground some distance from any other rocks, and had there become imbedded in the soil and stood in an upright position. It was about five feet high and round and smooth. The waters of the Missouri River had probably fixed it where it stood. Being a mile or more from other stones, it was a noticeable object. The Indians looked upon it as "good medicine," and they kept it painted in gaudy colors and surrounded it with offerings of various kinds: pieces of calico or red flannel, bows and arrows, etc., and amongst them it was a widely known landmark, and about it was a famous gathering place for their sun dances and great councils.

During my stay at Fort Yates, I was the Inspector of Supplies for the Standing Rock agency for the Sioux Indians, and I used to inspect all the goods received for them on contract: horses and cattle, etc. I had to attend the issue of beef to the Indians, and while the sight was a very picturesque one and highly interesting, it was at the same time disgusting at times. The cattle were weighed in bunches of five or six and then driven off the scales onto a narrow passageway where they were branded with a hot iron. Or, if they were to be issued to the Indians, they were simply turned into a pen and killed by the Indians themselves. The Indians were and always are entirely without any merciful feelings for a dumb animal, so that they were especially cruel at the killing time. We used often to see Sitting Bull and other noted Indians at the agency.

———

IN THE MONTH OF JUNE, 1887, I was ordered to Fort Mead in the Black Hills on a Court Martial. It was only about 250 miles across the country to Mead, but I was compelled to go around by way of Saint Paul to get there as there was no rail communication across the country to Mead. From St. Paul, I went to Missouri Valley Junction and thence through northern Nebraska to Chadron, south of the Black Hills, and then north to Rapid City, which was the end of the railroad. From Rapid City we went by ambulance to Fort Mead 25 miles further north. The trip through Nebraska and the Hills was all new to me so that I enjoyed it very much. It was interesting to see along the Elk Horn Valley, such a beautiful rolling prairie country with farms all along the way, and the regularly planted trees everywhere. The Black Hills were new to me also and very interesting.

At Mead we were received in the most cordial manner, and the hospitality extended was beyond anything I ever saw before. The garrison consisted of several troops of the 7th Cavalry with their headquarters, and four companies of the 25th (Colored) Infantry. The 7th is an elegant regiment and has long been known for its style. We were at the Post two weeks and we had a perfect round of entertainment: balls, card parties, breakfasts and dinners. On one occasion we were taken to Deadwood, the mining center of the Black Hills. My host was Capt. Thomas McDougall, and he drove me with his team. It was all the way uphill from the Post, and I saw so many interesting and amusing things that I enjoyed the trip very much. We went to the longest stamp mill in the world, and saw all the phases of mining and washing out the gold. It was 18 miles from the Post to Deadwood, and we returned to the latter not at all tired.

While I was walking on the street of Deadwood, a man came to me and said, in a maudlin sort of a way for he was drunk, "Hello Major, I know you." I said, "You have the advantage of me." He said, "Well I 'spose so, but I am Vennatten and used to belong to the 20th Ind. Regt. while you were Major of it."

So we sat down and had a chat of old war times. He was a well-to-do farmer living about 30 miles from Deadwood, and prosperous in every way. After our talk was over, I got up to go and he shook me warmly by the hand and said, "I do like to get up to Deadwood once a month or so and have a little Toot," and I bade him good-bye. He said, "So long, Major, the world ain't so infernally big after all, is it? We will bump up against one another, after all, once in a while."

I was surprised to see such an air of progress and thrift about the people of the Black Hills, and some of the stores in Deadwood were splendid. Soon as the Court Martial had finished its sessions, I left to go to Fort Yates by the same route I had gone to Mead, but decided I would go to Chicago and meet my daughter, Etta, who was coming out from Philadelphia, Pa., where she had been going to school. So at Chadron, I took a car for Chicago and had a pleasant journey through Nebraska, Iowa and Illinois to Chicago, where I stopped with my sister until my daughter had arrived.

On the way in from Fort Mead, I met a wholesale grocery man named Kingman from Chicago and, in talking with him of my children, he proposed that I bring my son, Will, to Chicago where he said he would give him employment. So I telegraphed my son to meet my daughter at Harrisburg and come with her to Chicago. They arrived there on the first vestibuled train which ran into Chicago. My son went to work for Gray Kingman & Co. and in a few days, I left for Saint Paul and Fort Yates where Etta and I arrived about the 28th of June.

We were astonished to receive an order in a few days to change station with our Regiment from Dakota to New York. I was very sorry I had not known of this before, as I would not have brought my daughter out from the East. But, we began packing up at once, and selling out all we could of our old things, and pictured many delights for an eastern station. We left Fort Yates in the last days of July, 1887, and were to go by boat to Bismarck, Dakota, and then take the cars. Lieut. Col. Bush was in command, and at Fort Lincoln we were to be joined by Company G., Capt. Noble. We took cars at Bismarck and so bade good-bye to the muddy waters of the Missouri along which we had served ten years. We now remember that service with much pleasure. Going into the country when it was all wild and uninhabited, we had watched the incoming of the people with much interest and we found many pleasures in our service.

From Bismarck we journeyed by the cars to Duluth, Minn., where we were to join the headquarters and the other companies of our Regiment. They had been serving at Fort Tully lower down the Missouri. At Duluth we met the 12th Infantry, with whom we were to change station, so that we had the two regular regiments at Duluth at one time. We put our companies on the *Vanderbilt*, a lake steamer, while all the officers and their wives, except one officer for each company, went on board of the steamer *Japan*. The two senior Captains, Sanderson and myself, got our Companies onto the *Japan*, where our Band and headquarters were also. The trip from Duluth to Buffalo was too nice to ever forget. The weather was perfect, and we sailed through Lakes Superior, Huron and Erie, stopping at all of the most important towns on the way.

We had a crowd of people on board, and every evening had music, dancing or theatricals, and a jolly good time.

At Detroit we met Col. Chipman whom I relieved at Fort Buford, and we stopped at Cleveland and many other places. The only storm we had was in Lake Huron and as it was at night and, not much of a blow, we did not notice it very much. I was ordered to Fort Wood, N.Y. Harbor, but got the order changed so that I went to Sacketts Harbor, New York, along with Headquarters of the Regiment. At Buffalo we took cars and rode the length of Lake Ontario to our station, while Company C, Capt. Sanderson and Company F, Capt. Read went to Oswego and Plattsburg. Company E and Company K went to Fort Niagara under command of Maj. Pugh. Lt. Col. Bush went with us to Sacketts Harbor. We were now in the heart of civilization as we thought and found a real old-time Post.

The men's quarters had been built in 1819 and some of the officers' quarters were equally old. I got a very good house and was very comfortably located. The Post was built on an arm of Lake Ontario called Black River Bay from the fact that Black River, heading in the Adirondack Mountains, here emptied into the Lake. It was the central one of three Bays with a single entrance from the lake. Chamoux and Henderson Bays were on the right and left of Black River Bay, and each of them was a beautiful sheet of water. There was lots of fish in all of these waters, and the fishing, sailing and bathing were superb during the summer, and ice boating, skating and sleighing on the ice was fine for those who like such sport. This part of the lake was really at the head of the St. Lawrence, and we made trips to the Thousand Islands as often as we liked.

COMMENTARY: *Fort Yates, Dakota Territory, was established in 1874 on the Missouri River as headquarters of the Standing Rock agency, heart of the Sioux reservation and home of chief Sitting Bull—who had led the Indians at the Battle of Little Bighorn in 1876. After that battle, he fled to Canada, then returned and was pardoned; in 1890 he was murdered near Fort Yates during the Ghost Dance uprising.*

When gold was discovered in the Black Hills in Indian territory in 1875, a gold rush ensued and the population of Deadwood soon topped 25,000. With renewed hostilities between Plains Indians and white settlers and miners, Fort Meade (named for Maj. General George Meade) was established in 1878 to protect settlers and gold miners.

By the 1880s, steel passenger steamers, like Vanderbilt *and* Japan, *were a common sight on the Great Lakes.* Japan *regularly operated between Duluth and Buffalo, a thousand-mile voyage.*

CHAPTER 16

SACKETTS HARBOR, NY

1888-1890

n the summer of 1888 we made our first visit to the Islands. We chartered a boat, and left the Post with all of the Officers on board and their families, accompanied by our band. The start was made at 8 A.M. We went out to the Lake and then down the St. Lawrence on the Canadian side as far as Alexandria Bay where we stopped for dinner, and then came up on the American side, stopping at several places, and reached home about 10 o'clock P.M. the same day. The Canadian side of the river, about the Thousand Islands, was then in a state of nature and was completely wild, while on the American side as it was called, or United States side, all the islands were in a high state of modern improvement with fine hotels and residences. The comparison was very interesting. We made one other trip while stationed at Sacketts Harbor, and both of these excursions were delightful.

We had a visit from two of our nieces whose homes were in Philadelphia, Pa., one from Baltimore, and a young lady schoolmate of my daughter Etta. These four girls had never seen anything of Army life, so they were very much interested in everything they saw. They went with us to the Thousand Islands. The town of Sacketts Harbor was an insignificant little town of about 700 people, about the deadest place I ever saw, and the country around about was so old-fashioned that one might think he had dropped into a past age. We were compelled to send our little daughter, Nannie, on the train to Watertown for school. She had to go from home on Monday morning, and return on Friday night, boarding in Watertown in the meantime.

IN 1889 I WAS SENT TO FORT NIAGARA with my Company for Target Practice and spent a few weeks there very pleasantly. The same year all of our companies were ordered to New York City to take part in the exercises in celebration of the 100th anniversary of the inauguration of George Washington to be President of the U.S. Our battalion, of four companies, was under the command of Lieut. Col. Bush, and our band was with us. We went from Sacketts Harbor via the Delaware and Lackawanna Railroad to Hoboken, N. J., and thence by boat to Governor's Island, [in N.Y. Harbor]. We slept on the floor in some of the offices on the Island, while the men occupied old Castle William. There was a procession made by President Harrison over the same route as that taken by President Washington from Elizabethport, N.J., to the foot of Wall St., to the Equitable Building, to the customs house, and old Saint Paul's Church.

There was a naval review, as the President passed up the Harbor, which we witnessed from the top of Castle William. The next day we marched up Broadway to Central Park, and thence to the North River where we went on board a boat to return to Governor's Island. The march up Broadway and Fifth Avenue was grand, as the entire route was lined with crowds of people, and at Union Square, President Harrison reviewed the column. National Guard Regiments were in the column from all of the original 13 colonies or states as well as the Governors of each.

After the review was over, we returned to Governor's Island and then to our Post, having passed a week away from it as pleasantly as one could wish. I was sent the same year, 1889, to Fort Niagara on a Court Martial and was accompanied by my daughter, Etta, who had a pleasant visit with Lt. Col. and Mrs. Bush who were then stationed at that Post.

———

IN 1890 I WAS SENT AGAIN TO FORT NIAGARA for Target Practice, which I finished in ten days, and on my return was ordered, with my Company and one other, to the camp of the Pennsylvania National Guard at Mount Gretna, Pa. Lt. Col. Bush was in command of the Battalion of two companies which were each made up of 60 men. The ride down through New York and Pennsylvania was delightful as we passed through the Wyoming Valley and that of the Susquehanna. Mount Gretna was a fine place for a camp on the property of Mr. Coleman who was a very public spirited individual, and gave his land free for the purpose, as well as furnishing floors for tents, water pipes conveying fine spring water all over the grounds, and many other comforts.

The Pennsylvania National Guard is a fine organization having 8000 men in the Camp, and it was an instructive lesson to most of our officers there, being only two who had ever seen so many soldiers together. The Regular Army was represented by two troops of Cavalry, two batteries of Artillery, two Companies of Infantry, and our little Brigade. We attracted a great deal of attention as all were well drilled. President Benjamin H. Harrison reviewed us at Mount Gretna also. We were in camp a week when we returned to Sacketts Harbor. One day I drilled my company in bayonet exercise in a level place between the hills. The National Guardsmen covered the high ground to the number of 5000, I suppose, and the drill was near to most of them, so that as my men, well drilled, went through the various movements, the onlookers cheered everything. It was a pretty sight, and they showed their appreciation of it by long and loud applause.

A cloud was cast over the pleasure of our stay at Gretna by receipt of the news that our Adjutant had suddenly gone insane and had died. Lt. Philbrick was his name, and he was esteemed by everyone.

After my return to Sacketts Harbor, I was again sent to Fort Niagara on a Court Martial, and this time Mrs. Gilbreath went with me. We stopped at Buffalo for a day or so and at Niagara Falls which we looked over fully. We were at the latter place while the work on the tunnel for the supply of water power was begun at the bottom of the tunnel. There was a great celebration. Fort Niagara is at the mouth of the Niagara River where it empties into Lake Ontario and is a very old Post, having been started first by the French and occupied by the British. There are many interesting points about the place on both sides of the river. Old Fort George on the Canadian side is only one-half mile away from the Fort on this side.

On the occasion of one of my visits there, the Canadian Militia was encamped at Fort George. They numbered about 3500 and presented a very fine appearance with red coats. They seemed to be well drilled, and their maneuvers were very interesting. We made up a party of our officers and called at their camp and were very hospitably received.

It had been decided in 1889 that later we should go from Sacketts Harbor to Fort Niagara by boat. I was sent in command of two companies on a very small steamer. The men had to be on deck most of the time, and the cabin was very small and stuffy. Soon after leaving Madison Barracks, about the time we got fairly into the lake, a storm came on and we came very near being lost. Everybody was very sick. My daughter was with me, and it was only by the most careful work that we got into Oswego. I then protested against going on so small a boat, and so they sent us the rest of the way on a much larger one where we were all comfortable.

During our stay at Madison Barracks, I was often sent on Courts Martial to Plattsburg and enjoyed such trips immensely. The road took us almost to Ogdensburg and thence east, and passed through a beautiful and highly cultivated country. Plattsburg itself was a very interesting, old-fashioned place and being of such historical interest was especially attractive. The Post was on the bank of Lake Champlain, and there were many ruins of old forts used in the war of 1812 on the reserve.

There were a few good churches in Sacketts Harbor, and we had a pew in the Presbyterian Church there and became very fond of Mr. Webber, the pastor. Old Col. Camp, an antiquated resident of the village, was a very amusing old bachelor who entertained us with long stories of the early days of Sacketts Harbor. During the war of 1812 this had been one of the principal ports on our side of the lake, and such a navy as we had made the bay there a rendezvous. A battle was fought there, and ships were built and outfitted there.

FORT HUACHUCA, ARIZONA

1891-1892

We had many rumors of a change of station for our regiment in the summer of 1891. A telegram was received from the War Department in September which seemed to put at rest all our rumors, saying that we would not go that year. So Mrs. G. and I went over to Watertown in a carriage to make some calls, etc., and had a right enjoyable time. We got back to the Post about dark, and the first greeting we received was from one of our friends who called out the orders have arrived. Sure enough orders had come for four of our companies to go with Headquarters, 11th Infantry, to Fort Huachuca, Arizona. We had hoped to stay another year so that we were a good deal annoyed. Mrs. G. and I would hardly have gone to Watertown that day, or have enjoyed our quail on toast so much if we had known we were so soon to take so long a journey. It was directed that we should change station with the 9th Infantry, and should take their transportation going back to Arizona. So we stirred ourselves and disposing of all surplus, packed up our goods to be ready. The day the 9th Infantry arrived, we marched out of the Post and embarked on the cars. The Companies going with us were H, F, B and G. Orders came that only two should go to Huachuca, the other two to Fort Apache. H, my company, and F were selected to go with the Colonel to Huachuca.

We had a special train for ourselves and another for our baggage, and we went first to Buffalo, then to Cleveland. At the latter place we stopped several hours and had a good chance to go up and see the city. It was Sunday but a crowd of us walked uptown. The next place of importance was

Chicago, and there we also made a good stay all day. My old friend Capt. Fowler of the 2nd Cavalry happened to be in the city right from Huachuca where we were going. I had served with him at Fort Custer in 1881, and was very glad to see him once again. He told me to go right into his house at Huachuca, and stay as long as we wished until we got settled in our own quarters. The next city was Kansas City from Chicago; we traveled all the way by the Atchison, Topeka and Santa Fe Railroad. It is a fine road, the eating houses being especially good. We passed through Kansas, Nebraska, Colorado and stopped for a few hours at Albuquerque, New Mexico. Here we were to separate from the companies going to Fort Apache, and we said good-bye with many regrets. We went on south while they went west. We crossed the Rocky Mountains at Ruicon and, for the first time in our lives, were over the Continental divide and on the Pacific slope. At Deming our trains were to go over the Southern Pacific to Benson and from the latter place we were to go south 30 miles to a siding, seven miles from Fort Huachuca. From the station to the Post we had to ascend the mountain all the way, and we found a very nice Post indeed at the end of the journey. The railroad running south from Benson extends to Guaymas on the Gulf of California.

Fort Huachuca, pronounced Wa-chu-ka, was almost 6000 feet above the level of the sea. The officers' quarters were all built of adobe or sun dried bricks, and were very comfortable. The Post was supplied with water from a mountain spring, and the wood from the live oak which abounded all about. It was 20 miles from Tombstone and about 8 miles north of the boundary between the United States and Mexico. The climate was perfect, although winds used to spin down from the mountains with great force sometimes. We soon settled in our own house, and Fowler came back from his leave. We had occupied his house as he requested and found everything in very fine order. He had a Chinaman cook who was a splendid one. The garrison was the pleasantest I had ever seen or served in. We had Fowler and Rowall's troops of the 2nd Cavalry, our two companies of the 11th Infantry with the band, and a fine lot of ladies and gentlemen with nothing to mar our enjoyment. We used to get fish and oysters from the Gulf of California, oranges from Hermosillo, Mexico. All these things were especially fine. Oranges were the best I have ever seen. After a while a Company of Indians came to the Post. They were from the Apache bands and were a hard looking crowd. They drilled very well indeed, and got to looking a good deal like soldiers

———

I COULD NEVER SEE ANYTHING GOOD IN AN INDIAN. They used to commit very serious offenses against each other, and occasionally seemed to be in an alarming state. In March 1892, I was ordered to go on a Court Martial to meet at San Diego, California, with Col. DeRussey and Maj. Bradford from our Post. It was a fine trip, and I especially enjoyed it as I had never been in California. We were 2½ days going to San Diego and on arrival there went to the Hotel Del Coronado. This Hotel was situated on a sandy peninsula in front of the City of San Diego and at the shore of the ocean, and the tropical growth of trees, plants and flowers delighted me.

I found in San Diego my old friend Mr. John Harbinson, who was a brother of William H. with whom I used to live at Newcastle, Pa. in 1855, and '57. He had made his fortune off the raising and sale of bees and honey. William Harbinson had packed and shipped 300 hives of bees to California in 1856 which I helped him put up. He took them via the Isthmus of Panama as there was no railroad across the continent in those days. Mr. John Harbinson received me very kindly, invited me to his house to dinner, and sent me to drive over the city with his daughter, who took me to all the points of interest about the city.

By the way, the Post was commanded my old friend Maj. Whitemore, 10th Infantry, with whom I had served at Fort Buford ten years before. He was just as eccentric as ever. He lived at the Coronado Hotel so I saw a good deal of him.

After a delightful stay of a week, we left for Los Angeles. At Los Angeles I met Genl. McCook for the first time. He was in command of the Department and received us very nicely indeed. He invited us to go to Redondo Beach with him, and as his guests there, we had a delightful time. Redondo was a very attractive place as the beach was perfect and beautiful. The Hotel was very fine. We were driven all about Los Angeles by a member of Genl. McCook's staff and found it a lovely city. After spending two days altogether in and about Los Angeles, we left for home at Huachuca. While I was at San Diego, my wife was at Huachuca, my daughter Etta with her, and my daughter Nan was in Philadelphia, Pa., so that, with my son in Chicago, we were pretty well scattered over the U.S. When we were ordered to Arizona, we sent Nan to school at Philadelphia.

The garrison was so harmonious and so pleasant in every way, that my old friend Fowler used to say, "Well Gil, it can't last, it can't last, this is too nice." So sure enough in May 1892, Headquarters, 11th Infantry, was ordered to go to Whipple Barracks at Prescott, Arizona, and I was ordered to take our two companies, F and H. to San Carlos. This was an agency for the Apache Indians, and there was a Post there of one troop of Cavalry and two companies of Infantry.

I was to be in command. I took the companies to Benson and to a station called Wilcox on the Southern Pacific Railroad, and from there we were to march 110 miles to San Carlos. It was a very barren desert-like country to march through. On leaving Huachuca, we had packed and stored all of our household goods except a few such things as we absolutely needed to use at San Carlos. My wife with all of the ladies stayed at Huachuca until we could get to San Carlos and get ready for them. The great difficulty about the march to San Carlos was to find water for camping places. It was 27 miles from Wilcox to Fort Grant, and water could only be obtained at one place six miles from Wilcox. I had to march along what was called Sulphur Springs Valley, and it was simply a dusty hot plain. I got contractors wagons and, having loaded on baggage, left Wilcox about 11 A.M. The marching was terrible, for although it was only May, every growing thing was burned up and the dust in the road was deep and fine as flour. I marched the men 50 minutes then halted 10, and got to the M Ranch about 3 P.M., and there found that the owner had dug two wells for watering stock and, having windmills, had an abundance of clear cold water. We camped and put up tents. A wind storm came up next morning and the dust just was unbearable. I decided to march at night, so left camp about 5 P.M. intending to get as near Fort Grant as possible.

The men marched well, and as darkness fell we kept spinning along. I knew I could not go all the way to Grant, so soon as I found the men getting tired, and judging by the time that we had been on the road that we had marched far enough. I had the wagons pull to one side of the road and made a halt. This was what we call a dry camp. That is camping without wood or water. It was about 12 o'clock at night when the men were all sound asleep having eaten the lunch which they brought with them. Next morning at daybreak, I had the reveille sounded and loading up, started for Grant. We had ascended on all our march during the night, and camped about six miles from Fort Grant. The prospect was beautiful as we marched along that morning as we could see far over the country, over the plain called Sulphur Springs Valley to the mountains beyond.

There was a little grass along the road, plenty of cactus and a kind of a palm looking plant which grew in abundance. We could see Fort Grant from the start and, the morning being pleasant, the men travelled rapidly. Before 9 A.M. we got to the Post and, having reported to the Commanding Officer, I was assigned to a camp near the Post and along the bank of a beautiful clear running mountain stream. The Post was garrisoned by the 1st U.S. Cavalry, and we were received by them in the nicest way. Col. Arnold and all of the officers called on us; Maj. Carroll, 1st Cav., with whom I had served at Fort Concho long before, being among them. The Colonel sent his band into camp to serenade us, and it was all very pleasant.

The next day we started again, and our road led us through about the roughest country I ever saw. It was up and downhill and very rocky. We camped that night at a miner's ranch called Shot Gun Smith's. There was no running water, but he had a fine well, and our camp was in a gulch with Mount Graham near by. Shot Gun Smith was a regular frontier character. He had served all through the War of the Rebellion, and then had drifted west having been stage driver and stage guard, cowboy, miner, and a little of everything. He came to the southwest country before the construction of any railroad, and first entered the employ of the great stage company which carried the mails across the continent from Fort Smith in Arkansas to San Diego and San Francisco. Indians were very bad in those days, and the stage drivers and keepers of stage stands or stations were in constant danger of losing their lives from a sudden attack by Indians. Smith's life was one of constant danger and adventure. After driving and guarding stages on the road for a while, he was placed in charge of a stage where the horses were changed, and his station was on one of the branches of the Gila River.

One occasion, he and his two companions had reason to suppose Indians about, so the two of them went out to see what they could find. It was very early morning, and their custom was for one man to go each day at dawn to look for Indian signs. These two went one-half mile from the station when they were suddenly attacked by a quite large war party and had to make a dash to get home again. It was a life and death race. His companion was killed while Smith got into the buildings without a scratch. The two then left alive continued the fight and, as they had plenty of guns and ammunition, one loaded while the other fired at anything coming into sight. The Indians took possession of one side of the corral yard and finally crowded the two white men into one corner building. Smith's companion was killed and he had to do the fighting alone. The struggle was kept up about 48 hours from the first attack, and ended only when a stage from the east and one from the west hove in sight. Both had been kept back by Indians, and Smith's life was only saved by a chance.

He was a bright intelligent man from New York State and had a mine near where we camped and he was working it, getting out a small amount of gold. The hills all about, and almost all the way from Fort Grant to the Valley of the Gila, were giving signs of gold, but in small quantity and so far from water, wood, etc., as to be of little use. Our march the next day took us to the first water at Cedar Springs, 14 miles. We passed that place after a short halt, and camped 3 miles further on at a place called Wham's Hill where we found a well with good water. This place was so named because of the robbery of Maj. Wham, the paymaster of the Army, a couple of years before. The robbers had a perfect trap laid for the paymaster. They were Mormons and desperate characters of the Gila Valley. The place at which this robbery took place was peculiar. After leaving Cedar Springs the road forked into three roads. The robbers had blocked up each of the three roads and prepared a regular breastwork at each obstruction. They put a man out to watch the road the paymaster should take. He signaled to them by firing a shotgun.

The paymaster took the inside road, and as he approached the valley, was compelled to go down a very steep hill, and a crooked road had to be followed. As he got down to a bend in the road, he found a very large boulder fallen from the bluff.

He stopped, of course, and his escort of soldiers got out without their arms to roll the stone away. As soon as the soldiers began work at the stone, the robbers right above the paymaster in the rocks, began shooting. They killed first two mules so that the ambulance could not be moved. Then two mules in the escort wagon were killed, and they began firing on the men. They wounded four of the soldiers and the rest, being without arms, ran to hide in the rocks on their orders and the paymaster was ordered off too.

They captured the safe and $29,000, and putting the booty onto a pack mule or mules went off into the mountains for a division of the plunder. The alarm was sent into the Post at Fort Thomas 17 miles away. They sent out detectives and finally arrested several men who were tried and acquitted. The two men tried as leaders were men who owned cattle, and they put their case into the hands of a sharp young lawyer who had been in that country but a year. He told his clients that in order to plead that they had no money in their possession, they must give him a mortgage on their stock, ranches, etc. Then he must have money to bribe witnesses, etc., so the money taken from the paymaster was given to him. As soon as the case was closed, this lawyer sold out all of the property of his clients and, taking what money he had saved from the plunder, he left the country in haste and went back east worth about $30,000 or $40,000 from this one case. He would not dare to show himself to his impoverished clients as, if he did, death would be his portion.

We marched next to Fort Thomas. It was on the banks of the Gila River and had been a very pretty Post. But owing to this robbery, the government ordered the Fort abandoned, and I was ordered to leave a Sergeant and a few men in charge there to take the place of the Company of the 25th Infantry, Capt. Wygants, which was the Company to be stationed there. We camped in the old houses and put our men into old quarters there. There was a small town just outside of the Post line called Maxoy, and it was the hardest place I ever saw in my life. It was filled with Mormons and colored people, a crowd of negro women of the roughest class. Gambling houses were open day and night, and altogether it was a terrible rowdy sort of a place. The Gila River is only a small stream at Fort Thomas, and the range of hills on the north side are void of any growth except giant cactus. They look like great piles of iron ore. I left a party in charge of the Post and, after one night's stop, started on the march down the Gila.

The road was terribly dusty and was crowded with teams going to and returning from Globe where there were silver and copper mines. Teams going carried coke and other supplies, and came back loaded with copper in 250 pound ingots. As the teams came up the valley, if they found themselves overloaded, they simply threw out a few ingots. The consequence of this was that all along the road we saw blocks of copper which had been left by passing trains. We camped 16 miles from Thomas on the Apache reservation, and the day following marched to San Carlos. It was not so bad a looking place, was rather pleasing in fact. The officers' quarters were small, of two and three rooms, each built of adobe. Near the Post was the Apache agency and two stores connected with it. We arrived about the 16th of May.

Our wives left Huachuca so as to get to San Carlos about the 20th of May, and we soon settled down in our new and novel home. I relieved the two companies of the 24th Infantry which were there. We could not keep house, so boarded at a Chinaman's mess. This I moved into, one of the sets of officers' quarters, and we lived fairly well. My wife and daughter Etta were with me. It was too hot even in May to have any cooking done about the house. We only put down a few rugs and opened a few of our oldest things. The climate was a great trial on the endurance of Mrs. G. and Etta, but it did not affect me at all. The water used was pumped from a well on the banks of the Gila and was fairly good. I soon got the ice machine, which had been at Fort Thomas, in good running order and we had ice every day. To keep water cool, however, we made some bags of heavy canvas to hold about ten gallons each. These, filled and hung in a shady place, were always cool enough to furnish water to drink. Each set of officers' quarters had a bathtub, and this we kept filled with water and bathed sometimes twice a day. The heat became terrible, and the record showed that during the months of June and July, the mercury was never below 85 either night or day. A great annoyance was the occasional dust storms which came to visit the valley. The wind would blow steadily and with increasing force from the east or west, and it brought with it dense and impenetrable clouds of dust which worked into every nook and crevice.

The Apaches used to crowd into the agency every week for rations, and we used to go to see them with a great deal of curiosity. They are the worst Indians in the country, and a treacherous, excitable lot they are. Their squaws are very expert in making baskets. They use willow for the frame or foundation, and then weave into the willow strips from the leaf of the Agave Americana or Aloe and a weed called devils claw. The former is white while the latter, being a permanent black, is used for making figures of various kinds. The squaws are very handy at making the ornaments to their baskets and show much ingenuity or skill in putting in the figures. They never have any pattern but weave in the pictures as they go along out of their head, so to speak. We saw the first Gila Monster which had ever come under our observation, and there were many kinds of snakes, tarantulas, etc., about.

In July 1892, Col. DeRussey commanding the 11th Infantry, wrote to me saying that if I wished to go on recruiting service for two years I could have the detail. I accepted at once, and the order was issued for me to report in New York, October 1, 1892. I sent my wife and daughter, Etta, off on the 2nd of August. They made the trip 110 miles to Wilcox station on the Southern Pacific Railroad in two days and went on east to Baltimore, Maryland. I remained in command of San Carlos until the 10th of September and then I followed my family east. I was four months in command of San Carlos and think I really enjoyed my stay there notwithstanding the extreme heat and the dust storms. I went direct to Chicago, and after a short visit, went on east to Washington and Baltimore. I reported in New York and on the 28th of September, 1892, I was ordered to take charge of the recruiting office at 1316 Filbert St., Philadelphia, which I did on the 1st of October.

COMMENTARY: *Posted to several camps and forts in southern Arizona, Gilbreath found himself in Apache territory. The Apaches were among the last of the Indians to be defeated by the U.S. Army and moved onto reservations, following the surrender of their war chief, Geronimo, in 1886. Travel in the Arizona territory was difficult, though the scenery and the local characters were colorful.*

CHAPTER 18

PHILADELPHIA & WHIPPLE BARRACKS, ARIZONA

1893-1895

M y brother-in-law, Dr. B. F. Betts, gave me the use of his house at Langhorne, Pa., 20 miles from the city, and we lived there until June 1, 1893, when we moved into the city. I sent my daughter, Etta, to the School of Design for women for a course in art, while my younger daughter went to the public or high school.

My main object in wishing to come east on recruiting service was to give my daughters a chance to go to school, so we were gratified to have so good an opportunity as Philadelphia gave us. We have lived in the city since June, 1893.

I remained on recruiting duty until October 3, 1894, when I was relieved by Capt. C.H. Potter, 18th Infantry. I left Philadelphia on the 4th of October for Chicago and, after spending a week there, went on to Whipple Barracks, Arizona, where I arrived on the 16th of October. My family remained in Philadelphia.

My length of service, my war service, and the rank I held during the war should entitle my wife to an increase of pension to $50 per month. I think Indiana Senators and Representatives would favor it and secure the passage of a bill to that effect.

THE POST QUARTERMASTER AT WHIPPLE FOUND, on going to his corral one morning, that one of his mules was missing. He began an investigation. He found that the stable had been properly locked and all the mules were in their proper places at the time.

The door of the stable was a double door with a division, and the upper half of the doors had been fastened open to admit the circulation of air as the weather was hot. The mule had disappeared and every search failed to disclose his whereabouts. Men were sent out of the Post in several directions but no trace could be found of the animal.

All day the search went on and, finally on the morning following, the Sergeant in charge went to an old shed where no one had looked and which had been unused. It was outside of the locked doors. He looked inside and there found the mule.

Further investigation showed the mule taken sick had broken his halter and then jumped over the double doors and so got out of the stable. He strayed into the shed and being sick with colic had lain down. The kicking about had kicked the door closed and so locked himself in.

It only shows the perversity of the government mule.

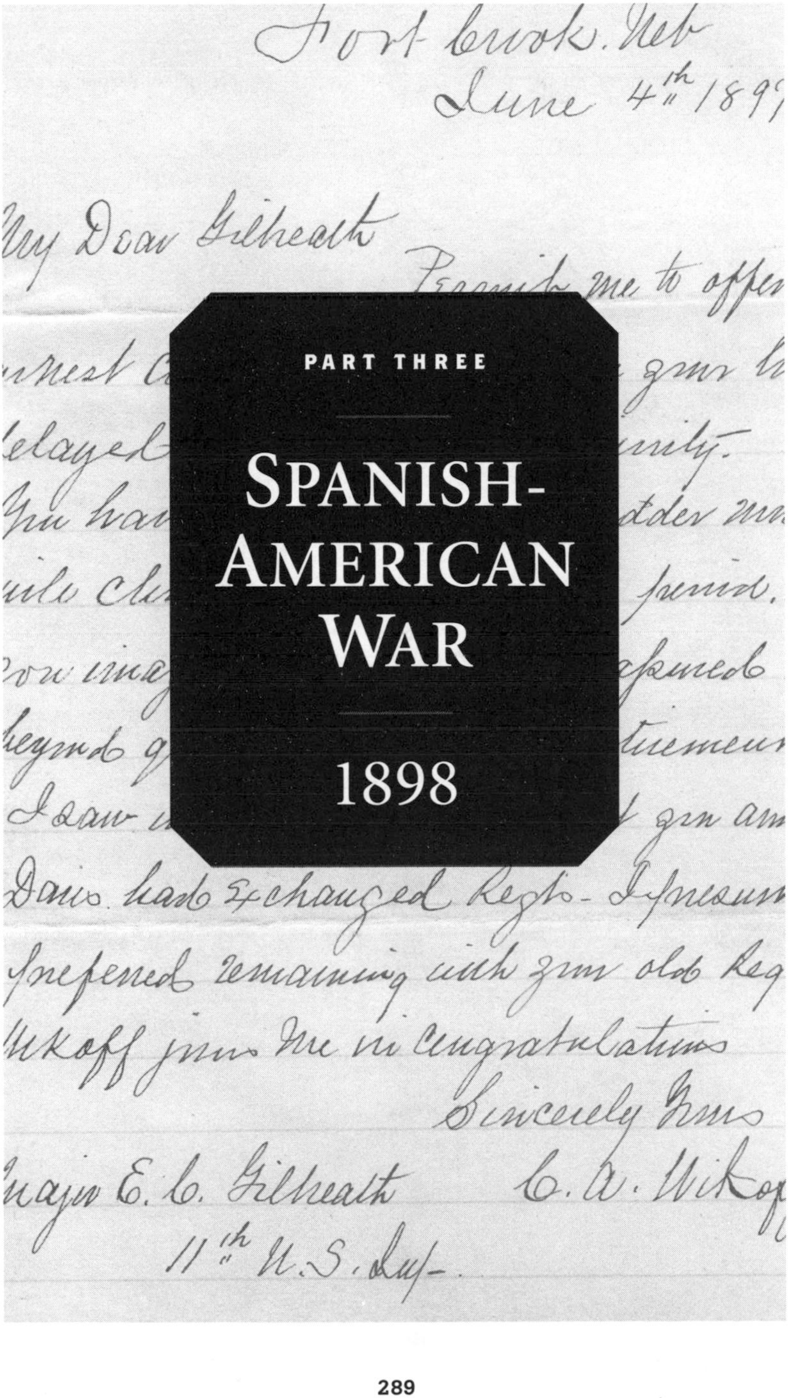

Fort Crook. Neb
June 4th 189

My Dear Gilbreath
Permit me to offer

Davis had exchanged Regts - I presume
preferred remaining with your old Reg
Wikoff joins me in congratulations
Sincerely Yours
Major E. C. Gilbreath C. A. Wikoff
11th U.S. Inf.

PART THREE

SPANISH-AMERICAN WAR

1898

This narrative is more or less disjointed or disconnected as I shall not have time or opportunity to put everything in exact order.

—E.C.G.

CHAPTER 1

MOBILE, ALABAMA, TO FLORIDA

June 1, 1898

In camp at Mobile, Alabama. Regiment ordered to go to New Orleans. Don't know what to follow.

June 2

Order changed so that the Regiment is to go to Tampa, Florida, presumably for the purpose of forming a part of a force to go to Cuba.

June 3

In preparation for the journey to Tampa. The 3rd Infantry, 20th Infantry, 2nd Company N left camp for boats to take them to Tampa.

June 4

Had a telegram from Susie wife saying Nan has had a severe reverse on the 3rd. I see no hope for the child. Been sick since April 26. Blood poisoning from inflammation of bladder. Telegraphed to Dr. Givaca in Dr. Arrell's name to find out her exact condition. Reply of Dr. G that niemic (sic) poisoning had probably set in. I cannot see why she should have such sorrow and pain as she has had since Feb 28. Scarcely a moment of peaceful rest.

June 5

Reveille at 5 A.M. General command 6:30. Martin around until 12:45 P.M. while tents and luggage were being loaded. At 1:10 left camp for cars and after marching about 1½ miles got caught in a storm of rain. Put the men on cars temporarily and at 3 P.M. started for Mobile where train was divided into two sections. 1st section carried Col. I. D. De Russey and the second battalion. The officers on our train were Capts. Nunsfilt(?), Huzt, and Novis, 1st Lieuts. Penuzs, Hirst, Alexan and Vance. 2nd Lieuts. Eammas, McEwen, Wells, and Maj. Gilbreath. Had a good sleeper and fine rest from Mobile. Passed Pensacola about 1 A.M. June 6th and as I woke up had a fine view of the Bay for a few miles by moonlight. Had breakfast at De Funiak Springs, Florida at 8 A.M. June 6th. Good breakfast. This is a winter resort with several hotels now closed, a lake near town. Crossed Choctawhatchee River about 9 A.M. and the Chattaboochee at 10:30. Pvt. Hise who looks after my horse got left from his train at Mobile but joined the animals at River Junction, Florida. We have one section loaded with horses, mules and wagons. It goes ahead of all as the Colonel says that he has made a mistake several times in leaving his baggage to follow him.

The second section is ours—12 cars. Then follows the 3rd Section with the 1st Battalion, Lieut. Col. Burke in command. He has with him, Capts. Nyer, Buchanan, Macklin and Enverz, 1st Lieuts. Davison, Guvointz, Ross, 2nd Lieuts. Child, McGinnis, Shelton.

Lieut. Blathbach is riding with the last train as he pays for all coffee and closes up accounts as we go along.

Lieut. B carries with him money to buy coffee. On the 5th the wives of several officers who have been following us stayed with us with the rain, mud and dust. We were so amazed that we did not know what to do as in the heat and all from rain and perspiration I as well as the rest were wet and dirty. They stayed with us until we left Mobile (the city) and finally at about 9 P.M. we were free to strip for comfort.

We got into the city of Mobile about 7 P.M. June 5th and were given permission to go up town to get something to eat.

At River Junction, Florida, we found a railroad car of some kind. We had come to this point on the Louisville and Nashville Railroad System but from here go two roads to Tampa and they are fighting for the traffic. Our first section left over the Plant System through Georgia, but before we pulled out news came that we were to go by the Florida Central so they had to send to have the first section with our horses and mules and wagons come back to River Junction.

The amount of monies paid to railroad companies is immense, and they are all fighting over it. At Mobile I bought a hammock for use in Cuba and on the 4th day of June spread it to see if all right. First swing the rope broke and came near driving my spinal column clear out. It has hurt me a great deal, but I borrowed some Ponds Extract from Lieut. Hirst and by the 6th it's getting better.

Had dinner served at Thomasville, Georgia. Poor meal at 4 P.M. Very pretty town. Arrived at Live Oak, Florida at 5 A.M. June 7 and find that Lieut. Col. Burke had gone on another line. We still have all the stock and baggage on the first section ahead of us and the four companies of 2nd Battalion on our section. At 8 A.M. June 7th had breakfast at High Spring Flat, 180 miles from Tampa.

This is a poor country. We passed the Suwanee River at Branford about 1 P.M., and a more unpoetic stream I never saw. It is about 50 feet wide, clear water but the bed of the stream is filled with logs and dirty drift. In the evening I saw the graves of those killed in the Dade massacre in the Florida Indian War.

June 8

We stopped at Sefferns, Florida, about 21 miles from Port Tampa to wait for orders and remained all night. Had a very poor breakfast which I rustled up at a house in the village. The man said that the crowd was too big for the town and while saying that he was too poor to get much, only charged 30 cents for breakfast. About 8 o'clock A.M. on the 8th of June, Col. De Russey left the train for Tampa. Lieut. Edwards [note: he was Nannie's husband] being anxious about Nannie asked and obtained permission to go also to Tampa for mail and telegrams.

We waited at Sefferns for a chance to get forward until about 10 o'clock A.M.

During the night the mail train from the north came in and stayed with us until we left. The railroad badly crowded. At about 10:20 we moved forward and at 11 had reached Ybra, a suburb of Tampa where we stopped and had coffee for the men and their luncheon or dinner and for the officers also. It was a curious town composed almost wholly of Cubans. It is rough and tumble sort of a place and is especially rough since the soldiers came here. It is interesting, however, to all of us in being a first sight of a strange people. Many of these Cuban women are pretty and there is an olive cast to the skin of the men and all which is quite attractive. All the signs and streets are with Spanish names.

I got Lieut. Hirst to get coffee for the men, and the 56 gallons having been delivered the men cooked their dinner and enjoyed it. The heat at 1 P.M. was excessive, and I marched the battalion of four companies through the town to camp which I found to be 2½ miles from the railroad. Found the camp rather better than that at Mobile. There was a fine Gulf breeze when we arrived, and the water from artesian wells was very good although slightly impregnated with magnesia.

The camp is in a fine grove of live oaks with some pine, and all the trees are filled with hanging moss. We found that many of the Regiments of the Regular Army had been compelled to embark on transports for some point in a hurry and that they had left their tents standing and much of the baggage of the officers still in the Camp.

We were ordered into the tents of the 13th Infantry, and I got the one which Col. Sinter of the 13th had left standing. We went to a restaurant near the camp for our meals at first but soon got our own mess started.

I engaged Pvt. Hise of Company B, 11th Infantry to work for me and brought along from Mobile also a young black man named Saint Clair Jenkins, my intention being to have Mr. Jenkins learn how to do things from Pvt. Hise when I shall let the latter go.

June 9

On the 9th of June got Lieut. Edwards to go to town to the Commissary and get some things for starting mess and we had beef, eggs, good coffee and bread for dinner. Edwards invested in a pie also and that tasted good although not having much filling.

Camp is full of rumors, and we don't know anything about where we shall go or what we are to do. Col. DeR. is "tanking" up again and filling himself.

At 3 P.M. the 13th Infantry which had gone on to transports for an expedition sent for their tents which we were occupying. We changed in a short time.

June 10

Got a letter from Susie dated the 6th inst. Had drill but still so sore from fall of hammock that it was not pleasant to ride. Col. DeR. sick but in command of Regiment still.

June 11

Policed camp by order of Genl. Coppinger. Received a letter from Mrs. G. dated 7th also one from Will who is at Saint Louis with his mother. Nan is improving in her health. Ordered to move camp to a new locality on account of measles at a Division Hospital.

Edwards and I went to the town of Tampa and bought something for the mess from the Commissary. The Commissary is well supplied with everything. Got some pea meal to make soup with—a new thing. Have first rumor of yellow fever being 30 miles from Mobile. We seem to be camped in a healthful locality and I do not fear sickness much. Colonel drunk. Letters from Mrs. G. this P.M. well and in good spirits. Answered it this P.M. Learned that Powell was to be retired.

June 13

Company B Capt. Tranisman ordered to Tampa Bay Hotel to act as a provost guard for the Division Headquarters. Also learned that the Brigade is composed of the 11th and 19th Infantry Regiments and that this is part of the Division 4th Army Corps. The Brigade is commanded by Col. DeRussey 11th Infantry. The Division by Brig. Genl Snyder, U.S. Vols. The 4th Corps is under Coppinger's command.

Everything about Tampa has been in a chaotic state as there seems to be no adequate head to manage things or to arrange the details even of this collection of troops.

Maj. O'Reilly, the Division Surgeon, established a Division Hospital, took all of the Hospital tentage and left the Regiment with only a sort of examining tent—a wall tent, but the medical officers attended to all cases at the Division Hospital from ½ mile to 2 miles from Regiments. The consequence was that if a man became suddenly ill or an accident happened to him, he had to be carried in the hot sun to and fro until the Division Hospital was found. As there was only a first aid place at each

Regiment if a man was taken sick and no doctor happened to be near, he had to go to Division Hospital without any proper attention.

Then Brig. Genl. Coppinger was made a Major General and assigned to command of the 4th Corps. Then our troubles increased.

The Surgeon General got all of his Captain Doctors almost made Majors of Volunteers and called Brigade Surgeons and our troubles still increased. The Corps Surgeon detailed one Doctor as an Aide or assistant. Then an Ambulance Corps was adopted, all Regular Surgeons were ordered to leave Regiments and go to Corps Hospitals, etc.

The consequence was that the Regular Regiments suffered a good deal. We came from Mobile to Tampa on a train of three sections, and had only a Contract Surgeon with us on one section. He has only had a contract for a few weeks, is about 24 years old and never has had any practice, no experience, and thinks his contract the biggest thing out. He is too elated over having such a position to pay too close attention to it so he has a new uniform coat and is on the fly most of the time—continual.

June 13

Measles has broken out, and about 50 men are in hospital from various regts from it. Two of the 11th Infantry were sent to Division Hospital last night with measles.

The Paymaster paid the men today, many received their first money from U.S.—Col. Burke is away all the time almost and is seemingly soured by the lack of promotion for himself. I don't feel soured at all but am cheerful and even happy. Have not been sick a minute since I left home.

Got a letter from wife today, in fact two, both mailed on the 10th inst. at one and 5 P.M. so I got one in the morning and one in the afternoon—a convenient arrangement for me.

There is not enough promptness in the supplies of the Quartermaster Departments yet or of the Ordnance. The officers are too slow and too independent as yet to supply the novas well. We have men today in the 11th Regular Infantry who have been a month enlisted and still wear citizen's clothes and have no tentage. The Commissary Department is the best supplied of any of the Staff Departments.

Lieut. Col. Hood of the 19th Infantry came into camp today to see Col. DeRussey.

The army of about 20,000 men under command of Maj. Genl. Shafter U.S. Vols which has been on transports in the harbor of Port Tampa, which is where Tampa Bay unites with the Gulf of Mexico, is said to be all in readiness to sail. Genl. Miles is at the Point and will have all of the vessels pass in review before him as they sail tomorrow the 14th of June.

It is freely talked about in Tampa that this Army goes to Santiago de Cuba to land and that we are soon to follow them either to the same place or to Porto Rico. Either will be a good landing place as both are very healthy.

June 14

44 Sick at Division Hospital and only 5 beds. Pvt. Cooper Company A very sick and compelled to stay in his own tent as there is no other place to put him.

Letter from Mr. Humphry today which I sent to wife.

June 15

Received a package of letters from Susie. Col. DeRussey gave up the command of the Regiment and Lieut. Col. Burke took charge. Col. DeRussey assumed command of the 1st Brigade.

June 16

DeRussey appointed Lieut. Edwards his Aide and Brigade Commissary. We hope this will give Edwards increased pay, mounted pay if not the pay of a Captain. Lieut. Ayer formerly of the 11th Infantry but now a 1st Lieutenant of the 12th Infantry is to be Actg Adjt Genl. on DeRussey's staff and Lieut. Dennison 11th Infantry is to be Brigade Quartermaster.

The formation of the staff for the Brigade was ordered from Headquarters of the 4th Corps in accordance with G. O. 30 from the Adjt. Genl Office. The new battalion is to be formed at once by making 4 new companies. This was ordered to be done Sat 26th inst but we have delayed till now for want of men. As we expect 180 recruits on the 18th the battalion will be formed at once. This will give us about 1000 men in the regiment and 12 companies 75 men or so each.

June 17

I had a very restless night last night. Could not sleep easily was rolling and trembling about all night. Feel first rate this morning though. Had drill from 7 to 8 and went off with Lieut. Wells to hunt a new drill ground. Found a good one. At 11 A.M. today received a telegram from Will at Jefferson Barracks telling me that Nannie had died at 3 this morning. It is philosophical to say Nannie's death was for the best and expected by me, but the pull at my heart of hearts no one knows but me.

June 20

Detailed on a General Court Martial to meet at 8 A.M. 25 inst. detail per SO 3 Headquarters 2nd Div. 4th Army Corps is as follows:

Maj. Gilbreath	11th Infantry
Capt. John G. Leave	19th Infantry
Capt. Albert L. Nyer	11th Infantry
Capt. Francis W. Nunsfich	11th Infantry
Capt. Alex McGuaca	19th Infantry
Capt. Wm. P. Edwards	19th Infantry
Capt. Francis H. French	19th Infantry
1 Lieut. C.W. Penrose	11th Infantry
1 Lieut. Edwin A. Root	19th Infantry
2 Lieut. Frederick G. Lawton	19th Infantry
2 Lieut. Oliver Edwards	11th Infantry
2 Lieut. John S. Battle	11th Infantry
1 Lieut. Wandbright Young	19th Infantry Judge Advocate

Arranged to pay servants as follows: to St. Clair Jenkins 15 per month from 1st of June. To Pvt. Hise for care of horse $5 per month. I found myself badly scalded from perspiration on my legs. Cannot ride. Am using talcum powder sent to me by Mrs. G. and find benefit from it.

June 21

Tried two cases before General Court Martial. Received Susie's letter of the 18th mailed at 8 A.M. As it is cheerful in tone or indicating that she is bearing up well under her great affliction. I am glad to get it as I have been so bothering over her troubles and her self-sacrificing love of Nannie, I don't know what to do.

June 22

Had a fine rain this forenoon. I am getting well of the chafing so that I think I may be able to ride tomorrow. This I have not been able to do for a week as the skin came off both sides of my seat. Sent a letter to Susie and to Will this morning.

Col. DeRussey came up to see me last night. He commands the Brigade still. Lieut. Col. Burke still commands the Regiment and really the latter amounts to a very small sum. His wife, a big fat Irish woman, follows him about from place to place and really keeps close watch over him, mends his clothes and looks out for him. Burke is inclined to be a little flirtatious and it is amusing to see how quiet he keeps when that mountain of flesh is about. We have a rumor that we are soon to go to Porto Rico, and we hope it is true as we or at least I would rather go there than any place else if we have to go out of the United States.

June 23

We have no news of any kind this morning. I got a letter from Susie this A.M. and that she is going to Chicago with Will to stay. Am sorry for this as I think that Saint Louis is the proper place for her and Etta. Have so far gotten over my chafing that I rode out to drill this morning. Got up at 5 A.M. had a good breakfast and a good ride. My colored man is getting to be a good cook, and caretaker, broils chops and does everything well.

June 24

Am detailed on a Board for the examination of candidates for the place of 2nd Lieut. in the Army. Some 200 are to be appointed, but I do not know how many we have to examine. We are to meet at the Tampa Bay Hotel at 10 o'clock on the 25th inst. tomorrow.

The detail for the Board is:
Lieut. Co. R. A. O'Reilly, Chief Surgeon 4th Corps

Maj. E. C. Gilbreath, 11th Infantry
Maj. Peter R. Egan, Brig. Surgeon
Capt. J. G. Leef, 19th Infantry
Capt. C. H. Watts, 5th Cavalry
1st Lt Alonzo Gray, 5th Cavalry Recorder

We meet at rooms 347, 349 Tampa Bay Hotel. This is one of the finest hotels in Florida and we will be in a swell crowd. The men are well contented. There are 950 men in the Regiment now. One at them in passing my tent today said to his comrade, "Well, it will take a good deal of this kind of war to kill me."

Another expression here in: If a man gets a good place or takes orderly or anything of that kind, others ask him, "How much did your rabbit foot cost you?"

We are pushing up the drill of these new men, and in fact all of them have 5 drills a day. I am glad I don't have to attend them as a Company Officer. Genl. Sydnor and his staff came to see Col. DeRussey today. Lieut. Edwards acts as Brigade Commissary and acts well. This place will give him pay of a mounted Captain.

June 25

The Board met at Tampa Bay Hotel and organized, then after deciding to select the questions to be asked each candidate, we adjourned to meet on the 29th of June when we will submit all the questions selected by each and decide which to ask. The candidates will be examined in Grammar, Arithmetic, Geometry, Trigonometry, Logarithms, Algebra, History and Geography. The friends of the candidates are about all ready and willing to talk to us of those they want to get through. 24 recruits came from Atlanta today. Lieut. Henry of our Regiment was in charge of them. He still has 137 at Atlanta not armed and equipped.

June 26

An order was received yesterday from Headquarters Army at Washington directing that our 2nd Division, 4th Army Corps should go to Cuba to reinforce Genl. Shafter as soon as possible. That the convoy would be at Key West within three or four days and we are not to delay. Capt. Buchanan is ordered to report to the Headquarters of the Army with his Company as Headquarters Guard and to go on board of the steamer *Louisiana*. We are all to carry 15 days' travel rations and 45 days' regular rations. It may be well to say now that a travel ration is composed of canned beef, cooked canned beans, hard bread and coffee, while the regular ration is composed of bacon and other things not cooked. In the evening today word came that the *Louisiana* on which Buchanan was to go had gone out of the harbor and his trip is thus off. We continue our preparations and are getting together the rations we need. It has been this way all through the Campaign so far, there seems to be no well studied plan of action. Orders are issued and revoked right and left. The most woeful inefficiency exists in the Medical Department.

June 28

The recruits of all the Companies went out for target practice. Amongst the colored men the rabbit's foot is supposed to be very lucky to bring good luck to the one who carries it. Pvt. Hise was telling Saint Clair Jenkins our colored cook that he, Hise, did not have to go on guard or do fatigue work or attend any roll calls because he was taking care of me and my horse. The cook looked at him a little while and then said, "Well, Hise, you are pretty lucky. How much did your rabbit's foot cost you?" Received a telegram from Washington relieving me from duty on the Board of Officers. Glad of it as it is not at all desirable to be on such a board. Bought fine ochra and a new thing to me, collia, a sweet pepper. It can be eaten in vinegar without cooking and is mild and pleasant to the taste. Cubans are very fond of this sweet pepper. Fine watermelons grow in this portion of Florida, but I was surprised to find that few other fruits except oranges grow here. One of the curious things I find is the camphor tree. It is a very pretty tree and grows in a good shape. Oleanders are very common and blooming beautifully at this time.

June 30

Had muster this morning. Lieut. Col. Burke ordered that the muster be made by battalion. My battalion now consists of A, C, L and M Companies with Penrose, Hirzt, Battle and Blotchford in Command of the companies in the order named. Did not sleep well last night or the night before. Examined by the Doctor. He orders me on to a strychnine diet as he says I need a heart stimulant. I am also to take Digitolin twice a day. After muster today I went to see DeRussey. He is half maudlin around all the time.

CHAPTER 2

FLORIDA TO PORTO RICO

July 1

Got some things to complete my outfit for the campaign. Arranged them. Beef Tea or Extract. Got a basket for the colored man to carry with a few cooking utensils and a small quantity of rations so that we might not be without something to eat at any time. Rumors of a great battle at Santiago, Cuba. No transports here for us yet.

July 2

More rumors of fighting in Cuba. Cannot tell anything about the losses or get head or tail to the stories. Wrote to Susie this morning.

July 4

Tampa - Genl. Schram took command of our Brigade this afternoon. He is very cordial with me being an old friend and having been Captain of Company G, 11th Infantry when I was 1st Lieutenant of it.

Letter from Susie dated 1st. List of some of the killed and wounded from Santiago—received friends. Regret the loss of many friends. Met on Court Martial this A.M.

July 5

Went to Tampa Bay Hotel with Lieut. Edwards.

July 8

Inspected by the Inspecting officer of this Division.

July 9

Had Regimental Drill this morning at 7. Heavy rain, we all got drenched.

July 10

Genl. Schram came to see me this A.M. Went to church and heard a fine sermon at the M.E. church in Tampa. Mr. Carpenter was the minister. Rain.

July 11

This is the worst any of rain we have seen since we started from home. It was a downpour all day. Man of A Company shot himself in the foot.

July 12

Tuesday had a General Court Martial at Brigade Headquarters. No drill. Rain and showers all day. This is the Florida rainy season.

July 17

Nothing has occurred here since last entry. Last night orders came to be prepared to go to Porto Rico. The prospect now is that we might get on board a ship some time this week. As we have been ordered several times before to be ready to go we hope there will be no miss fire this time.

July 21

On the 21st of July I was ordered by Col. DeRussey under Schram's order to go to Port Tampa to see the *Mohawk*, a vessel on which we were to go to join Genl. Miles. I asked to have Capts. Hyer and Hansfield to go with me as they both commanded Battalions or were the next in rank to me. We inspected the boat going by rail nine miles from Tampa to Port Tampa. The latter place is curious as there are miles and miles of docks and a very large number of steamers can load at the same time. The *Mohawk* is a very large vessel, and we are expected to take 1000 men and 1000 horses on her. We inspected the boat all over and find that the men will be fairly comfortable. We got new latrines and some coffee boilers put up for men to make coffee during the trip. The Captain's name is Cannon, and the whole vessel is one of five purchased from the company for use during the war. This vessel was used with others of equal size to carry beef cattle from New York to London. It is 450 feet long. I got awfully wet while at Port Tampa, but nice on train. Was sent to Port Tampa without any orders to report to anyone. In trying to get the matter straightened out I got wet and then in trying to get any clothing I got wetter. Capt. Mansfield asked me to dine with him at Tampa Bay Hotel which I did and enjoyed it very much. Genl. Schram ordered Col. DeRussey to send my battalion of Companies A, C, L & M on board the *Mohawk* on the 22nd. DeRussey sails on the 23rd. Company F went on the *D. H. Miller* with a battery of Artillery, and Company G on the *Whitney*. The whole of the 19th Infantry was boarded on the *Cherokee* and some other boat.

July 23

On the 23rd I dined with Genl. Schram at the Port Tampa Inn, and he told me of his efforts to get rid of Col. DeRussey. Saw his boy at the Inn.

July 25

On the 24th of July six more companies of the 11th Infantry came on board of the *Mohawk* and about 3 P.M. we sailed from Port Tampa. We have on the boat 1416 men all told and 877 animals. A pilot took the steamer out about 15 miles where we anchored for the night. At 7:30 A.M. the pilot left our boat after bringing us from our anchorage. We passed the Quarantine station on our right and a Fort on the left, and at 9 A.M. were out of sight of land on our way to Porto Rico. Our route is to be around Point San Antone, Cuba, and along its southern coast through the windward passage to Samana Bay, Santo Domingo. All the vessels are to rendezvous in that Bay. We are then to sail on the north of Porto Rico through the Virgin passage to the west of Virgin Islands and thence to the west of Humacao, Porto Rico, where the landing is to be made. It is said that Genl. Miles is already there.

July 26

On the *Mohawk*, July 26, 1898. We have sailed about 300 miles from Tampa and are now at 10 A.M. west of Dry Tortugas. Our route will be about west, a number of miles west of Cape Antone on the west end of Cuba. Amused ourselves looking at flying fish, porpoises, black fish etc. Steamed 261 miles in the 24 hours ending at 12 o'clock noon. Observation taken showed that we were about 75 miles northwest of Point San Antone, Cuba.

July 27

Steamed 270 miles in 24 hours ending at 12 o'clock noon today and at that hour were south of the Isle of Pines. Saw a large English war vessel steaming west. The sea has been perfectly calm ever since we left Tampa. No sickness on board the *Mohawk*. I am a good deal worried about Edwards as he seems so despondent all the time and so hopeless. I took six pills of chamomile yesterday and am feeling the effects today. Have a fine salt water bath every morning, and my prickly heat is almost all gone.

July 28

Got up at 5:30 after a good night's sleep. Perspired a great deal during the night. Took a bath in salt water in the ship's tub and feel fit as a fiddle. Saw a *New York Journal* of the 22nd inst. which Col. Burke had. Rained heavily at 7 P.M. Wind from N. E. Observation taken at 12 o'clock. Run for 24 hours 160 miles. Paid board on boat to include Friday, July 29th.

Friday, July 29

Got up at 5 A.M. Saw coast of Cuba about 40 miles west of Santiago and 20 miles away.

Saturday, July 30

Sailing in sight of Santo Domingo all day. Paid $5 for meals on ship to include today the 30th of July.

Sunday, July 31

Samana Bay, Santo Domingo. We arrived at our anchorage in this Bay at about 11 A.M. The day since 12 yesterday was very interesting to me in many ways. All yesterday was windy and with a heavy sea so that our progress was slow. As night fell last night we were sailing along the north shore of Santo Domingo. We passed Turtle Island early in the morning, and it seemed to be a continuation of the coast line. Our Captain set his course for the night for Bank and sailing due east, or about that, he found the Bank at 12 o'clock midnight. There after lying at a rest on the waves until he sounded and sounded to make sure, he headed due south for a land he had never seen and at 7 o'clock we sighted land and the mouth of Samana Bay was before us. This bay is not buoyed to mark channels, and the Captain could only get in by his soundings and his observations. But thanks to him we 1500 men were at anchor at last.

A pilot boat put out and brought us letters for the Commanding Officer. Genl. Miles has come and gone, and Genl. Schram had also gotten in and left on the *Comanche* with the 19th Infantry, and they had proceeded to Porto Rico two days ago. I am awfully disappointed as it shows one thing to me and that is that we are to have no chance for a fight or any glory in the first capture of a landing or anything. Col. DeR. has stood in our way all through. He has shown his unwillingness to cooperate with those over him and even goes to the extreme of not fully obeying orders. Hence the officers over him will have no confidence in him and the Regiment gets left behind. Genl. Schram on getting here found that Genl. Miles had gone on to Porto Rico. So he at once left Samana Bay and went to join Genl. Miles. Schram has the 19th Infantry with him and they get in first work while we wait for a few transports here and then go on to sea. I am disgusted.

Sunday, July 31

We left Samana Bay at 7:30 P.M. for Porto Rico, landing to be on the eastern end of the Island. We received orders, and Col. DeRussey directed all the vessels at Samana Bay to go together. We have the *Florian* with 5 Cos 19th Inf on board and the *Whitney* with Buchanan's Company G and Hopper's troop of 2nd Cav. on board to go with us. The *D. H. Miller* is in Samana Bay. She got on a coral reef and did not get off till 5 P.M. Then she had to get water from shore, and so she can not go with us. Just before we left a gunboat belonging to Santo Domingo came to order us out of their neutral port. She was a small vessel and danced about with her colored officers and crew at a great rate trying to look as important as a man-of-war. She is the entire Navy of Santo Domingo.

CHAPTER 3

Porto Rico

August 1, 1898

We were sailing all night in company with the other boats and at 6 o'clock we were overhauled by the war vessel *Annapolis*. All was excitement to see what she had to say. The officer in command came with orders from Genl. Miles to say that he had taken Ponce on the south side of Porto Rico and its largest city and wanted all the troops to meet there. We changed our course therefore soon as we could get orders to the other vessels and are going around the west end of Porto Rico. We got no particulars of the taking of Ponce by Miles.

August 2

We sailed to the south of Porto Rico and then from the southwest point to the east. At about one o'clock this A.M. we were not far from Ponce and had sailed in sight of land since about one P.M. on the 1st of August. The Captain hauled to, and we lay at rest for several hours in fact until day broke when the Captain again steamed ahead, and about 10 A.M. we sighted war vessels and finally about 20 minutes more sighted the landing at Ponce. There was a forest of masts as many transports were at the landing. We got a pilot who could talk no English, and we could not talk Spanish to him. He took us in to the harbor, and we went to an anchorage about one mile from shore.

The sight from the deck of the vessel was the finest I ever saw. There were several islands on three of which were lighthouses. All of the latter were most beautiful white and as clean and pretty as could be. The hills all showed a very fine green and were dotted with cottages and houses far as the eye could reach up and down the island. Coconut groves covered some of the hills, and all in all it was very attractive indeed in more ways than I can find words to describe. At about 1 P.M. orders came on to the boat for the Colonel to send one of his battalions on shore before night. So Col. DeR. ordered me to go ashore with my battalion. The only way to do this was to go in lighters which are great wide deep boats used to unload vessels. It was a difficult undertaking as there were no lighters of value and we had to use the life boats of the *Mohawk* and such native boats as we could pick up. I got two companies ashore and into camp before dark. Hoyt's men first, then Blatchford's. I went with the first load of the latter's. We camped 2 miles from the landing place which is called the Playa or Port. There is a fine road lighted with lamps and regularly sprinkled from the town of Ponce to the Playa or Port, and in peace times it is a delightful drive for the residents of the town, 17,000. It is one of the most curious places I ever saw. There are no windows to the houses only shutters and doors.

August 7
We camped at Ponce until August the 7th when I left with the last of the companies of the battalion by rail to Yanco. It is a queer little narrow-gauge road owned by a French company. The engines are small affairs made in France. We made the trip in ½ hour being 21 miles in all.

Monday, August 8
Left Yanco at 10 A.M. and marched to Sabana Grande and were welcomed by the Mayor and Priest.

Tuesday, August 9
We marched from Sabana Grande to San German and beyond. At about 1 P.M. we heard shots fired in front of us and pushed on. At 3 P.M. we found our advance guard attacked as they were marching to the road and I was pushed on to the front. The advance guard was composed of Hoyt's and Penrose's companies. We had a fight, carried a bridge and a ridge. Lost 1 killed and 17 wounded.

August 10
Camped on the ground the night of the 10th of August.

August 11

On the 11th marched on into Mayaguez. Took possession of the towns and camped on the outskirts. I was very sick all day from wet and cold on the 10th.

August 12

On the 12th was made field officer of the day. Still in camp. Sent in report on the action of the 10th at Rio Rosario.

August 13

On the 13th of August Lieut. Col. Burke left Mayaguez for Los Marias and marched about 10 miles when he came in contact with a fleeing force of the enemy. He camped and reported. We left Mayaguez on the 13th to follow Lieut. Col. Burke. We marched in a body 12 miles with 2 batteries of Artillery 4 Gatling Guns, 6 Company S of Infantry and a long train. Genl. Schram back on order for Col. DeRussey to send forward 4 Companies of Infantry at once to aid Burke. I started but Col. DeRussey retained command so that I only got about 6 miles before another order came from Genl. Schram for us to bivouac. Thus I am sending back Blatchfords' and Dentlers' companies to build roads. We have a good camping place but passed a miserable night as we had no tentage—no rations and nothing for the comfort of officers and men. Lieut. Edwards and I gave the officers each a meal from stores we had carried in our saddlebags. We had supper and breakfast in that way without any bread or hard bread.

August 14

I have been sick since the 11th so it was quite a surprise to me that I should feel first class after a slight breakfast on the 14th. We got a note from Genl. Schram saying that peace negotiations had so far progressed that all operations should cease. 10 guns of the artillery had joined me during the night of the 13th so that I had quite a large camp. We were ordered to go back via the road towards Mayaguez. I left camp about 10 A.M. August 14th and marched six or seven miles and went into camp with the rest of the six companies.

August 15

On the 15th I was very sick, but at 9 A.M. we started back on the road cheered up at the idea of peace coming on. We had marched halfway to the train or about 4 miles when we were ordered to go back to our old positions of the night before. So we turned about to start to the front again and had no sooner done so than on came one of the heaviest rains I ever saw and it rained and it rained. The mud was awful, and we got to camp again just before dark drenched and red with mud.

August 16

Got some lunch and supper and sleep and feel very well this morning the 16th. Lieut. Col. Burke had further to go than we, and he did not get to Marias until noon of the 16th. He camped on the 15th at my old camp on the coffee plantation of Quetio Cobraro. Mr. Cobraro is a fine man, talks English well and is thoroughly American in sentiment I think. He would accept no pay for anything. He gave me two beef cattle for the men for nothing and he brought us a gallon of the most delicious coffee I ever tasted so that the officers all had a good cup. I had with me Company H Mansfield and Company F Emery. The officers in the bivouac at Cobraro Creek were for the night:

Artillery	Capt. Thorpe
	Lieut. Callan
	Lieut.
Infantry Company F	Capt. Emery
	Lieut. Child
Company H	Capt. Mansfield
	Lieut. Maginuss with the 4 Gatling Guns
	Lieut. Edwards and myself

August 17

I got up very sick this morning. Camp still on top of a red hill at Maximo Gomez Coffee plantation, and I wish the hill and all were someplace else. It has rained all the morning and the mud is awful. Everything is red in my tent. It appears that peace negotiations are still in course of finish and that it was not the intention to withdraw us from our advance place pending the closing of the terms, hence we came here. We put up a great white flag to indicate that peace was on and tell all citizens. The men have not been dry for several days but are all in the best of spirits. Getting rested and full of grub makes a great difference in their spirits.

Thursday, August 18

We are still in camp at the Red Clay Hill about 7 or 5 miles out of Mayaguez. It is awful red mud, and we often are very uncomfortable indeed. We hope for a change of some kind very soon. I feel better today but had an awful night of it. We got a mail today, the second since we came on the island. My letters were from wife of 25, 27 and 30th of July—one from Will and one from Etta. I feel like a new man getting them. Last night Col. Goto, a prisoner, passed through camp swung in a stretcher. He had his leg broken and is helpless. Is a fine looking man. His wife also passed in a regular Bull suit with a Sister of Charity for Company. We were enabled to send off letters today at 12:30 as the Steamer *Morgan* sails for New York tomorrow. Capt. Emery went to the hospital, and I presume has gone north sick.

Friday, August 19

Am feeling a little better today but still have most awful nights from lack of breath. Lieut. Col. Burke did not come back from Mayaguez yet, and when he does we hope he will bring orders to go some place. I was amused to see Edwards on his first battlefield on the 10th of August. He rode a slow going old mare and she looked like a plow horse. The bullets were flying on all sides, and he was so cool and indifferent as possible. We had to get off our horses as they shot at us. So Edwards trudged along through mud and water with bullets kicking up every minute. He was indifferent to them. He came on Hirst who skulked as low as he could in the mud and water and the action of Edwards shamed Hirst. This is an awful camp because of the red clay mud which covers everything. It rains every afternoon regularly so that the mud is always in evidence.

Here he passed on.
(Written in the hand of his son, William Sydnor Gilbreath)

HEADQUARTERS ELEVENTH INFANTRY.

Camp at Rio Gana, P. R. August 24th. 1898.

General Orders No 81.

The regimental Commander announces
to the Regiment the death from _apoplexy_ of Major E. C.
Gilbreath, on the 22nd. instant.

Major Gilbreath was born in Ohio, May
13th. 1841, he entered the military service as 1st Lieutenant
20th. Indiana Volunteers on X July 22nd. 1861., served with
bravery and distinction through-out the war of the Rebellion,
rising to the rank of Major and was mustered out of the
service July 28th. 1865.

On February 23rd. 1866, Major Gilbreath,
was appointed 2nd. Lieutenant 15th, U. S. Infantry, promoted
1st. Lieutenant same date, transferred to the 24th. Infantry
September 21st 1866 and to the 11th. Infantry, April 25th.
1869. He was promoted to his Captaincy December 23rd. 1873
and to the grade of Major April 30th. 1897.

Major Gilbreath was a most energetic
officer and well informed in all the details of his profession,
in his death the service has lost a most valuable Officer.

The Officers of the regiment will wear
the usual badge of mourning for thirty days.

By order of Colonel De Russy:

(sgd) Charles P. Russ,

1st. Lieut. & Adjutant 11th. Infantry.

Official.

Edgar A. Macklin -

1st. Lieut. & Batt. Adjutant 11th. Infantry.

Adjutant.

313

GLOSSARY

Abatis: An obstacle to slow or block an enemy charge, often consisting of felled trees or piled logs and sometimes including sharpened branches or stakes.

Adjutant: Staff officer responsible for transmitting orders.

Artillery: Cannon or other large-caliber gun in which a controlled chemical explosion—usually of black powder—propels a projectile. Also, the name of the army unit armed with such weapons.

Battery: An artillery position on a battlefield. Also, a unit of artillery.

Bayonet: A long metal knife that can be attached to the end of a rifle barrel, for use as an antipersonnel weapon and wielded like a pike.

Bivouac: To camp temporarily in the open, usually during an action or a troop movement. In the Union Army, two-man tents were often issued, but temporary shelter might consist of whatever could be found on site.

Blockade: A naval strategy of deploying ships of war for the purpose of intercepting enemy ships of war or merchant ships in coastal waters to prevent their reaching enemy ports.

Blockade Runner: A ship specifically designed for the speed and stealth that can enable it to penetrate an enemy blockade and elude capture while delivering arms or other cargo.

Bombproof: A rifle pit or foxhole that is strongly roofed over, often with logs and earth, to protect against mortar fire or other artillery fire.

Bounty: Payment to volunteer enlistees by state or federal governments.

Breach: A break or gap in a defensive position, usually created by artillery or a charge by cavalry or infantry.

Breastworks: Any kind of breast-high barricade, earthen or consisting of logs or other materials, to provide shelter from enemy fire.

Breech-loading Gun or Cannon: Firearm in which the explosive charge and the projectile are loaded from the rear rather than from the muzzle.

Brevet: Temporary promotion in rank, granted in wartime, sometimes in combat. Often given to officers in volunteer units, the higher rank did not carry over if the officer transferred into the regular U.S. Army.

Buck and Ball: A musket load, associated with the Confederate smoothbore. It consists of three buckshot balls packaged with a .69 caliber musket ball—usually employed in close-range defensive situations.

Caisson: Two-wheeled ammunition-carrying cart, attached to a horsedrawn artillery limber.

Caliber: Diameter of the bore of a gun, and of the corresponding ammunition, measured in fractions of an inch and usually expressed as a decimal figure, e.g., .57.

Campaign: A series of engagements or military operations that constitute a distinct phase of a war, e.g., Stonewall Jackson's "Valley Campaign."

Canister: Antipersonnel artillery ammunition consisting of a tin cylinder packed with several dozen iron balls (or random pieces of scrap metal or even stones) designed to scatter like the shot used in shotguns; employed at close range, often to break up an enemy charge.

Cap: On a rifle or musket, an essential element of percussion cap system of firing. The cap is a small brass container of fulminate of mercury, which ignites when struck by the weapon's hammer. Its flame in turn ignites the black powder that explodes and propels the ball or bullet.

Car: Railroad passenger or freight car.

Carbine: A light-weight long gun, usually carried by cavalrymen.

Cartridge: A type of ammunition for rifle or carbine, with the explosive powder and the bullet packaged in a single container, which is much simpler and faster to load than earlier forms of long-gun ammunition.

Case Shot: Another type of antipersonnel artillery ammunition, usually consisting of a spherical iron shell loaded with iron balls or scrap metal along with a powder charge. Designed to explode after firing and scatter its contents.

Cavalry: A military unit mounted on horseback for mobility. Often employed as advance scouts to learn of enemy troop movements or as shock troops in sudden raids or flanking attacks to disrupt enemy movements. Cavalrymen often fought dismounted.

Colors: Flags, either national or unit (e.g., regiment), deployed in combat lines of battle, to identify and show the position of various units. Valued by soldiers as important symbols of their units.

Contrabands: A Union army term for freed or self-liberated African-Americans who made their way into Union army–controlled territory. Term first employed and acted upon by General Benjamin Butler at Fort Monroe, Virginia, in 1861, who considered runaway slaves as "contraband of war," to be rightfully kept by the conquering Union forces.

Defeat in Detail: To fight smaller enemy units one at a time and defeat them piecemeal.

Demonstration: A small-scale aggressive movement on a battlefield, often to determine enemy strength by provoking a reaction or conducted as a feint to distract the enemy from a major attack elsewhere.

Dog Tent: A two-man tent carried by infantrymen as a temporary shelter.

Earthwork: A dug-in defensive position, involving throwing up a protective barrier of earth from a trench.

Enfilade: A flanking maneuver to get into position to fire directly into the length of an enemy line.

Engagement: An act of combat between opposing forces, generally considered larger and more significant than a skirmish but smaller than a battle. Often associated with an unexpected or surprise encounter between opposing army units.

Entrenchment: A form of defensive work consisting of one or more long trenches dug in the earth, with dirt and rock thrown up in front as part of the protection for the forces occupying the trench.

Envelopment: Usually a large-scale strategic maneuver designed to encircle an enemy formation and cut it off from retreat or reinforcements; considered a risky but less costly mode of attack than a frontal assault.

Flank: The sides or wings of a battle formation that extend outward from the central position. Often a defensive position to protect the main body of troops. Also, an action to attack the ends or sides of a battle position or line. In the Civil War, both sides frequently sought to flank or outflank the opponent's position.

Fortification: Any type of more or less permanent construction of earth, logs, masonry, or other materials to form a strong defensive and protective military position.

Friendly Fire: Episodes in which army units mistakenly fire on or attack individuals or units of their own army. In a famous friendly-fire incident, Stonewall Jackson was mistakenly shot and fatally wounded at Chancellorsville by soldiers of his own army.

Furlough: A leave granted to an enlisted soldier, usually for a specified length of time.

Garrison: A military post, often a minor location, or the unit of soldiers stationed there.

Gatling Gun: An early form of machine gun consisting of six rifle barrels mounted in a circular pattern. Invented by Richard Gatling in 1862, it boasted a high rate of fire but was rarely used in the Civil War.

Guidon: A small flag carried by a company or cavalry troop used to identify the unit.

Haversack: A canvas shoulder bag usually carried by Union army soldiers for rations and other personal items.

Howitzer: A short-barreled cannon employed to fire shells in a high trajectory over obstacles or in difficult terrain.

Instant or Inst: Immediate or at this time or on this day.

Kepi: A round and visored cap of French origin, worn by soldiers of both armies in the Civil War.

Limber: A sturdy two-wheeled cart used by artillery units to carry ammunition.

Militia: An army unit of volunteers, often engaged for a specific term of service, as distinct from a regular army unit of full-time soldiers.

Minié Ball: A soft lead bullet of French origin. For use in a rifled long gun with greater accuracy than round-ball ammunition; it accounted for a very high percentage of gunshot wounds in the Civil War.

Mortar: A heavy-duty type of artillery with a very short barrel, designed to lob large explosive shells high over fortifications. A smaller, more portable variation was called a Coehorn Mortar.

Musket: A long-barreled smoothbore gun in common use early in the Civil War. An old design, it was not nearly as accurate or effective as the newer rifled weapons.

Muzzle-Loader: Any weapon, whether shoulder fired or cannon, that was charged with powder and ammunition from the muzzle.

Parapet: A defensive work often atop a fortification, designed to protect guns and gunners.

Parole: Release of prisoners of war upon agreement that they would no longer bear arms against their captors. The agreement was widely ignored, and the parole system was dropped late in the war.

Picket: Soldiers who were posted out front of a camp or battle line as guards who were to give early warning of an enemy attack. Often the first ones in the field to exchange fire with the enemy.

Quartermaster: A staff officer with responsibility for logistics, providing equipment, supplies, clothing, lodging, and transportation.

Pioneer: A specialized army unit, similar to today's combat engineers, responsible for construction of roads, bridges, and fortifications.

Pontoon Bridge: An old form of temporary bridge, usually for river crossings, which utilized a series of heavy barges to support a timber roadway.

Redoubt: A temporary enclosed field fortification, usually defensive.

Rifle: A shoulder arm weapon with long barrel and internal spiral groove—"rifling"—in the barrel that imparts a spin on the bullet, improving accuracy, consistency, and range.

Rifle Pit: A defensive pit or short trench dug to provide protection for riflemen.

Salient: A fortified occupied position that juts out ahead of a battle line, often vulnerable to enemy attack.

Shrapnel: Metal shards or small metal balls loaded into spherical case shot to be fired by field artillery. With a short time fuse, the shell explodes, scattering the shards or balls. It is an effective and much-feared antipersonnel weapon, named for its inventor, British Army artillery officer Henry Shrapnel.

Siege: A prolonged assault on a fortified enemy position or town in which the objective is surrounded and isolated from supply and reinforcement, usually subject to bombardment. Famous Civil War examples include Vicksburg, Mississippi, and Petersburg, Virginia.

Skirmish: A small-scale armed fight, usually among detached soldiers not with the main forces. Skirmishers are generally outliers out front of a major position or on its flanks. When more than a few soldiers are thus deployed, the formation is called a skirmish line.

Straggler: A soldier who has, on his own, temporarily left his regiment, often during an arduous march or to avoid combat. Most stragglers return to their unit in a day or so.

Strategy: Large-scale operational plan for a campaign or battle, often specifically directed toward overall victory.

Sutler: Civilian merchant who travels along with regiments for the purpose of selling items to soldiers that are not supplied by the army, e.g., tobacco and food. Sutlers' behavior and practices were regulated by the armies.

Tactics: The deployment and direction of troops in combat.

Torpedo: A large explosive device, essentially a mine used either on land or in water.

Units: Organizations of soldiers in an army (similar in both Union and Confederate armies). In order of size, from small to large numbers of soldiers:

Squad = 10–25 men or 25% of a company.

Company = 100 men commanded by a captain.

Squadron = 2 companies of cavalry.

Battalion = 2 companies for special duty, e.g., pioneers or sharp-shooters.

Regiment = 10 companies of infantry or 12 companies of artillery or cavalry, totaling some 845–1,025 men.

Brigade = 4–5 regiments plus a headquarters staff, often accompanied by artillery or cavalry and commanded by a brigadier general.

Division = 3 brigades commanded by a major general.

Corps = 2 or more divisions with some 12,000–25,000 soldiers, commanded by a major general. Designated by number, e.g., III Corps, but also identified by the name of the commander.

Army = Largest unit, named for river or region in theater of operations. Commanded by a full general.

Works: Large defensive field fortifications of earth and other local materials, often designed by engineers.

List of Officers of the 11th United States Infantry, from the
back of the photograph on page 215 (bottom)

ACKNOWLEDGMENTS

"Dignity of Duty" Team
Colonel (IL) Jennifer N. Pritzker, IL ARNG (Retired): Executive Editor
Kenneth Clarke: Executive Editor, Creative Director
Wendy Palitz: Designer, Creative Director
Susan Gilbreath Lane: Editor
Michael Robbins: Consulting Editor
Sharon Brinkman, Patricia Curtis: Copy Editors
Stephen Callahan: Indexer
Keith A. Grogan: Image Production
Helen Rae Kennedy and Consolidated Graphics: Printing

Pritzker Military Museum & Library Board of Directors
Colonel (IL) J. N. Pritzker, IL ARNG (Retired), Founder and Chair
Tyrone C. Fahner
Lieutenant Commander Arie Friedman, MD, USNR-R (MC) (Retired)
Scott Murray
Master Sergeant Ginny Narsete, USAF (Retired)
John W. Rowe
Robert E. Sarazen
John H. Schwan
Captain John A. Williams, PhD, USNR (Retired)
Kenneth Clarke, Ex-Officio

Pritzker Military Museum & Library Staff
Kenneth Clarke, President & CEO
Teri Embrey, Chief Librarian
Becky Krueger, Office Manager
Kat Latham, Director of Collection Management

Megan Williams, Director of External Affairs
Ben Altensey, Development Associate
Nate Barnes, Public Relations Coordinator
Martin Billheimer, Library Clerk
Olivia Button, Digital Collections Coordinator
Noel Carroll, Development Services Assistant
Dustin DePue, Special Collections Librarian
Paul W. Grasmehr, Reference Coordinator
Brad Guidera, Production Manager
Tina Louise Happ, Associate Chief Librarian
John LaPine, Collection Services Manager
Chris Meter, Administrative Assistant
Aaron Pylinski, Production Coordinator
Christy Stanford, Volunteer and Intern Coordinator
Katie Strandquist, Special Events Manager
Lindsey Sturch, Librarian
Thomas Webb, Oral History Coordinator

Editor's Acknowledgments

I AM MOST GRATEFUL THAT MY GREAT-GRANDFATHER, Erasmus Corwin Gilbreath, wrote these journals so that his descendants and many others can learn from his fascinating experiences.

I want to thank my friend, Anne D. Gordon, the chief editor of the Susan B. Anthony and Elizabeth Cady Stanton papers, who kindly passed on much practical information that helped me with the edits I made to Erasmus's journals.

The staff of the Detroit Public Library has been supportive and offered help when needed. In a time before easy access to copiers, they arranged for me to have copies of the Civil War Journal. Paige Plant has been especially helpful with all my research efforts.

I would like to thank Laura Ashley Cooper, who provided me with a copy of the book, *The Green Rose of Furley*. Laura's great-great-grandmother, Esther Sinclair, was my great-grandmother's sister.

My cousin Bill gave me unlimited access to his large collection of family archives. Our fathers had received from their fathers scrapbooks filled with fascinating photos, letters, and documents. That material has been extremely useful.

My cousin, Tom Chandler, was one of the first recipients of a copy of the Civil War Journal and was very enthusiastic about it. His enthusiasm was motivating to me. He discovered and provided me with copies of the application that my great-grandmother Susan made for a military pension.

Not long ago, my brother, Steve, who had read the journals, asked if I had read them. I had not, but he convinced me to read them and I learned at last what a treasure I had unearthed. Steve has spent lots of time research- ing information in the journal and passing on important suggestions.

My brother Jack, using his attorney's eye, reviewed the agreement I signed with the Pritzker Military Museum and Library.

Years ago when I first learned about Craig Dunn's book, *Harvest Fields of Death*, a story of the 20th Indiana, I contacted him to ask his opinion about what to do with Erasmus's journals. In his experience, Craig knew of only a few men who had begun as Civil War volunteers and continued after the war to have military careers and even fewer who documented their histories. The journals, he thought, were worth publishing. I value his help and encouragement.

During our condominium book club meeting, I mentioned my proj- ect to the group. When I asked if anyone would be interested in reading the journals, Susan Youdovin took me up on my offer. She found them very interesting and urged me to show them to her friend Colonel Jen- nifer Pritzker, the founder of the Pritzker Military Museum and Library. After I sent them to Colonel Pritzker, she emailed to say that she had found them fascinating and suggested that I submit a proposal for their publication. With the valued help of Susan and Barbara Schiacchitano, a great friend and historian, we created a proposal.

I don't know how I can possibly thank the Pritzker Military Museum & Library enough for agreeing to publish the journals. This is a thrill for our family and a thrill to know that Erasmus's voice will be heard.

I have had the pleasure of becoming acquainted with the President and C.E.O. of the Pritzker Military Museum and Library, Kenneth Clarke. With great enthusiasm he has proceeded with a team of associates to help realize my dream of getting Erasmus's story to a larger audience. I appreciate his efforts to include me in the process every step of the way. It has been a pleasure.

I have spoken to countless people about the Gilbreath journals, and it has happened that their comments have led to important insights and changes in the process. Because I have talked with so many people, I run the risk of omitting someone from this list of acknowledgments. Thanks to you all for your time and interest.

To Lee, my husband, who has volunteered countless hours reading the journals and providing me with insights, I owe great thanks. Your help and encouragement have been invaluable.

—*Susan Gilbreath Lane*

Fort Crook. Neb
June 4th 1897

My Dear Gilbreath

Permit me to offer my earnest congratulations upon your long delayed promotion to a majority.

You have your foot in the ladder now. and will climb to the top. in a less period. than you imagine - a colonelcy is assured to you. beyond question, before your retirement

I saw in some newspaper that you and Major Davis had exchanged Regts - I presume you preferred remaining with your old Reg. Mrs Wikoff joins me in congratulations

Sincerely Yours

Major E. C. Gilbreath   C. A. Wikoff
11th U.S. Inf.

Letter of congratulations from Colonel Charles A. Wikoff congratulating Gilbreath on his promotion to major. Wikoff and Gilbreath served together in the 11th U.S. Infantry. Colonel Wikoff was killed during the Battle of Santiago, Cuba, while in command of the 22nd Infantry during the War with Spain.

INDEX

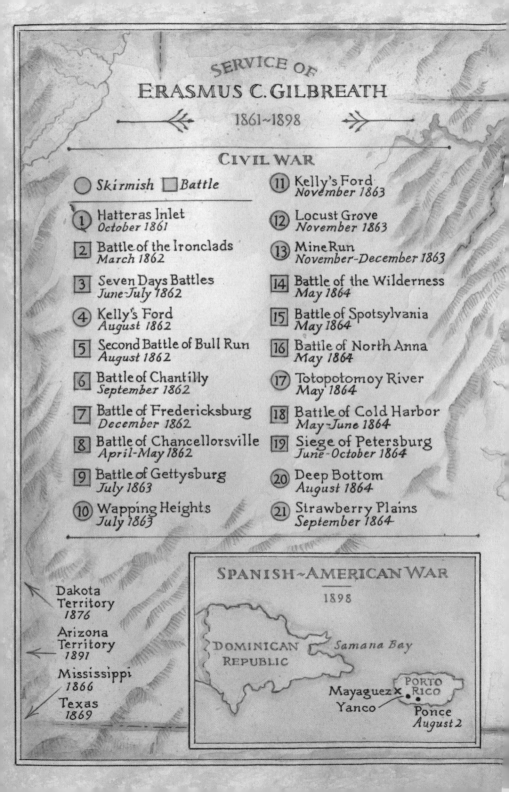

SERVICE OF
ERASMUS C. GILBREATH
1861~1898

⟵ ⟶

CIVIL WAR

◯ *Skirmish* ▢ *Battle*

① Hatteras Inlet
October 1861

② Battle of the Ironclads
March 1862

③ Seven Days Battles
June-July 1862

④ Kelly's Ford
August 1862

⑤ Second Battle of Bull Run
August 1862

⑥ Battle of Chantilly
September 1862

⑦ Battle of Fredericksburg
December 1862

⑧ Battle of Chancellorsville
April-May 1862

⑨ Battle of Gettysburg
July 1863

⑩ Wapping Heights
July 1863

⑪ Kelly's Ford
November 1863

⑫ Locust Grove
November 1863

⑬ Mine Run
November-December 1863

⑭ Battle of the Wilderness
May 1864

⑮ Battle of Spotsylvania
May 1864

⑯ Battle of North Anna
May 1864

⑰ Totopotomoy River
May 1864

⑱ Battle of Cold Harbor
May-June 1864

⑲ Siege of Petersburg
June-October 1864

⑳ Deep Bottom
August 1864

㉑ Strawberry Plains
September 1864

Dakota
Territory
1876

Arizona
Territory
1891

Mississippi
1866

Texas
1869

SPANISH~AMERICAN WAR
1898

DOMINICAN
REPUBLIC

Samana Bay

PORTO
RICO

Mayaguez ✗
Yanco

● Ponce
August 2